The Business of Ballet

The Business of Ballet

Diaghilev's Ballets Russes between Profit and the Avant-garde

Ira Nadel

LEXINGTON BOOKS
Lanham • Boulder • New York • London

Published by Lexington Books
An imprint of The Rowman & Littlefield Publishing Group, Inc.
4501 Forbes Boulevard, Suite 200, Lanham, Maryland 20706
www.rowman.com

86-90 Paul Street, London EC2A 4NE

British Library Cataloguing in Publication Information Available

Library of Congress Cataloging-in-Publication Data

Names: Nadel, Ira Bruce. author.
  Title: The business of ballet : Diaghilev's Ballets russes between profit
    and the avant-garde / Ira Nadel.
  Description: Lanham, Maryland : Lexington Books, [2024] | Includes
    bibliographical references and index.
  Identifiers: LCCN 2023050693 (print) | LCCN 2023050694 (ebook) | ISBN
    9781666945805 (cloth) | ISBN 9781666945812 (ebook)
  Subjects: LCSH: Ballets russes--History. | Ballet companies--Finance. |
    Diaghilev, Serge, 1872-1929.
  Classification: LCC GV1786.B355 N34 2024 (print) | LCC GV1786.B355
    (ebook) | DDC 338.7/617928--dc23/eng/20231107
  LC record available at https://lccn.loc.gov/2023050693
  LC ebook record available at https://lccn.loc.gov/2023050694

For Gideon, Levi, and Coby,
dancers all

Contents

Preface

The Blue Shadow

This multifaceted study narrates the transformation of Russian dance from the Imperial Ballet of St. Petersburg to the Ballets Russes of Paris and the political, social, artistic, and most importantly, the economic challenges involved in reshaping ballet from the Imperial style to the avant-garde. Or more directly, the interplay between magic and money. How new music, set designs, and choreography remade European ballet emanating from Russian traditions and culture is the focus. Supporting this is the theme of money and modernism, or economics and modern social transformation. Diaghilev had to make his company a financial success while seeking to remain a cutting-edge leader of the new. The interaction of dance and economics is the subject of this study or, more prosaically, the business of ballet.

Art and money converged with the Ballets Russes. This meant balancing the aesthetic drive to create original productions through the union of tradition and innovation. The result was a radical art that quickly defined the modernist ethos while striving to appeal to the box office. But this posed a challenge: How to sustain the avant-garde with profit? What would be the formula to attract audiences curious to see and experience new forms of movement through the unification of seemingly disparate arts while not losing money?

Innovation was the answer. In the "blue shadow" of a theater's wings, dancers prepare to enter an artificially lit stage and offer new movements. It is a moment of "concentrated expectation" in the "hothouse" atmosphere of ballet shaped by the imposing, if impetuous, Serge Diaghilev.[1] It is the anticipation of the new which lured audiences in an effort to encourage public interest and financial solvency as the Ballets Russes struggled to meet the challenges of being an artistic as well as commercial enterprise. But money and art soon joined, creating a synergistic cultural economy seemingly eliminating an ideological dichotomy between innovative dance and commerce. Audiences knew it was expensive to produce ballet but were prepared to support it either through patronage or the box office. Inescapably, money became as fundamental an aspect of dance as art. What was new was the funding of radical, not traditional, forms of dance.

The wish to experience avant-garde theater was the very enticement for audiences to attend, prompted by marketing, promotion, advertising, publicity, scandal, and almost always, controversy which worked to attract crowds. Popularity did not mean aesthetic compromise but its opposite: reconfirmation of the individualistic, iconoclastic, original, the very source of the company's appeal. This meant pleasure for Parisian audiences eager to experience "luxuriant opulence" and radical forms on stage.[2] To maintain the company's stability, however, a new, popular aesthetic emerged which undermined its original goals, but if the company was to continue, such a compromise was required. Expensive costumes and sets suddenly amplified the richness of the characters and performances, creating scenes that dazzled, seduced, and intoxicated viewers. But it was costly.

The Ballets Russes evolved from inciting riots to shaping a new method of dance. Through its artistic innovations, which by necessity had to become less challenging to meet audience's demands, it nevertheless shattered the idea of ballet. Their radicalism generated cultural debate and social reaction, although over time not always box office returns.[3] But its impact was large, marked by the author of *Peter Pan*. In 1920, J. M. Barrie's one-act play, *The Truth about the Russian Dancers*, was at the London Coliseum for a month. It was a hit.

NOTES

1. Prince Peter Lieven, *The Birth of the Ballets Russes*, trans. L. Zarine (1936; London: Allen & Unwin, 1956) 355, 354, 359. "In the wings everything is hidden in . . . bluish darkness," Lieven adds (355). Hereafter Lieven.

2. Lynn Garafola, *Diaghilev's Ballets Russes* (New York: Oxford Univ. Press, 1989) 46. Hereafter Garafola, 1989. Also see Ilyana Karthas, *When Ballet Became French: Modern Ballet and the Cultural Politics of France, 1909-1939* (Montreal: McGill-Queen's Univ. Press, 2015) passim; and Oleg Brezgin, "Sergei Diaghilev: A Centennial Bibliography," trans. Oleg Minin, *Experiment* 17 (2011): 459–687. In English and Russian.

3. In commenting on the dialogue between money and modernism, the critic Robert Jensen has written that "the two partners remain alien to one another, though always, endlessly intertwined." The commercial benefits of Ballets Russes performances were both acknowledged and dismissed by critics. Jensen also recognizes the

"ubiquity of market discourse" in the ideological defense of avant-gardism. In short, the avant-garde sells. Robert Jensen, *Marketing Modernism in Fin-de-Siècle Europe* (Princeton: Princeton Univ. Press, 1994) 10.

Acknowledgments

To study the Ballets Russes is to enter a multi-layered world of dance, music, art, and action. Diaghilev's company, the leading modern dance company in the world from 1909 to 1929, was a mix of originality and instability, especially from a financial perspective with shaky fiscal resources that spanned continents and languages. Autobiographies and accounts such as Serge Lifar's *Ma Vie*, Prince Lieven's *The Birth of [the] Ballets Russes,* and S. L. Grigoriev's *The Diaghilev Ballet, 1909–1929* are as revealing as Alexandre Benois's *Reminiscences of the Russian Ballet* or Richard Buckle's *Diaghilev.* Expanding this has been ongoing scholarship including such recent work as Lynn Garafola's *La Nijinska*, Jennifer Homans's *Mr. B: George Balanchine's 20th Century,* and Rupert Christiansen's *Diaghilev's Empire*, all appearing in 2022. Publications on Stravinsky, Nijinsky, and Picasso have been equally important, all part of an increasing library of materials relating directly or indirectly to Diaghilev and the life of the Ballets Russes. Although I met few of these authors, I feel I have shared with them a curiosity and desire to understand more clearly the story of the Ballets Russes and its dynamics. And all have been helpful in my effort to assess the economics of the company and Diaghilev's financial profile which existed in a productive tension with his art.

Archives at the Jerome Robbins Dance Division of the New York Public Library for the Performing Arts at Lincoln Center, the Harvard Theatre Collection, and Ballets Russes materials at the Library of Congress, from photos to costume designs, posters, and printed materials, including Diaghilev's autograph notebook of 1926–1929 (with lists of ballets, sketches, and details for music and casting), plus Nijinsky's dance notations for *L'Après-midi d'un faune*, as well as the dance collection at the Vancouver Public Library, have been inestimable resources—as have been those who encouraged and listened: Jennifer Homans, Anne MacKenzie, Dara, Jon, Gideon, Levi, and Coby Pavlich, as well as Ryan Nadel and Isabelle Rash.

Introduction

Magic and Money or "Étonnez-moi!"

"Astonish me!" was Serge Diaghilev's challenge to a disheartened Jean Cocteau as they walked through the Place de la Concorde one evening in 1912 behind a dejected Nijinsky.[1] Diaghilev, the Russian impresario and founder of the Ballets Russes, was offering a challenge to all his dancers, artists, composers, set designers, and musicians to continue the originality and excitement of his company. It had become the embodiment of the new, the unexpected, and the surprising.

"Audiences do not insist upon a story or a situation to appreciate the movements of a dance or the strains of music" wrote the critic Robert McAlmon in an introductory essay to what would become *Finnegans Wake*.[2] This is precisely the modernist aesthetic Diaghilev and his company would develop, ballet becoming a work of, and for, itself, expressing a new freedom in the arts where meaning did not matter, only expression.

In dance, the new meant not a revision of the real as much as a replacement and a turn away from the classical style and content promoted by the Imperial Ballet of St. Petersburg. The story of the Ballets Russes is how the impact of the new affected audiences, critics, dancers, and other companies and led to the Ballets Russes becoming the leading exponent of modern European dance coinciding with developments in Russian avant-garde art during the "Silver Age." But while adhering to Cocteau's belief that "rebellion is indispensable in art," Diaghilev also realized that ballet was entwined with economics.[3] There could be no Ballets Russes unless the bills were paid. Any rebellion would fail unless the company was solvent. The tension between the artistic and commercial was continuous. On one hand, he enhanced the popular awareness of ballet and cultivated a new marketplace for dance. But on the other, in commodifying the ballet, he may have become a slave to an uncultured audience. But that overstates the case. Diaghilev, uniquely, did not sacrifice artistic integrity to the checkbook. This reaffirms his individuality in the ballet world.

The tension, however, is of course not a new problem. The economics of ballet in a market economy has always been perilous. Unless government or institutional support was forthcoming, the existence of private ballet companies was always questionable. Occasionally, wealthy patrons supported their own companies but for the most part, during Diaghilev's time and following, ballet companies depended on three sources for economic survival: ticket sales, an affiliated ballet school, and (in today's terms) development: donations and grants. Reports entitled *The Performing Arts: The Economic Dilemma* (1966) or the "Untenable Economics of Dancing" (2014) are as prevalent today as they were during the period of the Ballets Russes.[4]

In a market economy, the financial demands on ballet never disappear; in the performing arts crisis is a way of life. With dance, costs per performance rise faster than that of the general price level. But the cause is not inflation but the economic structure of live performance itself. The gap between income and costs never shrinks. The only thing assured is the increase in deficits. Ironically, as Baumol and Bowen show in *The Performing Arts*, while the costs of labor productivity in manufacturing over the last two hundred years declined, in the performing arts, it increased. And while growth in productivity output is accompanied by a rise in wage rates as production costs diminish, the reverse happens in the arts. A rise in the wages of performers, unavoidable over time, means adding to spiralling costs without an increase in productivity which translates into an increase in income. There was also an inverse curve: as society grew wealthier, the amount spent on the arts stagnated or declined. The chart for production costs of the arts only moves higher.

This narrative outlines, however, the imaginative, persistent, and original ways Diaghilev was able to navigate the difficult waters of ballet economics and for twenty years maintain not only a first-class company of dancers and musicians, but sustain his troupe of more than one hundred through cultural wars, a World War, economic upheavals, rivals, and difficult personalities. Yet it was always a struggle between his desire for artistic independence and yet dependence on patrons, managers, audiences, and banks. The story of the Ballets Russes is fundamentally economic, becoming a model of financing the arts in the late 19th and early 20th centuries. Cut off from government or institutional support, Diaghilev had to be creative off stage as well as on. He succeeded, combining his cultivation of his audiences with an astute, sociological sense of Parisian society, essentially conservative but with liberal artistic leanings.

The artistic solution for Diaghilev was a paradox: while the innovative and complex became the very draw for new audiences, he needed box office receipts to sustain the novel and experimental. This meant the regular inclusion of the traditional, or at least the acceptable, in dance. This was in response to the prevailing turn-of-the-century performance culture in Europe.

But for Parisian audiences in 1909, the conventional became the passport to the avant-garde, relating to an important question: Was what Diaghilev did actually new? His financial solution relied on cultivating the social elite, from aristocrats to the wealthy *nouveau riche* whether industrialists or newspaper magnates. To both groups he appealed to their wish to appear cultured and desire to be thought patrons of the arts.

The first Ballets Russes Paris season balanced the traditional with the new and included the Louis XIV–styled *Le Pavillon d'Armide* and *Les Sylphides* with music by Chopin and Anna Pavlova in a long white tutu. For Berlin, it was *Carnaval,* which evoked the Biedermeier era; for London, narrative classics such as *Swan Lake* and *The Sleeping Princess,* interspersed with experimental, new ballets. These recursive, restagings relate to the idea that the new is only "the hybrid offspring of recurrence and recombination."[5] Metaphorically, it is the young man in *Don Quixote* who recombined his three outfits in such a way so that others thought he had ten.[6] But the new is always a threat because it corrodes the existing, often conservative, values. The avant-garde as understood in the arts is at first a curious attraction, but it soon loses its appeal because it cannot remain new when repeated. It suddenly seems old. Newness, in the full sense of the word, is not creative; it is just a recombination of the already there. Re-staging *The Firebird* in 1926 in London lost the impact of its original 1910 production, despite new costumes and sets with a dramatic backdrop of stylized Russian city towers in red and blues with golden domes by Natalia Goncharova.

Stravinsky demonstrated this in 1928 with his allegorical ballet *The Fairy's Kiss* commissioned by Ida Rubinstein. Based on a fairy tale by Hans Christian Andersen, Stravinsky relied on Tchaikovsky who stood for Europeanized Russia for the composer. *The Fairy's Kiss* was in many ways an homage to Tchaikovsky, borrowing melodies and orchestration, as well as harmony and overall structure blended with Stravinsky's own additions. Again, the new is the old which critics, other than Diaghilev (jealous of the work), valued. The émigré critic André Levinson praised the ballet as Stravinsky's return to the classical ballet tradition, the music offering "a concentrated extract of what was at its apogee the *ballet d'action.*"[7]

When it overstays its welcome, the new degenerates into fashion, exactly the story of the Ballets Russes in the last third of its career. Reports of its performances in the 1920s largely skipped any remarks on dance and focused only on the style and behavior of the audience. Disenchantment became the critical position of the press and public. Despite his encouragement and desire for the new in music and dance, the source of the early reputation of the Ballets Russes, Diaghilev knew that the public retained a taste for the old. The challenging new modernist motto at this time was not Pound's "Make It New," itself a restatement of a Confucian saying, but "Redo" (North 148).

How to unite the commercial with the artistic without sacrificing the traditional or the excitement of the new was Diaghilev's dilemma in an effort to
unite art and money. One, he believed, would make the other possible.

Founded in Paris in 1909, for the next twenty years the Ballets Russes com-
plexly embodied modernism on the stage through its choreography, costumes,
dancers, sets, and music. This volume tells its story against the backdrop of
finance to highlight how the personalities of those who gave the company
its international renown, originating in its thrilling and experimental visual
narratives, were also attuned to the cost of such ventures. It considers the
in-fighting, economic struggles, and reactions to its unconventional ballets
offered in establishment venues throughout Europe. But ironically, what initially created the biggest sensation was not the new movements or even new
music but the highly eroticized primitivism mixed with refinement expressed
through costumes and decors in shocking colors and fabrics. This was drastically different from the nature of traditional dance costumes or theater sets
with their flat, monochromatic colors. These changes met the demands of
cosmopolitan Paris, a city which constantly valued the progressive and modern, becoming at this time "the capital of the future."[8]

The Ballets Russes started by resurrecting classical ballet but in a novel
way. Their first season presented a program inspired by historical periods
favored by Russia's *World of Art* journal (started by Diaghilev): *Cléopâtre*,
Egyptian; *Polovtsian Dances*, ancient Russia; *Le Pavillon d'Armide*, the eigh-
teenth century. The journal's enthusiasm for Greek arts resulted in *Narcisse*
in 1911, followed by *L'Après-midi d'un faune* and *Daphnis et Chloë*. Ballet
for Diaghilev should be entertainment stressing drama, while movement
becomes an emotional and aesthetic experience. He engaged audiences in
allegories or even fairy tales which appealed to their love of myth, while
simultaneously challenging them to re-imagine what a ballet might be. His
stagings were almost symbolist experiments where the moving parts, from
décor to costumes to music and dance, worked together while projecting an
undercurrent of sensuality and eroticism.[9] What he sought was *passion à la
Russe,* mixing a meditative, romantic sadness with physical and visual intensity expressed experimentally. He believed that his early Parisian audiences
wanted to be transported, not punished (Bridgman 41). He also showed the
pagan origins of Russian nationalism through captivating movements and
music as in *Le Sacre du printemps.*

The Ballets Russes made ballet an intricate theatrical experience and in
so doing created a new visual and musical discourse that equally thrilled
and displeased audiences eager to replace tradition with innovation. Proust,
as well as Virginia Woolf, André Gide, and John Maynard Keynes, attended
performances to watch Nijinsky leap and Pavlova dance which occasioned
both riots and applause. T. S. Eliot, in Paris in 1910–1911, most certainly

saw them and witnessed how early productions generated controversy but everyone still went; the performances could not be missed. They were a cultural sensation even if the music by Stravinsky, Satie, and Prokofiev mixed the dissonant with the discordant. But how did such radical innovations in ballet theater become the compass for the modern? And what was the role of money in this process?

The answer in part lies with its founder, Sergei Diaghilev, and his vision of ballet as a total work of art incorporating elements of often radical forms of musical, artistic, and physical expression. The result was the remaking of ballet through the avant-garde drawing on Futurism, Symbolism, Dadaism, neo-primitivism, and other artistic forms.[10] A reshaping of the European and Russian dance aesthetic, first understood as threatening, reactionary, and decadent, resulted. Its originality insured its misunderstanding and yet it became the critical definition of the modern by dismantling the past. But Diaghilev also knew that the secret of sustaining the avant-garde on stage was the box office—and to keep that going, he had to be both experimental, challenging and even threatening, while not sacrificing the traditional. One depended on the other.

Reforming dance rather than opera at this time was also an increasing preference for composers and artists. The European tradition of blending music and voice supported an operatic tradition but one Diaghilev and others soon believed to be too expensive to produce despite his success with *Boris Godunov* in 1908 Paris. Stravinsky agreed on aesthetic grounds, claiming in 1912 that "opera is a lie, aspiring to truth, but I want a lie aspiring to a lie. Opera is a battle against nature."[11] Radicalizing the anti-mimetic became a principle of Diaghilev's troupe which continued with select operas but with a difference. *Le Coq d'or* (1914) illustrated the change: singers were no longer part of the dramatic scene but sang offstage in the wings, while the dancers performed under the direction of Fokine. The singers were not visible, nor did they attempt to act. Yet despite the originality of the production, the origin of the ballet was a fairy tale by Pushkin with the stage showing Russian folk scenes. The past and the future appeared to merge.[12]

Diaghilev was responsive to new movements and changes, the years 1914–1917 perhaps the most dramatic in defining his modernist aesthetic. Much of this reorientation occurred during a period with the company (much smaller in size) in Switzerland.[13] His absorption of Futurism, neo-primitivism, and a kind of pre-Romantic artistic heritage created a set of styles that would distinguish the postwar Ballets Russes. He appropriated the artistically new and fused it with ethnic content while not entirely sacrificing the traditional. He broadened the modernist experiment, remaking the company in the image of the avant-garde itself which meant replacing a neo-Romantic sentimentality with an assemblage of styles presented through ironic detachment.[14] A remade classicism became a counterpoint to the sentimentality of the past projected in conventional ballets, but the success of a work like *The Three-Cornered Hat* (1919) showed the importance of his commitment to modernism. The work possessed an artistic unity matching *Schéhérazade* or *Petrushka:* "modernist ballet had finally grown up" (Scheijen 347).

But these shifts in orientation meant an economic as well as aesthetic reorganization which occurred outside the demands of the box office during six months in Switzerland (1917–1918) that saw Diaghilev finally install a new economic program eliminating distinctions in salary. Regardless of rank, dancers received four hundred Swiss francs a month. For artists like Larionov and Goncharova, a stipend replaced payment for work performed. And from this period of renewal, modernism and internationalism became signposts of the company's new identity.

The impact of the Ballets Russes on the modernists was profound. The visual contest between innovation and tradition astonished Proust, Woolf, and Joyce. Proust was so impressed that he included references to the *au courant* aspect of the Ballets Russes in the fifth volume of *Remembrance of Things Past*, "The Captive." Not only does the aged Mme. Verdurin have a box at Ballet Russes performances but enthusiastic friends would appear at her apartment after a performance to debate the excellence of *Schéhérazade* or the dances from *Prince Igor.* In the novel, her sumptuous post-performance suppers were often attended by the dancers themselves, as well as a fictitious Stravinsky or Strauss.

Proust's admiration of Diaghilev's art resulted from firsthand knowledge.[15] This came about through his friend, the composer Reynaldo Hahn, who wrote the music for the one-act *Le Die bleu* with a libretto by Cocteau. Proust socialized with Diaghilev, Bakst, and on at least one occasion, Nijinsky. Proust was also aware of a new subjectivity conveyed by the body in its movement with novel gestures and forms projected by the dancers' bodies. Proust soon assimilated this new poetics of dance into his work.[16]

Suddenly, the vogue for the Ballets Russes expanded beyond the theater and literature, impacting fashion, art, and design.[17] The vocabulary of culture, as well as dance itself, changed. Attraction to the Ballets Russes even took personal form: Picasso, as well as John Maynard Keynes, would marry Ballets Russes dancers.[18]

The Ballets Russes showed how aesthetic experience is not only the result of a culture but works to influence and shape it. On a national level, the Ballet Russes created a version of Russian culture for export at the same time it articulated a national tradition at home. Ironically, in the early twentieth century, Russian culture was a story written largely outside of Russia and its influence was broad. The impact of *Schéhérazade* (1910), for example, was so great that for at least a decade after, French fashion (led by the designer

Paul Poiret) imitated the harem pants and flowing silks worn by the dancers. Diaghilev, Poiret, and even Matisse (who had visited Russia in 1911) eroticized the female body. Criticisms that the Ballets Russes dances were frenzied, barbaric, or voluptuous were actually reactions to ballet sexualizing the body and flooding the stage with color and movement. Unsurprisingly, Coco Chanel's modern bathing suits for *Le Train bleu* (1924) created a new, captivating style sought by many, especially on the Riviera. Even perfumes appeared confirming Diaghilev's idea that ballet was a living, contemporary practice and that artistic change meant social change.

But Diaghilev, ever eager to capitalize on the appeal of the new, also knew his weaknesses. To his stepmother in 1895 he wrote that he was a "charlatan, albeit *con brio*" but also a "great charmer" blessed "with a great deal of cheek." He possessed logical thought but lacked principles, he claimed. He was also without talent. His quest, he discovered, was to "lead the life of a patron of the arts. I have everything one needs to that end except for money."[19] Money, in fact, would become the great aim and obstacle of his career.

NOTES

1. Sjeng Scheijen, *Diaghilev: A Life,* trans. Jane Hedley-Prôle and S. J. Leinbach (New York: Oxford Univ. Press, 2009) 323. Hereafter Scheijen.

2. Robert McAlmon, "Mr. Joyce Directs an Irish Word Ballet," *Our Exagmination Round His Factification* (1929; New York: New Directions, 1972) 105.

3. Cocteau in Garafola, 1989: 98. Cocteau added that the "spirit of creation is the highest form of the spirt of contradiction" and that "a work of art should . . . be an object difficult to pick up."

On the economics of dance see Garafola, 1989: 159–63, 171–73, 177–200, plus Scheijen, *Diaghilev: A Life,* passim, and Jennifer Homans, *Apollo's Angels: A History of Ballet* (New York: Random House, 2010) passim. Hereafter Homans.

4. William J. Baumol and William G. Bowen, *The Performing Arts: The Economic Dilemma* (New York: The Twentieth Century Fund, 1966); Baumol and Bowen provide an analysis of the economic challenges for the performing arts from the composition of audiences to costs, income, organizational structure, and contracts. They indicate that the cost per performance and per attendance has always risen faster than an economy's rate of inflation.

Andy Horowitz, "Untenable Economics of Dancing," Culturebot (March 27, 2014). https://www.culturebot.org/2014/03/21361/the-untenable-economics-of-dancing/. Horowitz indicates the unsustainable incomes of young choreographers and dancers, noting that on average a dancer working with an early career choreographer can expect an income anywhere from $100 to $500 for a three-month development period. Depending on the number of performances, they might earn $1,500 for 3–4 months' work. Debt becomes inimical.

Dancemakers, a 1993 report from the National Endowment for the Arts, and their 2012 report, *How Art Works,* are two further studies of art and economics. A more recent but parallel analysis is "Economics" in Susan Manning, et al., *The Future of Dance Studies* (Madison, WI: Univ. of Wisconsin Press, 2020) 339 –412.

5. Michael North, *Novelty: A History of the New* (Chicago: Univ. of Chicago Press, 2013) 75. Hereafter North.

6. For the *Don Quixote* reference see part 1, chapter LI of the novel.

7. André Levinson in *The Cambridge Stravinsky Encyclopedia*, ed. Edward Campbell and Peter O'Hagan (Cambridge: Cambridge Univ. Press, 2021) 152. Hereafter, the *Cambridge Stravinsky*.

8. Davinia Caddy, *The Ballets Russes and Beyond: Music and Dance in Belle-Époque Paris* (Cambridge: Cambridge Univ. Press, 2012) 124. Hereafter Caddy.

9. See Elena Bridgman, "Mir Iskusstva, Origins of the Ballets Russes," *The Art of Enchantment: Diaghilev's Ballets Russes, 1909–1929,* ed. Nancy Van Norman Baer (New York: Universe Books with the Fine Arts Museum of San Francisco, 1988), 38 –40. Hereafter Bridgman.

10. On the specific role of Futurism, see Lynn Garafola, "The Making of Ballet Modernism," *Dance Research Journal*, Vol. 20.2 (1988): 23–32.

11. Stravinsky interview, *Peterburgskaya gazeta*, September 27, 1912 in Scheijen 297.

12. The production itself united classical ballet technique for the temptress Queen Shemakha and the golden cockerel with energetic Russian folk dances for the peasant girls and men.

13. Diaghilev's retinue was often immense. For his first season in London, taking place at the Royal Opera House, he had 100 dancers, 200 supernumeraries, plus singers. For the 1914 Paris season, he headed a company of twenty principal dancers, eleven principal singers, a corps de ballet of one hundred, and the chorus of the Bolshoi Opera. Garafola, 1989: 205.

14. Lynn Garafola, "The Making of Ballet Modernism," *Dance Research Journal* 20.2 (1989): 30.

15. See Proust, "The Captive," *Remembrance of Things Past*, trans. C. K. Scott Moncrieff, Terence Kilmartin, and Andreas Mayor, Vol. III (New York: Random House, 1981) 237–38.

Ballet, in turn, responded to Proust. Roland Petit produced a ballet of *À la recherche* in 1974 at the Opéra de Monte-Carlo. It entered the repertoire of the Opéra National de Paris in 2007. See Marion Schmid, "Proust at the Ballet: Literature and Dance in Dialogue," *French Studies* 67.2 (2013): 184–98.

16. On the impact of the Ballets Russes on Proust's writing, see Marion Schmid, "Proust's Choreographies of Writing: *À la recherche du temps perdu* and the Modern Dance Revolution," *Marcel Proust Aujourd'hui*, *Swann at 100*, Vol. 12 (2015): 91–108.

17. On the vogue for the Ballets Russes style and its social impact, see Samantha Vettese, "The Ballets Russes Connection with Fashion," *Costume* Vol. 42.1 (2008): 130–44; Jane Pritchard, "A Giant that Continues to Grow—The Impact, Influence and Legacy of the Ballets Russes," in *Diaghilev and the Golden Age of the Ballets Russes*, ed. Jane Pritchard (London: V&A Publishing, 2010), 187–205; Mary E. Davis, *Ballets Russes Style: Diaghilev's Dancers and Paris Fashion* (London: Reaktion, 2010); Davinia Caddy, *The Ballets Russes and Beyond: Music and Dance in Belle-Époque Paris* (Cambridge: Cambridge Univ. Press, 2012).

Selfridges in London announced a Russian season for its department store in 1911.

18. A further sign of the closeness of the Ballet Russes community is that the young composer Igor Markevitch, who was a late infatuation of Diaghilev's in Paris, would marry Nijinsky's daughter Kyra.

19. Diaghilev in Ada Raev, "Working for Diaghilev: An Introduction," *Working for Diaghilev*, ed. Sjeng Scheijen (Netherlands: Groninger Museum, 2004) 8. Also see Scheijen, *Diaghilev* 74.

Chapter 1

Diaghilev

A Russian in Paris

The instigator of the revolution in modern ballet was the Russian-born impresario, promoter, and *bon vivant* Serge Diaghilev. Entangled with the history of modern dance is his story and his choices in commissioning new works and following them through their creative execution. But he had a paradoxical view of money: it was secondary to the artistic goals of his company at the same time it was essential if they were to be realized. The result was a redefinition of the cultural space of dance, music, and art made possible through capital. Modernism's ideology superficially seemed at odds with capitalist practices but needed to rely on them, especially in costly theatrical enterprises like opera and dance.

The rise of Diaghilev to become, in the words of the dancer Serge Lifar, "Art personified," began in St. Petersburg with a successful art journal, the *World of Art*, and then a show of Russian historical portraits and the realization that Europe would be eager to see works of Russian culture.[1] He quickly mixed ambition with cultural politics. He undertook to promote Russian art and music (first opera, then ballet) in Paris with limited Russian and French financial support. But he was a marketer who from the start understood the value of public relations, promotion, and publicity, plus political support. In 1906, for example, he organized five Russian concerts at the Grand Opéra in Paris with the Czar's brother, Grand Duke Vladimir, as one of his backers. A Dutch rubber merchant living in St. Petersburg was another supporter, indicating that Diaghilev had not only cultivated international connections but knew who had the money at home (Scheijen 153).

Le Maître

Born on March 31, 1872 in Selishchi in northwest Russia, Diaghilev initially grew up in St. Petersburg but moved to the family home in Perm near the

Urals. The death of his mother shortly after his birth and financial challenges for his father necessitated a return to the family home in 1879. In Perm, his father remarried and the household became a center of culture with music, literature, and art regularly performed, read, or exhibited. The home included a ballroom. Young Diaghilev learned to play the piano, as well as speak French and German. His grandfather had been a successful vodka distiller, his father an army officer, although one with debts.

But the grandfather's tottering vodka monopoly in Perm led to the company's decline in the face of competition and then a failed attempt to file for bankruptcy in 1879. His failure to modernize may have contributed to the firm's weakness, a lesson Diaghilev never forgot. The grandfather then left his overseer to operate the estate and manage the collapsing distilleries. The overseer proceeded to defraud the grandfather and Diaghilev's father of any remaining assets, committing suicide in 1884 after murdering his sister and wife (Scheijen 31–32).

The family kept the scandal out of the papers but Diaghilev's father had to immediately find 50,000 rubles to cover newly emerging debts caused by financial mismanagement. This undercut the family's high social standing enhanced by their eager promotion of classical music and singers. Nevertheless, Pavel Diaghilev was able to raise the funds (Scheijen 31). In 1885, Diaghilev's father took out a five-year mortgage of 125,000 rubles on his entire property (the distillery and homes). The terms were complete repayment by the end of the period or all would be forfeited. And then new creditors appeared. By the end of May 1889, the lender went to court to order a public auction of the Diaghilev properties and their contents. The father had four months to repay the full amount or face financial ruin. The result was ruin. His son never forgot this breakdown but also how loans may see one through, if only temporarily.

Nevertheless, these events did not stop Diaghilev from venerating Russian culture, annually visiting Pushkin's grave and meeting Tchaikovsky, a family acquaintance. The same year as the collapse, Diaghilev returned to St. Petersburg to study law, quickly forming a circle of friends who shared similar artistic ambitions including Alexandre Benois and Lev Rozenberg, later known as Léon Bakst, both to have roles with the Ballets Russes. They called themselves the Nevsky Pickwickians. The group outlined new aesthetic goals in opposition to the conservative, academic values of the day and staged readings and musical performances. They opposed simplistic realism and sought to restore beauty, artifice, and order. The French 18th century was their ideal. They admired classical ballet, while Benois venerated Versailles and had a mannequin of Louis XIV on his desk. The young Diaghilev studied singing and music at the city's Conservatory of Music.

Well-read and well-educated in Russian culture, Diaghilev, nonetheless, felt a constant need to sustain a cultural awareness of Europe. His St. Petersburg student group debated Ibsen, Zola, Maeterlinck, and Maupassant, as well as Tolstoy and Dostoevsky. He and his cousin Dimitry Filosofov even concocted a meeting with Tolstoy, visiting him in Moscow in 1892. Money facilitated their appointment. They had written to Tolstoy with the ruse of student contributions to the author's current charitable project. This caught Tolstoy's interest and a meeting took place in February, Tolstoy embodying "truth and naturalness," as Diaghilev wrote to his stepmother (Scheijen 47). Warmly greeted by Tolstoy because of their charitable intentions, the two students spent time outlining possibilities and at their departure were hugged by the writer at Dimitry's request. Days later, Diaghilev sent a photo of Tolstoy to his daughter for the author's autograph. Several days later, it was returned signed. Flattery and admiration, useful habits for an impresario, were here on display (Scheijen 44–49). A year later in a letter to Tolstoy written when he was twenty-one, Diaghilev wrote that his dream was to "work creatively in the realm of the arts" (Scheijen 49). This unwittingly foretold his future.

Diaghilev's money hoax was not a surprise since money soon dominated his life, although he did have some funds to travel, although his immediate goal upon graduation was a career in the Imperial bureaucracy. In 1892, for example, he traveled in pursuit of Wagner with whom he had become fascinated. At the time, however, his music was unpopular, although Diaghilev would often sing and play his compositions. On his 1892 trip to Germany, Diaghilev repeatedly sought performances of Wagner's work, while simultaneously seeking out the "greats." Visiting Brahms, he requested an autograph; Brahms signed a visiting card. But in a letter home, he described the composer's distressing apartment which was akin to an "old tavern," presciently adding that with the well-known, it's "better to imagine them than to see them." This anticipates his later view that omission is the key to art and that illusion and suggestion have more impact than showing (Scheijen 58).

Compositionally, Diaghilev began to see the value of cutting, removing "what is antiquated and boring" in order to improve and streamline musical performances. He would soon shape dances and music to provide what he felt would be the artistic essence of each work, an approach shared with a number of his artists, notably Stravinsky and his choreographer Massine (Scheijen 59). Returning to St. Petersburg after his musical excursion, Diaghilev devoted himself to composing, believing in his own talent, writing at one point, "Damn it, I am not a completely ordinary man (!!!)" (Scheijen 60). Friendships with Tchaikovsky and Rimsky-Korsakov did not hurt, although the latter thought poorly of Diaghilev's early musical compositions. He also began singing lessons twice a week.

At the time, Diaghilev joined several musical circles with other young composers who sought to break away from academic traditions and return to a native Russian musical idiom incorporating authentic folk tunes. This foreshadowed some of Stravinsky's most original work for the Ballets Russes. The founding group was loosely known as the Five, referring to five St. Petersburg composers who sought a national style of classical music. They included Mussorsky, Rimsky-Korsakov, and Alexander Borodin. They would play an important role in the new Russian music and influence the music composed for the company which differed in a formal way: previously, the choreographer ordered music from the composer bar by bar after a dance was structured. For the Ballets Russes, complete pieces for a ballet became the practice, the composer working together with the choreographer to integrate the movements with the music.[2]

Money and Art

The family bankruptcy cast a shadow over Diaghilev's plans: he needed an income to support himself and his two half-brothers then living with him in St. Petersburg. His artistic ambitions, coupled with his family's history, taught him that one could only promote culture with money: only with proper backing could one support artistic enterprises. He began to fashion a scheme: getting underway with a Paris exhibition of Russian art and then a season of Russian music and, finally, the Ballets Russes, Diaghilev matched private funds with government support, all the more necessary as government subsidies diminished (for political as much as economic reasons). Increasingly, he turned to private sources, often Russian art collectors, connoisseurs, and industrialists, and then French aristocrats and English noble men and women.

Family insolvency initiated a determination to succeed, encouraged by his stepmother, and he tried work as a researcher, critic, editor, publisher, and exhibition organizer. He also sought a governmental position and in 1901 even proposed to reorganize all of Russia's art galleries, a result of his growing knowledge of Russian art and its principal collectors. This partly emerged from his founding Russia's first lavishly illustrated art magazine, *World of Art* (*Mir iskusstva*), with backing from others which ran from 1899 to 1904.[3] Inception of the journal coincided with the opening of the Russian National Museum in St. Petersburg (associated with the Imperial Court and the goals of Tsar Alexander III) but the journal stood in opposition to the museum's emphasis on national, figurative, realistic, often plot-driven paintings in an effort to create a national cultural identity. The *World of Art*, with its preference for controversy and search for authenticity in Russian painting, quickly attacked the museum's collection, generating a counter-discourse that created public interest (Dianina 186–88).

Diaghilev, particularly upset at the museum's failure to represent the historical development of Russian art, was himself only a self-taught critic (several happily dismissed him as a dilletante) but that did not stop him from challenging the authorities. He wrote and spoke confidently, a quality that marked his entire career, but it also made him vulnerable to jests, satire, and comedy (see Dianina 267–68). Such ridicule, however, did not curtail his ambitions, at one point approaching Chekhov to become the journal's literary editor. Coincidentally, *The Three Sisters* (1901) was set in Perm. But despite a series of solicitous letters, Chekhov declined (Scheijen 128–29).

Diaghilev's prefatory essay, published as a four-part manifesto in the first two issues of the *World of Art*, was "Complicated Questions. Our Imaginary Decline" and set the tone of his appeal and position. It declared war on the Academy and its followers. The goal was to turn the public away from the realism found in Russian art toward more subjective styles that had emerged in Western Europe loosely grouped under the term "symbolism." Up until then, art was to be Russian in subject matter, accurate, and socially useful. But realism had become sentimental and indifferent to formal values, unaware of the artistic debates occurring in European circles. For Diaghilev, the strength of art was that "it serves only itself" and that it is free from obligations to the actual world.[4] Artists did not have to seem sincere, nationalistic or embrace any social or political purpose. They only had to paint.

Attached to these principles was the journal's effort to propagate Russian culture and art from the past, as well as promote ideas from the present, the so-called "Silver Age." Despite the journal not being widely read, its provocative editorials attracted journalists who wrote about it frequently in mass circulation dailies where "scandalous publicity" promoted the publication "no less than its attractive reproductions" (Dianina 233). The cultural wars it instigated contributed to animated debates on the visual arts in Imperial Russia, all led by Diaghilev who revolted against the idea of socially "useful" art in contrast to beauty and artistic freedom. Art should not pursue messages; such concerns only debase the medium. One should search for a nationalism that is "unconscious" and "in the blood." It must be for the artist "a constant reflection of indigenous nationality." The artist must bear within him "the characteristics of the nation."[5]

The *World of Art* movement contributed to the early aesthetics of the Ballets Russes.[6] But its policies soon jeopardized the 10,000-ruble annual grant from the Tsar; furthermore, the Sino-Japanese war of 1904 was endangering funds and after eleven issues, the magazine ended. Diaghilev had also lost interest in overcoming the financial, artistic, and interpersonal problems dogging the magazine. But he still had debts and was forced to sell a number of his best paintings to cover expenses.

At the time of the journal, Diaghilev also worked on special assignments for the Imperial Theatres including the theatres' Yearbook. He had become special assistant to Prince Sergei Volkonsky, director of all Imperial Theatres. Through Volkonsky, Diaghilev soon gained production power but the two fell out over Diaghilev's elaborate plans for the ballet *Sylvia* and he left two years later. He had decided to become an entrepreneur of art and his ideas on marketing art, opera, and ballet blossomed. But while he still sought a government placement (dependent on the tsar), the 1905 revolution, initiated by the "Bloody Sunday" of January 22, 1905, derailed his plans. In the events that followed, the artistic world was swept up in the maelstrom of revolt and disruption. During this period and after, artistic partisans battled each other: Constructivists confronted Suprematists, while neo-Classicists challenged Surrealists. Liberals and anarchists, as well as reactionaries and progressives, constantly attacked one another. Unrest knew no limits.

Nevertheless, Diaghilev began with an early success: in February 1905, his wide-ranging Exhibition of Historic Russian Portraits was opened at the Tauride Palace in St. Petersburg by no less than Tsar Nicholas II. It was the product of his extensive search throughout the country resulting in an exhibit of over 4,000 important Russian paintings dominated by portraits of the tsars and aristocracy, all commanded by Diaghilev who oversaw every detail and was eager "to do everything himself," from selecting to hanging.[7] The show was a summing up of Imperial absolutism at a time of turmoil anticipated by the death, by a terrorist bomb, of an uncle of the Tsar, Grand Duke Sergei Aleksandrovich, within the grounds of the Kremlin only seven weeks earlier.

At the conclusion of a banquet speech at the Metropole Hotel to mark the success of the show, Diaghilev translated the politics of the day into artistic discourse declaring that Russia was witnessing "the greatest historic hour of reckoning, of things coming to an end in the name of a new, unknown culture." A new aesthetic will emerge, he predicted, unknowingly anticipating his own later triumph throughout Europe with the Ballets Russes.[8] His mix of Russian nationalism with avant-garde artistic goals and entrepreneurial savvy would create a new modernism affecting art, dance, music, and even literature in the East and West. But how did this restlessly ambitious man, a failed composer, musician, and artist, succeed? And what social politics were involved in his sustaining a Russian dance company in a world of revolution and uproar?

Paris I

Without a preferment, Diaghilev was at loose ends. But in 1906, while on a tour of Greece, Turkey, and Italy, he revived the idea of bringing Russian art to the West, specifically Paris, initially tried by Benois. "I'll show them the real Russia," he confided to Benois (Scheijen 149). The idea was to exhibit the most progressive art schools in Russia with Moscow painters like Larionov, supported by a selection of academy and 18th-century art, plus various Russian icons from the collection of a historian, Nikolay Likachov. Icons were not considered fashionable works of art at the time and their inclusion was a gamble.

A month later, Diaghilev was in Paris introduced by Benois to a series of curators and organizers. He secured twelve rooms at the Salon d'automne in the Grand Palais and selected Léon Bakst as the designer. But even this event caused friction, with Bakst and Benois often at odds on arrangements, artists, and décor. Diaghilev avoided the conflict by spending hours hanging and rehanging works himself, while chaos reigned until the final hour when everything seemed to fall into place. Walter Nouvel, soon to become Diaghilev's secretary, joined him at the time, as well as Prince Argutinsky-Dolgorukov, a rich collector and connoisseur. Opening the exhibition of nearly 750 works on October 6, 1906 was the president of France.

The goal was to show that Russian art was not provincial. Diaghilev featured Larionov, Goncharova, Vrubel, Sapunov, and Sudeykin. Larionov, at Diaghilev's insistence, attended the opening. The exhibition made an immediate impression, but its novelty was greater than its importance. But could these artists equal Cézanne, Gauguin, Matisse, and Picasso also on display? Not yet. Diaghilev knew how to capitalize on the public's curiosity. At the end of the show, the works traveled to Berlin and, in a reduced version, to the Venice *Biennale.* By Christmas, Diaghilev was back in Paris with a new set of friends including the poet Robert de Montesquiou and the Comtesse Greffulhe, a wealthy patron. Both saw life as art, the former the model for Baron Charlus and the latter the prototype for the Duchesse de Guermantes in Proust's *À la recherche du temps perdu.* More importantly, the contacts and money of de Montesquiou and the Comtesse were essential for Diaghilev's future projects as he combined the knowledge and behavior of an aesthete with the action of a businessman and entrepreneur.

The success of the Russian art show inaugurated a series of Parisian hits for Diaghilev, establishing his reputation as an innovator, impresario, and man-about-town. The next year, 1907, saw Diaghilev and Rimsky-Kosakov organize a set of five Russian music concerts with opera excerpts beginning May 16, 1907. Chaliapin starred (for ₽1,200). This was a sensational triumph, the first experience of Russian opera for the French. Attending were four grand dukes, the Russian ambassador, and Richard Strauss. The ovations would not end, resulting in a scandal when the conductor sought to continue the program but the audience would not be silenced. In disgust, he stomped out of the orchestra pit (Buckle 97–99). The concerts were a sellout but the enterprise still lost Frs. 100,000, covered by Nicholas II (Scheijen 160). In

1908 came the impressive *Boris Godunov* directed by Alexander Sanin and produced by Diaghilev with a chorus composed of singers from the Bolshoi Theatre performing for the first time at the Paris Opéra. This, too, was a sensation.

In 1909, Diaghilev planned a second opera season and at first did not intend to include ballet. In fact, he was not particularly interested in ballet but his collaborator on the *World of Art*, Benois, was keen on the form which had survived in Russia but declined in other countries. He suggested, and then insisted, that Diaghilev present ballet along with opera for two reasons: there was an exceptional company of young male and female dancers at the Mariinsky, including someone named Nijinsky, and a new form of choreography was emerging, that of Michel Fokine who succeeded the recently retired *maestro*, Marius Petipa. Fokine's *Le Pavillon d'Armide* embodied a fresher, more original style. Diaghilev was curious and soon attended Fokine's productions. But only after much persuasion, and even pressure from Benois and others, did Diaghilev agree to include ballet in his forthcoming season and offered Fokine the position of *maitre de ballet.* He appointed S. L. Grigoriev, an associate and assistant of Fokine's, as his *régisseur* or manager.[9] In his account of their first meeting, Grigoriev noted a certain physical habit which suggested a certain puzzle: whenever he smiled, Diaghilev's mouth alone would smile while the rest of his face remained entirely serious. Such a "polite but cold" image suggested a doubleness about the man, Grigoriev wrote (Grigoriev 5). In a later interview, Grigoriev noted that you could never anticipate Diaghilev's reaction; collaboration was always difficult; he changed his mind often (in Lieven 360–61). He presided "czar-like over his productions," monitoring rehearsals, generating publicity, booking theaters, and irritating artists.[10]

In planning the season, Diaghilev worked by committee. Invited to the master's apartment in St. Petersburg, Fokine and Grigoriev joined a group around an oval table in the dining room. A samovar took center stage, manned by his valet, Vasili, who poured out tea. Pencil and paper were set before every member of the committee, while Diaghilev held a large exercise book. Collaboration was for Diaghilev his preferred method, although it contradicted his desire for authority and need for control. Notebooks from Diaghilev record his thoughts, diagrams, costs, revisions, and evolution of individual ballets and programs plus his decisions.[11]

But Diaghilev could be temperamental, his views autocratic even if his knowledge was underdeveloped and he appeared to seek committee input. The creative teas he held almost nightly in his St. Petersburg apartment on Zamiatin Street were known as much for their outbursts as for their creativity.

One time, he angrily dismissed Bakst, throwing his overcoat and boots after him on the street. Two weeks later, he was warmly invited back.

Benois and part of the *Mir iskusstva* group was the start of Diaghilev's committee projects, expanded with the Ballets Russes as he worked with Massine, Bakst, Stravinsky, Picasso, and Satie, to name a few, and of course the dancers, whether Nijinsky or Pavlova. As Diaghilev explained to Benois in a letter of June 14, 1898, the façade of any building was the result of his artistic associates; he was concerned largely with the technical and practical but the façade mattered more to him than the building. According to Benois, Diaghilev spent most of his life building facades, not solid structures. He was not an architect but a "pyrotechnist" and his palaces often crumbled shortly after their construction (Lieven 235–36). Nevertheless, Benois would play an important role in publicizing the Ballets Russes in Russia. His updates on the Russian seasons in Paris appeared as a column in the newspaper *Speech (Rech)*. His and others' reports allowed Russians to share in a national pride generated by Diaghilev's company at the same time he advanced a pan-European culture (Dianina 273).

Surprisingly, Diaghilev did not attempt to create anything of his own in music, his early passion, or ballet but he responded deeply to both, often cutting, rearranging, and revising dances and musical scores with an authority that disguised his lack of technical knowledge. His genius was connoisseurship, Stravinsky calling him "a *barin*," a *grand seigneur.* This meant the reassertion of aristocratic values and taste in contrast to the realist and nationalist schools that had dominated Russian art and music, becoming stale and sentimental in their expression of artistic nationalism.[12] The values of the past guided his conception of an artistic present. What Diaghilev could do technically resembled an assembly, a form of *bricolage*, as in the music for *Cléopâtre*, an assortment from the works of Russian composers. Nevertheless, the remade piece was a success. But soon, after his first season, critics urged him to bring his music up to the level of dance and design displayed in 1909. The music had to match the originality of the designers and dancers.

The Franc, the Ruble, and the Ballets Russes

The relationship between money and ballet is the key to understanding Diaghilev's rise to international acclaim and controversy, underscoring his reliance on patrons, bankers, friends, cheats, and officials. As early as 1898, Savva Mamontov put up five thousand rubles (30 percent of the capital) necessary to launch *Mir iskusstva* with Princess Tenisheva another supporter. But the following year, Mamontov's financial collapse erased any support and in 1900, with the withdrawal of Princess's patronage, the journal faced its demise.[13] But two additional merchant princes stepped in: Ilya Ostrukhov and Sergei Botkin. Both were collectors of the *Mir iskusstva* artists and would soon contribute to Diaghilev's successful 1906 Paris exhibition of Russian art, more specifically the Russian Section at the 1906 Paris *Salon d'automne* which initiated Diaghilev's program of exporting new Russian talent to the West.

The show, designed by Bakst with introductory essays by Diaghilev and Benois, opened six months after Sergei Witte obtained a French-subsidized loan that kept Nicholas II's government in power. The exhibition had political implications in its repackaging Russia, a country that had sought stability after the 1905 revolution, for Europe. Financially, the "Salon Russe" received partial government support but not enough to meet all the expenses. Diaghilev raised some thirty thousand additional rubles in Moscow, a portion from Vladimir Hirschmann, another collector of *World of Art* painters. The exhibit's three honorary chairmen were also contributors. Flattery, recognition, and public notice worked financial wonders.

But critical reception to the art was cool to negative, questioning the existence of an actual Russian art. By 1913, however, critics responded positively to Diaghilev's campaign, favoring his exotic designs in his productions summed up by a new colloquialism: *"C'est très ballets russes."*[14] Many of these figures continued to back Diaghilev as he turned to opera and then ballet, each production having its own patronage committee. Prince Vladimir Argutinsky, for example, personally guaranteed a last-minute loan from an English bank that allowed Diaghilev to complete his preparations for his 1909 Paris season. The prince repeatedly co-signed or signed loans on behalf of Diaghilev and his company, his backers a mixture of the aristocracy and merchant capitalists who united in their support of Diaghilev's ventures (Scheijen 159–61). These included André Benac, managing director of the Banque de Paris, the Turkish-born oil and shipping magnate Basil Zaharoff, and Baron Henri, associated with the Rothschilds. Further patrons emerged as a result of Diaghilev's earlier Russian concert series of 1907 in Paris and included Nikolai van Gilse van der Pals and the St. Petersburg grocery magnate Eliseyev with his distinctive emporium at 56 Nevsky Prospekt.[15] Later supporters would be English, Lady Juliet Duff and Lady Ottoline Morrell two prominent examples. But all this support remained uncertain: no fixed sums existed making budgeting and programming precarious.

But new patrons seemed almost magically to appear. A mysterious Mr. K., the head of a galoshes business, supported the Ballets Russes as part of a quest for a Patent of Nobility, an official designation as a "noble" permitting certain social and tax advantages. Indeed, many of Diaghilev's new backers sought a notice in the press, a name in a program, a Patent of Nobility, or other public acknowledgment through Diaghilev's aristocratic connections, all in the name of "merchant philanthropy" (Garafola 1989: 162). And Diaghilev knew how to cultivate these figures, often inviting them to dress rehearsals encouraged by caviar and champagne. On occasion, he entertained his guests by singing. In a strong baritone, he would perform Rubinstein, Schubert, and Wagner. But ironically, these merchant patrons, key to display their support for the arts and ballet in particular, failed to transfer their business acumen to the arts. Neither the Moscow Art Theater, nor Mamontov's private opera company, nor the Ballets Russes would be self-sustaining or a commercial success. They always remained on a financial precipice (Garafola 1989: 162–63). Diaghilev's solutions ranged from soliciting funds from aristocrats to arranging gruelling overseas tours for his company, always making prosperous managerial arrangements.

The Paris theatrical producer Gabriel Astruc (originally a music publisher) was one of Diaghilev's most important sponsors. But from the start, the promoter knew that money always mattered: the success of Diaghilev's 1909 season in Paris rested on the Russian's promise to raise Frs. 300,000 from Russian sources. This did not happen and set a pattern that saw Diaghilev often in debt to Astruc and others. The first season of the Ballets Russes in Paris, while a critical triumph, was a financial disaster. The gap between production costs and supporting capital left a debt of Frs. 86,000 for Astruc to collect (Garafola 1989: 178). But this was not unusual: throughout his career, Diaghilev never seemed free from debt or financial calamity. Yet he never hesitated in asking for new funds, appealing to the ego of his patrons and the needs of his art. In this manner, he was able to produce revolutionary productions with revolutionary, often (at the time) unknown artists, whether Stravinsky, Picasso, or Satie.

Diaghilev returned to Russia deeply in debt after the Ballets's first Paris season. His efforts to return to Paris succeeded only with the financial help of the wealthy including the Parisian Misia Sert, Polish pianist and widow of a Parisian newspaper magnate, Alfred Edwards; she would later marry the Spanish painter José-Maria Sert.[16] Without such assistance from her and others, it is unlikely Diaghilev and the Ballets Russes could have continued. But within years, the company and Diaghilev were known the world over. By 1917, in the wake of the February Revolution, various factions were even suggesting him as Russia's new Minister of Culture, which found favor with the then prime minister, Kerensky. However, intrigue and influence interfered; the appointment did not happen.

Paris II

Importantly, Diaghilev began to shape his new Parisian audience before his first Ballets Russes season began. His early successes meant partisans and supporters quickly formed, a cultural coterie eager for his new productions. Critics, patrons, journalists, and publicists worked to promote his works, culminating in his 1909 *Saison russe.* What he brought to the theater was a mix of Russian modernism, radical forms, and traditional dances summarized by the dancer Lydia Lopokova: "Diaghilev had the cunning . . . to combine the excellent with the chic, and revolutionary art with the atmosphere of the old regime."[17] Such a blend satisfied public impatience with the moribund found in other, institutionalized dance companies.

The first season of the Ballets Russes opened at Paris's Théâtre du Châtelet using ballet dancers on summer leave from the Mariinsky and Bolshoi theaters to form, but not formalize, the Ballets Russes. Politically, the Tsar was eager to encourage cultural relations with France and allowed Diaghilev to borrow dancers from the Imperial Theaters for his hastily organized new company. In the spring of 1909 the following joined Diaghilev for the assault on Paris: Fokine, Pavlova, Karsavina, Nijinsky, Benois, and Bakst. He returned with his company in 1910 for a second, revolutionary season premiering Stravinsky's *The Firebird,* which became an international sensation. By 1911, many of the dancers ended their formal connection with the Mariinsky to join Diaghilev.

Diaghilev's first ballets in his early Paris seasons de-emphasized a Russian atmosphere, replacing an exotic mystique with something definitely French. The sumptuous and courtly décor by Benois for *Le Pavillon d'Armide* is one example, while Fokine's *Les Sylphides* is another, recalling earlier 19th-century productions. The *Saison russe* of 1909 consisted of a number of one-act ballets, mostly reshaped but standard *pastiches* from the Russian Imperial ballet repertoire. The company was thought a novelty as Romanticism and stylized movements ruled, echoed by *Giselle* in 1910. The French roots of Russian ballet dominated through Fokine's interpretation of the tradition. But Diaghilev knew, as he wrote to the composer Anatoly Lyadov, that a Russian ballet was missing: "I need a *ballet* and a *Russian* one—the *first* Russian ballet, since there is no such thing." There are Russian operas, symphonies, songs, and dance but no ballet, he stressed.[18] This was a crucial statement implicitly outlining the agenda of the Ballets Russes.

A new, Russian ballet—Eastern, mysterious, primitive, *and* modern—did not exist until Diaghilev and company invented it, an evolution which started with Stravinsky's *The Firebird* premiering on June 25, 1910 at the Palais Garnier. This, as Benois understood, was a Russian ballet created to express neo-nationalist arts for export to the West, depicting a world of art inspired by Russian folk traditions arranged as a *pastiche.* What Diaghilev accomplished was not to restage Imperial Russia, which he sensed was dying, but a newly imagined "Slavic ur-Russia, exotic, primitive, modern" and purposely styled for export to the West (Homans, *Mr. B* 113). Importantly, while classical ballet was not new to France, Russian exoticism was. What fascinated Parisian audiences was not the ballet dancing but the "exotic display of Russia."[19]

Tcherepnin was originally to compose the music for *The Firebird* but he declined and then Lyadov was invited but he delayed. Diaghilev briefly considered Glazunov but then approached the younger and less established student of Rimsky-Korsakov, Igor Stravinsky; he accepted. While writing *The Firebird* score, Stravinsky studied ethnographic accounts of native groups, the folk sound of the piece a homage to Russian folk traditions in art and music. This reflected a trend towards the primitive, paralleling the art of Gaugin, African art, and even Picasso. Léon Bakst and Aleksander Golovin created the costumes in a nationalist style with references to peasant arts and crafts. The ballet had no antecedent in Russian art and was expressly (and ironically) created for a non-Russian audience.[20]

Importantly, the Firebird itself was not a woman, although danced by Tamara Karsavina, but an idea. She was a commanding mystery with magical powers, not the eternal woman but eternal Russia as Diaghilev imagined the West conceived her to be (Homans 302). This differed from the exoticism sought by French audiences, but Diaghilev ensured that at least one or two of his ballet slots included a ballet with a dramatic Eastern or Russian theme: *Schéhérazade* and *The Firebird* in 1910, *Sadko* and *Petrouchka* in 1911, *Thamar* and *Le Dieu bleu* in 1912, *Legend of Joseph* and *Le Coq d'Or* in 1914. The public loved sensation and Diaghilev obliged (Garafola 1989: 43).

But why Paris as the incubator of the Ballets Russes? What made it embrace the gossip, dancers, controversies, disputes, and even battles about the company and its productions? What encouraged its promotion of avant-garde music, dance, and design? Was it an eagerness for the experimental, a drive for the new, or simply boredom with the old? Did it have something to do with the nearly 70,000 Russian emigres to Paris after the 1917 Revolution?[21] The importance of the Russia Abroad movement cannot be overlooked. This exile society of uprooted Russians, beginning as early as 1905 and lasting until 1939, formed the basis of a vibrant Russian culture in Berlin and then Paris. And despite geographic distances, they remained in contact with each other sustaining a cultural identity institutionally and individually.

Through newspapers, libraries, social clubs, political organizations, and even neighborhoods, the Russians abroad sustained a Russian culture in exile. Collectively in Europe, but especially in Paris, they provided the bulwark of Diaghilev's Russian supporters and his strenuous efforts to encourage Russian art, opera, and ballet.[22] Diaghilev was by default very much a part of this émigré culture. By the end of 1921, those who lived abroad such as Diaghilev and Stravinsky were stateless, deprived of their citizenship by

Soviet decree. Both had settled in Europe before the revolution but their continued residence meant the loss of their Russian citizenship.[23]

Diaghilev suited Paris and Paris suited him: by 1910 and his second ballet season, he was recognized as an exciting impresario, as well as a cultured *boulevardier,* prima donna, and celebrity who knew how to culturally excite the public. He was at home with the aristocratic high society and the public, putting on an act of supreme intelligence, preferring to sweep into a room rather than merely enter. Part of this might originate in Diaghilev's determination to erase his provincial origins in Perm and eradicate the aura of an outsider. In Paris, he became the ultimate "insider," cultivating the elite and transforming the political economy of ballet into an activity for the middle class. He also remade its operation from a disciplined, conservative practice to something imaginative, creative, intuitive, collaborative, and often disorganized. But it also had spark, inventiveness, and excitement, backstage as well as front-of-house. Publicity was his mainstay, performances his *raison d'etre.*

Le Nouveau

Paris constantly welcomed the new. The socialite Mme. Verdurin in Proust's *À la recherche* declares that she is not "afraid of daring innovations," prompting Mme. de Cambremer to reply that it's "splendid to be advanced, one can never be advanced enough."[24] In simple terms, in Paris it was fashionable to throw off the past. Being *au courant* meant being modern and Paris was determined to be modern.

This Diaghilev offered, challenging the established traditions of Parisian ballet at the same time he acknowledged its cosmopolitanism summarized by the dance critic Louis Énault: "In Paris one learns to dance quickly and well; all the world's *steps* meet there."[25] Diaghilev's charm, taste, and ability to raise money initially convinced his coterie to support original, unorthodox programs expressed by his painters, musicians, and choreographers. Diaghilev's quest for shorter ballets also met with acclaim (and criticism), breaking away from spectacle with its lengthy, tedious music and stilted action. Ballet became compact, tight, more focused and vivid but with a loss of narrative. Detached turns or short scenes replaced dramatic narratives, Diaghilev at one point instructing an American composer to write the music without regard to story or action (Garafola 1989: 137). He also presented ballets with contemporary settings, something novel but which appealed to French tastes.

Diaghilev soon came to embody the avant-garde itself with a retinue of experimental artists, composers, designers, and world-class dancers—but not at once. In fact, he may have embraced them only because he sensed the public's eagerness to be part of the artistically new within a Russian frame.

He was at first hesitant but the attention and publicity of the new work was irresistible. The stage soon became a canvas for the most original and innovative productions yet seen in Paris offered to a public eager to be part of the experiment.

The Ballets Russes always made an impression and the success of Diaghilev's 1910 Paris season, with dancers like Nijinsky and works like *The Firebird* and *Schéhérazade,* brought the ambassadors from America, Russia, and Spain, plus the Vanderbilts, the Rothschilds, and the Armenian oil millionaire, Calouste Gulbenkian; musicians and writers included Ravel, Proust, Gide, and Claudel. All attended and raved about the performances, Proust writing to a friend that Bakst's *Schéhérazade* was unique: "I never saw anything so beautiful." And Diaghilev's social circle widened: Misia Sert introduced him to Debussy, Ravel, and Cocteau.[26] His success was so great that he decided to establish a permanent company in Paris the following year.

But there was also friction, the French feeling exploited by the Russians who occasionally satirized the conservatism of not only the French but the West. Benois made this clear in his reports on the success of the Ballets Russes and the seeming capitulation of the French to the new ideas of the Russians. He belittled French performers and institutions in the *Journal de Saint-Pétersburg* and a Russian newspaper *Speech* (*Rech*). He stressed the success of the Barbarians (the Russians) conquering Rome (the French). "After our stagings," he wrote, "the stagings of the mighty Opéra and the Opéra-Comique will only appear as absurdities from a fairground stall" (in Caddy 132).

The French were not happy. A special sixteen-page edition of a satirical journal presented a comic strip about a "Marianne" who had succumbed to the Russian ballet and Wagnerian music. These "dangerous infatuations" created delirium and the behavior of a madwoman (Caddy 134). This expanded to a critique of cosmopolitanism, embodied by the Ballets Russes and Wagner, both imagined as dangerous and demoralizing. The anxieties aroused by Diaghilev and his company related to issues of national identity now threatened by the Russians who embodied the state of alterity or otherness.[27] A negative discourse grew around the company, extending the fear of a subversive culture. The primitivism once celebrated became a sign of aesthetic decomposition. The unnatural contortions, irregular rhythms, and stamping feet of *Le Sacre* became evidence of artistic deconstruction. The body seen swooning, jumping, falling with knock-kneed angularity was as threatening as it was distorting. Stravinsky's music, some suggested, confirmed the end of music as art (Caddy 146).

Often criticized as being frenetic, untamed, or chaotic in style, the Ballets Russes was also celebrated as decadent and decorative, brutal and civilized. An article in *Vogue* for 1913 neatly summarized this combination stressing their disciplined energy and link to a sophisticated Orientalism. The "message of this art may be semi-Asiatic; the method is more than semi-European. The material may be barbaric; the craftsmanship, if anything, is super-civilized." There was no doubt that in their constant staging of modernism, the company triumphed through its multiple artistic forms.[28]

But the mix of the primitive with the elegant, the erotic with the refined, was impossible to resist and the French found it fascinating. Erotic luxury might be a term for what the Ballets Russes often staged, creating Oriental ballets that drew on a European taste for the exotic. *Schéhérazade* was especially known for its barbarism and refinement. Such works staged savagery and sophistication, and possessed a psycho-sexual appeal which the erotic contained. Embellishing the Oriental provided an undercurrent of the sexual marked by the choreography and body movements of the dancers satisfying a fantasy of entangled bodies enmeshed with jewels, bracelets, and golden fabrics. Freud's "Theory of Psychosexual Development," describing the contest between frustration and pleasure, appeared only four years earlier. The performances of the Ballets Russes may have provided the visual and psychological release of tensions projected in the pent-up sexual energy of the audience. Dance would both release and re-charge.[29]

The Ballets Russes was unusual: it was unaffiliated with either an opera house or commercial theater. Its artistic identity alone defined it. Over time, the company became more international because Diaghilev's many dancers, designers, and musicians were from various countries. His initial group was hesitant to leave the Mariinsky or Imperial Theaters and he had to recruit outside those sources. He turned to the Wielki Theater, Warsaw, or the private Moscow studio of Lydia Nelidova. London theater schools also helped. The turmoil of the First World War, however, jeopardized even this group and led Diaghilev to seek Paris-based artists and composers. Between the debut of Picasso's ballet *Parade* in 1917 and the closure of the company in 1929, almost every well-known Parisian artist and composer designed or wrote for the Ballets Russes including Braque, Gris, Matisse, Ernst, Miró, and de Chirico, plus Strauss, Satie, Ravel, Stravinsky, Prokofiev, and Milhaud.

Emphasis on the male dancer displacing the ballerina furthered interest in the company. It began with Diaghilev's promotion of Nijinsky and the demand for ballets that featured male solos. For Fokine this was an issue; he preferred to create for women offering only small parts for men. But beginning with *Schéhérazade*, Nijinsky took precedence over ballerinas. After *Firebird*, originally conceived for Pavlova, only *Thamar* had a woman as its protagonist. Later male stars like Léonid Massine, Serge Lifar, Anton Dolin, and Adolph Bolm triumphed, controlling the works selected.[30]

Male stories soon dominated: *Petrushka* is about a male puppet, *L'Apres-midi d'un faune* about a god of the forest, part beast, part man. The title characters in *Apollo* and *The Prodigal Son* by Balanchine are male-centric. And the male dancers like Nijinsky astounded with their leaps and delicacy. *Prince Igor*, with its corps of virile men, was so powerful that in reaction to the raw male energy on stage, the audience was reported to have ripped off the orchestra rail in the theater.

Ballerinas were suddenly eclipsed by the virility and power of the men. While Pavlova, Karsavina, and Rubinstein danced to great acclaim with the Ballets Russes, the men excited the audiences more. Ballet no longer centered on the female body or dancer. Pavlova soon left to start her own troupe. Fokine put Karsavina in pants in *The Firebird* and confined her movements. Bronislava Nijinska, Nijinsky's sister, a dancer and choreographer, danced as a male fox in *Le Renard* of 1922. That same year she strapped her breasts down to dance Nijinsky's role in *L'Après-midi.*

The power and athleticism of men could not be overlooked, the hard lines of primitivism turning into the sharp, angular movements of the male dancers. No longer the florid shapes of Art Nouveau, but the Cubist angles and dissonant forms of Picasso's *Les Demoiselles d'Avignon* echoed in Stravinsky's *Le Sacre du printemps*. The masculine character of the Ballets Russes sprang out into the modern culture.[31] But the creation of a male audience of the culturally informed was no accident. Diaghilev's sexual orientation promoted this aura when Nijinsky, Massine, and Lifar became his stars and often his lovers. The stage offered a gay world of sensory pleasure. The Ballets Russes dissected human experience in terms of gay sexuality as no other theater had done. And the escalating male dancer—Rudolf Nureyev, Mikhail Baryshnikov, Yury Grigorovich, and Valery Panov—found their origins in the Ballets Russes. The male body became the embodiment of agency in modern ballet. Importantly, this deviated from what were the traditional gender constructs on the ballet stage in that it merged male and female characteristics. It framed the body, in the words of Ilyana Karthas, "as a powerful social and political tool," offering a platform: "Competing representations of gender identity could be expressed and disseminated in the press" (Karthas 113).

Painters (largely male) were also part of this drive to the new, moving easily, with Diaghilev's encouragement, from the studio to the ballet stage: Golovin and Bakst designed *The Firebird*; Benois designed *Petrushka*; Roerich designed *Le Sacre du printemps*. Their art found dramatic expression and new admirers as Diaghilev continued with significant commissions, such as Picasso's drop curtain for *Le Train bleu,* two expressive giantesses exuberantly running on the seashore.

Musically embodying the pull to the new were Satie, Ravel, and Stravinsky who composed seven ballets and operas for Diaghilev. Dance or ballet music was, in fact, *the* artistic constant in Stravinsky's career. Almost one third of all his music was written for the ballet or ballet-related productions.[32] Most importantly, writing for ballet gave Stravinsky an opportunity to investigate multiple extra-musical sources for composition. He also worked as a sometime musical editor for Diaghilev, re-orchestrating Chopin's *Les Sylphides* for the 1909 season and later Tchaikovsky's *Sleeping Princess* (1921).

New scores were now being written expressly for ballets, movement commanding the notation. Parisian audiences had never before seen such visually exciting Russian exoticism. *The Firebird* drew on an explicit Russian musical tradition yet radically interpreted: human characters were represented diatonically, otherworldly or spiritual ones chromatically. But leitmotifs still distinguished the characters, with the piece containing a larger proportion of narrative music than in Stravinsky's later ballet scores. The work was transitional yet modern with one further radical move: the elimination of applause breaks in order to sustain the audience's involvement. What followed—*Petrushka, Le Sacre du printemps,* and *Le Rossignol,* for example—extended this new aesthetic originating in the folk song technique of distorting normal verbal stress, where sound, itself, became distressed. Characterizing such a practice is the union and disunion between the aural and the visual. The parallel is ritual, rather than straight narrative, shaping the story.

Working with Stravinsky, a new disjunctive mode (especially between costume and design) without conventional dance rhythms occurred, while also drawing on a neo-classical musical style.[33] What evolved to underscore the modernity of these changes is a new equality between the composers, designers, and dancers.

Art and Movement

The innovations of the Ballets Russes subsumed the traditional visual and musical features of ballet, replacing them with the new demands of choreography. Diaghilev, with Fokine, sought a new "alliance of dancing with other arts" in Fokine's words, adapted from Wagner's idea of the total work of art.[34] Artistic coherence was a further goal achieved by Diaghilev by assigning only one artist to a production, although others occasionally joined. Diaghilev's designers ranged from Bakst's colors and fantasies to Picasso and his unique shapes for *Parade.* On multiple levels, Diaghilev broke with convention, while also seeking dramatic and formal consistency. The style of movement must reflect the subject, not the opposite. He generally rejected the *danse d'école* method, although found it useful for training but renounced the structured *pas de deux* supported by an opening adagio, solo variations, and then coda. The bravura dance had no place in his productions, nor the full turn-out, modified by all his choreographers beginning with Fokine who began to substitute parallel positions.[35]

The stage itself was renewed, becoming a spatial forum where artists interacted with other arts and where visually and conceptually modernism went on display. Physically, space was being expressly designed for ballet. And in his overall effort to glamorize his company, Diaghilev chose glamourous theaters, although they were purposely built for opera, not dance. While the stages were deep and wide to accommodate up to fifty dancers plus supernumeraries, they were counter to the new practice of the Ballets Russes: limited dancers and shorter ballets preferring smaller spaces. Newer theatres also had up-to-date lighting with sophisticated front-of-house amenities principally to flatter the crowd. But Diaghilev understood that the questionable status of ballet at the time meant audiences wanted to be seen in such impressive performing spaces as the Paris Opéra, the Royal Opera House, Covent Garden, or the Metropolitan Opera House in New York.

But if such space was not available or pliable, Diaghilev altered existing theaters. In 1919 at the London Coliseum, he had extra lighting installed to supplement spotlights and floodlights. He also insisted that sequins on the front curtain be removed. Their glitter would spoil the lighting effects he had designed, one of his greatest concerns. But without a permanent home, the company needed to tour to maintain income, which meant theaters of varying sizes and adaptability, especially once they left the major cities. In Britain, they often performed in variety halls where there was mixed entertainment. Sightlines and sound were often compromised. Only rarely in the variety halls were their performances presented as independent, if brief, ballet seasons, separate from the variety acts. The Alhambra and Empire in Leicester Square were two theaters where this happened.

But the avant-garde in dance, Russian and otherwise, exploring new forms of movement and sounds, began to enter mainstream entertainment and commerce. Through promotion, publicity, and advertising, it became popular with Parisian audiences filling major theaters, not small or underground venues. Box office receipts alone measured the general interest in the new or experimental which became fashionable. This shift to making the avant-garde central was inescapable, encouraged by the performances of the Ballets Russes which shocked less but surprised more. It also paralleled such developments as Fauvism, Cubism, Futurism, Dadaism, Constructionism, and Expressionism.[36] Newness was unavoidable. Audiences were eager to see original work on stage. The Ballets Russes gained from its association with the artists of the day, Diaghilev's union with these figures enlarging the reputation of the company as part of the cutting edge of the avant-garde.[37]

Diaghilev and his collaborators reframed modernism, which in order to maintain public interest, if not curiosity, had always to be more outlandish and surprising, beginning with *Parade* in 1917 and continuing through the Constructivist production of *La Chatte* in 1927. But even if the reputation

of the company suggested experimental and unique productions, it needed
the support of the *la rive droit* which was more artistically conservative and
bourgeois. Associated with *la rive droite* was elegance, wealth, and a certain
panache in contrast to the more bohemian *rive gauche*, the world of the
artistes who led irregular if creative lives. But what Diaghilev sought in terms
of audience, support, and praise resided in the pocketbooks and checkbooks
of the rich.[38]

Proust

Among Diaghilev's many Parisian admirers, perhaps none was as committed
as Proust who attended the opening night of the Ballets Russes's 1910 season. With his close friend the composer Reynaldo Hahn, Proust saw the
first performance of the opulent *Schéhérazade* choreographed by Bakst and
Fokine, with music by Rimsky-Korsakov (June 4, 1910). Nijinsky was the
slave, and Ida Rubinstein the Sultan's favorite wife. The stage was a green
tent with shadowy blue doors and a large orange carpet. The modernist pageantry thrilled him and he was infatuated with the athletic, eighteen-year-old
Nijinsky who, as the Golden Slave (actually painted gold), acrobatically died
on stage following various sensuous movements. The Orientalism of the ballet was unrestrained and erotic.

Proust would soon celebrate the company through multiple references in
À la recherche du temps perdu, often through Mme. Verdurin who acts as
an "accredited representative in Paris of all foreign artists . . . an aged Fairy
Godmother . . . to the Russian dancers" (Vol. III, 237–38). At one point in
Sodome et Gomorrhe, the narrator refers to Baron de Charlus as a manager
of music who contrived to "place his virtuosity at the service of a versatile
artistic sense. . . . Imagine a purely skilful performer in the Russian ballet
trained, taught, developed in all directions by M. Diaghilev" is Proust's ironic
remark.[39] Mme. Verdurin was also a strong supporter of Wagner, Nijinsky, and
Stravinsky, all direct or indirect contributors to Diaghilev's artistic vision.[40]

To celebrate the premier of Stravinsky's *Le Renard*, on May 18, 1922, the
British writer Sydney Schiff and his wife Violet, friends of Diaghilev, held
a gala dinner at the Majestic Hotel on Avenue Kléber in Paris. It became a
memorable, modernist "after-party" because of five remarkable guests. In
addition to Diaghilev, Picasso, Stravinsky, and Joyce was Proust, the only
time all five ever gathered together. Joyce came late and was tipsy; Proust
came even later at 2:30 a.m., elegant in black with white kid gloves and a fur
coat. According to one account, he possessed "an insinuating air" with "eyes
like Japanese lacquer."[41] But reality deflated the anticipation of such an elec-
tric gathering of these modernist masters. Their meeting fell flat.

At the dinner, Proust spoke effusively to Stravinsky about Beethoven's late quartets (Proust sat between Sydney Schiff and Stravinsky) but found Stravinsky an anti-admirer. Proust and Stravinsky had met before following the 1913 premiere of *Le Sacre du printemps* at a supper party given by Misia Sert who became the model for Princesse Yourbeletieff in *À la recherche*. In the novel, Sert's party becomes a supper held by Mme. Verdurin under the auspices of the Princess with Ballets Russes dancers, Diaghilev, Stravinsky, and Strauss. Proust already knew Diaghilev, having twice attended productions in 1910[42] followed by an intermittent correspondence. The behavior of Charlus in *Sodome et Gomorrhe II* (published only a few weeks before the Majestic evening) has been partly attributed to Diaghilev, notably Charlus' pride over his protégé lovers and autocratic manner. At one point in the novel, he advises Mme. Verdurin on the arrangements of her musical evening "in a peremptory tone which blended the rancorous pride of a crotchety nobleman with the dogmatism of the expert artist in questions of entertainment."[43] These are the characteristics of Diaghilev.

At the Majestic dinner, Proust reluctantly spoke to Joyce, whose most repeated word was "no" to Proust's inquiries, often about acquaintances. Joyce was nervous (partly because he had no evening clothes) and may have been jealous since Proust was touted in Paris as *the* quintessential modernist writer. Schiff's own enthusiasm was for Proust, not Joyce. A coda to the encounter was Joyce apparently forcing himself into Proust's cab, opening a window, and lighting a cigarette before the asthmatic Proust who also hated fresh air. Schiff snatched the cigarette from Joyce's lips and threw it out (D-Hines 39–40, 43)! Ostensibly a party to honor Diaghilev, the evening at the Majestic saw the one and only meeting of the modernist giants of literature, art, and dance. That no fireworks occurred does not diminish the brightness of the gathering. Six months later, Proust would be dead. Diaghilev attended the funeral.

Modernism and Modernity

A modernist tenet is its supposed resistance to commodification. Its own complexity and obscurity ensured its severance from everyday culture. But Diaghilev and the Ballets Russes found it necessary to commodify its art in order to fill its theaters and pay its bills, something Diaghilev learned from his previous efforts with his art exhibits and operas. You need people to pay, even for the new. The challenge for Diaghilev was adapting his art to capitalist modernity where competition and the free market determines the nature and reception of the modern, guided by the desire for profit. But Diaghilev also understood that scarcity drives not only demand but the sense of the new. The innovative and the new "sets and keeps the capitalist engine in motion," the economist Joseph Schumpeter explained.[44] This is what links Diaghilev's drive to be original and the appeal of the box office. The double bind, however, was that while novelty was necessary, it was also impossible in absolute terms. Yet novelty remains "one of the most basic requirements of the capitalist market . . . to be new is necessary" (North 149).

This contradiction—the need to transform the modern into a product while denying such claims—is the paradox at the center of the Ballets Russes story. The public could not stay away because of its eagerness to see the groundbreaking dances, costumes, colors, and art of the company even if they could not understand it. But to see, they had to pay, enticed by the company's promotional methods, often relying on flamboyant posters, elaborate programs, and constant publicity. Ironically, the disavowal of the commercial, according to modernist practice, masked the need for economic success, while generating symbolic capital (reputation, prestige) and actual capital (funds to continue).[45] This in fact alienated several of his most important musical contributors, Stravinsky writing to Benois in 1914 that this Diaghilev

> business isn't for me. Precisely because its artistic life is over, and is now pure commerce—which is the one thing that stops me (since I survive on it) from breaking with this international soldier's club.[46]

Furthermore, Diaghilev and the Ballets Russes could not avoid the social, political, and artistic upheavals of the early 20th century. Its new directions in dance, underscored by modern steps, forms, and notations, was partly a response to social and political changes in the culture at large. The backdrop was the emergence of other new art forms: cinema, radio, photography, musical recordings, and mass printing. Modernism was contradictory, disorienting, and confusing; the world was no longer orderly or fixed. A minimalist narrative satisfied as much as a realist one. Inspired by Isadora Duncan's St. Petersburg performances in 1904, 1907, and 1909, a dance without a plot emerged. Her performances in the Hall of Nobles with the cream of St. Petersburg's fashionable and artistic society showed Diaghilev that art could appeal and succeed even when the performance lacked a story. Ida Rubinstein was another revolutionary figure in *fin-de-siècle* Russia who wished to dance free of her clothing and re-appropriate her body.[47] She was best known for her provocative role as Salomé not in a controversial 1908 St. Petersburg production of the play (shut down after a dress rehearsal) but as a Salomé/Cleopatra figure in Diaghilev's 1909 *Cléopâtre* premiering in Paris. In her dance of the veils, emerging from a casket on stage and unwinding a lengthy shroud, she became a threatening, destabilizing femme fatale.[48]

For Diaghilev, passion for artistic innovation often meant provocation which he repeatedly sought: he encouraged controversy because it would bring more supporters, critics, patrons, and audience members. This was part of his circular double vision: be more provocative in order to attract larger audiences and generate more funding which would, in turn, allow him to be more artistically intimidating. But to do so, he had to exert more artistic and professional control, overseeing the programming, contracts, publicity, casting, music, and dancers, assuming full creative responsibility. In other terms, he revolutionized new media techniques, fulfilling Benjamin's call for the remaking of artistic modes of production itself. The revolutionary artist is concerned with not only a revolutionary message but altering the mode of production itself. The way a dance was produced was as critical as its content, although that could have several contradictory possibilities of interpretation. This form of "complex seeing" (the term is Brecht's) both invited and alien-ated audiences.[49] Diaghilev's principal agent for conveying such changes was publicity: for his season of twelve ballets in Paris in the spring of 1922, he had not only the support of two papers, but of the Prince and Princess of Monaco who attended a rehearsal of *Les Biches* on May 24, described at length in the press. Other attendees, duly noted, included Prince Edmond de Polignac, the Duchesse d'Ayen, Lord Berners, and Picasso, plus Poulenc and Milhaud (Buckle 428).

The postwar period of the Ballets Russes saw its cachet, and that of Diaghilev's fame, fade as its programming became less revolutionary and finances less dependable. After the war, an anti-Romantic direction emerged in productions with a new athletic aesthetic, what Cocteau called *choses en soi* ("things in themselves"). This might be dance in itself without musi-cal consistency such as *Les Femmes de Bonne Humeur* (1917) and later Poulenc's *Les Biches* (1924). These changes were efforts by Diaghilev to get Paris "to recognize the European Russia he loved" (Taruskin 211). Patrons now played an even more crucial role, Sir Joseph Beecham in England per-haps the most generous, although audiences, not finding the excitement of the earlier years, declined. An "aesthetic malaise" settled on the company as artifice replaced dramatic tension. Diaghilev produced what he called "musiquettes" demanded by the *faubourg*.[50] He was unable to keep up with changing Parisian taste.

The box office now seemed more critical than ever and began to more directly fashion the programming. Indebtedness and obligations to Beecham and others soon ruled as pressure intensified to produce works for an audience Diaghilev needed to support the company. The public still admired shock and color but not the experimentation that brought the company its early renown. Ballet still had to astonish but also satisfy middle-class expectations.

With less startling and revolutionary performances, the company itself weakened. By June 1918, Russians comprised a minority of the dancers. Of the thirty-nine dancers, eighteen were Russian with only ten trained at the

Mariinsky or Bolshoi. Twelve were Polish, with four Italians, two Spaniards, and two Englishwomen. No longer could the company legitimately be called a Russian enterprise (Garafola 1989: 96).[51] What did save the company was Monte Carlo where increasing support and box office success allowed Diaghilev a reprieve from growing debts, fewer productions, and declining public interest. A short season of twelve performances in April 1922, however, was a challenge because the company had to rehearse works which had not been performed for a year; dancers had forgotten their steps (Grigoriev 176). But Monte Carlo was home: as early as 1911, the company had visited, using the Monte Carlo theater, designed by the architect of the Paris Opéra, as their rehearsal and performance space (Grigoriev 48–50 passim).

Money and Style

Although "terms like cost-effectiveness and productivity rarely enter discussions of ballet history," writes Lynn Garafola in *Diaghilev's Ballets Russes*, such matters are the core of the Ballets Russes story (Garafola 1989: 262). Without attention to contracts, fees, production costs, and bank accounts, the company could not continue. Neglect of such matters would often end up in court. Rastorgoueff, Mrs. Bewicke, Gulbenkian, and Nijinsky all brought lawsuits against Diaghilev, mostly for failure to execute contracts. He, in turn, brought actions against Fokine, and Ksenia Makletzova.

Declining wages and arbitrary personnel decisions created tension and occasional, if limited, disruptions with dancers threatening to strike or carpenters refusing to work. Dancers initially fared well with wages above their contemporaries at the Paris Opéra but pay scales soon declined during and after the war years. The depreciation of the franc between 1923 and 1926 did not help as the cost of living rose and the value of the franc declined (Garafola 1989: 262). Within the company, a divide emerged between the seeming aura of wealth among the stars and company leaders, and the impoverishment of the dancers. In the spring of 1924, for example, the dancers threatened to strike unless they received a 25 percent raise; reluctantly, Diaghilev agreed to 20 percent. In 1925, forty-two dancers petitioned Diaghilev to raise salaries further: they were unable to pay rent for hotel rooms in Paris or Monte Carlo. Diaghilev addressed them with a mix of threats and a plea for sympathy for his financial plight. He won them over (Garafola 1989: 263–64).

But financial tensions meant the forfeiture of Slavic intensity, collective creativity, and a belief in the importance of art because receipts, not aesthetics, now fashioned their vision. "Market values sapped imaginative energy," Garafola summarizes (Garafola 1989: 311). One had to produce works for which an audience already existed. Diaghilev faced such challenges as early as 1914 with indebtedness causing a shift to productions that substituted spectacle for artistic challenge. Business and art solidified their union but with debilitating consequences for the Ballets Russes's originality.

And Diaghilev? He was still a presence but after the war more backstage than front-of-house.[52] He increasingly depended on patrons but they were sparse, especially postwar. Lord Rothermere became pivotal: his liaison with the dancer Alicia Nikitina encouraged company support. In reality, however, Diaghilev actually used his dancer Sokolova to solicit funds from Rothermere. She spoke English and was acquainted with him. At a late March 1926 dinner, in Paris, he ordered her to dance with Rothermere. She told him she had no experience extracting large sums from rich men. But at the Carlton Hotel, Diaghilev told her now was the time to dance with the lord. She obeyed and after two dances, summoned the courage to ask. Rothermere hesitated but agreed only after he made it clear that he would underwrite a London season *not* for Diaghilev's sake but for hers. But at the same dinner, he also began to pursue Nikitina (Buckle 465). Diaghilev used his dancers as emissaries to find money from approachable (and usually older) men.

But Rothermere's largesse, designed to spotlight his current dancer favorite, was mercurial. When he suddenly withdrew his support, Diaghilev faced another crisis. To gain more funds, he at one point sold portions of Picasso's hand-brushed curtain for *Le Tricorne* to a German collector for Frs. 175,000 (Garafola 1989: 260). But he also realized he had to acquiesce to Rothermere's demands. When *Apollo* was to open in London in June 1928, Diaghilev asked the dancer Danilova if she would object if Nikitina could dance the part of the Terpsicore on the first night. "Otherwise, I shall lose £3,000," he told her. She agreed (Buckle 502). Another sponsor at this time was Cole Porter, partly because of his infatuation with Boris Kochno.[53] But the views of many were turning against the impresario, Lydia Lopokova remarking that Diaghilev was a "wicked prima donna with intrigues."[54]

During and after the war, audiences shifted—from the *haute-monde* to middle-class music and theatre lovers. Audiences had become democratized and the six prewar years of greatness for the company were fading, especially as it became more and more evident that Diaghilev, who had built his career and company on shifting credit and an unpredictable box office, needed more financial security from audiences that demanded less, not more, artistically. He tried to economize using cheaper materials for sets and costumes while engaging less costly and lesser-known conductors and dancers.

But the Ballets Russes did not go out of vogue, nor disappear without a flourish. They stayed in the public's eye but more for fashion than dance. Critics covered the dance programs but the focus was on décor, stage design, and costumes. Sonia Delaunay, costumer and set designer, transformed a remounted 1918 production of *Cléopâtre*'s Oriental heroine into a chic Parisienne, more a modern art work and fashion model than Egyptian priestess. Her outfit drew attention to her costume, not the ballet, turning the audience into shoppers rather than ballet fans as the stage became a store window. Publicity soon featured the outfits, dancers, and décor. Attention went to Coco Chanel and her radical costumes for *Le Train bleu* of June 1924 rather than to the music or the dancers.

Soon, what people wore to the ballet, not the ballet itself, became of greater interest. The society pages featured who, not what, went on at the Ballets Russes, British *Vogue* especially, between 1924 and 1926, featuring the social not artistic side of the company. The ballets had only a glancing interest as commerce edged out art. Rather than pursue an audience of dance partisans, Diaghilev chose to seek consumers of the new who wanted to show that they understood and imitated the latest styles and habits seen on stage. But this vanguard was too small and could not support his enterprise; guided by the whims of the marketplace, his supporters soon moved on, ironically anticipated by Proust. In "The Captive," he writes that "society is like sexual behavior, in that no one knows what perversions it may develop" (Proust 236). Or as the British composer Constant Lambert wrote, "Before the war Diaghilev created a vogue for Russian ballet, after the war he created merely a vogue for vogue."[55]

Funds were now in short supply as Diaghilev came in for criticism over his *jejune* music, unexciting productions, and sense of artistic fatigue. "Parisian" became a pejorative term. A scathing 1927 review of *La Chatte* claimed that it lacked originality but not fashionableness; instead of art, there was only novelty. Between 1918 and 1922, Diaghilev anglicized ballet; afterwards, it took a French turn but never recovered. Café society and the Cote d'Azur reigned. A reviewer of his last Paris season (May 1929) devastatingly wrote that the Russian ballet was no longer to be "regarded as a serious manifestation of contemporary art." André Levinson went even further claiming in the 1929 *La Danse d'aujourd'hui* that "no one has served, or betrayed, Russian ballet like Serge Diaghilev."[56]

But as Diaghilev aged and his artistic impact diminished, he did not lose his presence: dining with the impresario in London after a performance of *Le Fils prodigue* in July 1929, Harold Acton wrote that "the ageing magician was feverishly gay" and resembled King Fuad of Egypt who had attended the performance. Both, he added, "had the same tyrannical eyes, the same air of Oriental opulence" (Buckle 534–35). But within a month Diaghilev would be dead, dying penniless in Venice at the Grand Hotel des Bains. Misia Sert and Coco Chanel paid for his funeral. Lifar attempted to jump into the grave, a tragic but theatrical end for the "Napoleon of the arts." Within months, the company disbanded.[57]

NOTES

1. Serge Lifar, *Ma Vie from Kiev to Kiev: An Autobiography*, trans. James Holman Mason (London: Hutchinson, 1970) 26.

2. Richard Buckle, *Diaghilev* (New York: Atheneum, 1979) 160. Hereafter Buckle.

3. Katia Dianina, *When Art Makes News: Writing Culture and Identity in Imperial Russia* (DeKalb, IL: NIU Press, 2013) 28. Hereafter Dianina.

4. Diaghilev, "The Eternal Conflict," in Joan Acocella, "Diaghilev's 'Complicated Questions,'" *The Ballets Russes and Its World,* ed. Lynn Garafola and Nancy Van Norman Baer (New Haven: Yale Univ. Press, 1999) 72–73.

5. Diaghilev in Dianina 272.

6. For parallels to the Silver Age, see John Bowlt, *The Silver Age: Russian Art of the Early Twentieth Century and the "World of Art" Group* (Newtonville, MA: Oriental Research Partners, 1979) 272.

7. Scheijen 132–33. The art historian Igor Gabar vividly wrote that Diaghilev "possessed a unique visual memory and an iconographic nose, and . . . put the rest of us to shame" (in Scheijen 133).

8. Diaghilev in Geoffrey Marsh, "Serge Diaghilev and the Strange Birth of the Ballets Russes," *Diaghilev and the Golden Age of the Ballets Russes 1909–1929*, ed. Jane Pritchard (London: V&A Publishing, 2010) 15. Also useful on Diaghilev and a new aesthetic is Peter Wollen, "Fashion/Orientalism/The Body," *New Formations* 1 (Spring 1987): 21–22.

9. S. L. Grigoriev, *The Diaghilev Ballet 1909–1929*, trans. Vera Bowen (London: Constable, 1953) 3. Hereafter Grigoriev. Grigoriev provides a detailed and important chronicle of the ballet company's twenty years beginning with his surprise selection as *régisseur* (4–5). He was to be in charge of multiple business aspects, beginning with contracts for the dancers but not finances. They remained with Diaghilev. Grigoriev's volume is one of the most valuable narratives for its details on the daily operation of the company and Diaghilev's habits.

10. Jennifer Homans, *Mr. B: George Balanchine's 20th Century* (New York: Random House, 2023) 113. Hereafter *Mr. B.*

11. His so-called "Black Notebook" is at the New York Public Library for the Performing Arts, Lincoln Center. His notebook for 1926–1929, which includes notes for his revision of Balanchine's *The Triumph of Neptune*, is at the Music Division of the Library of Congress, Washington, DC. Another useful notebook is Massine's from 1917–1918 at the Victoria & Albert Museum, London. It deals with *Le tricorne* and contains choreographic diagrams plus other notes. The ballet premiered in London on July 22, 1919 with sets and costumes by Picasso.

12. Richard Taruskin, "The Antiliterary Man: Diaghilev and Music," *On Russian Music* (Berkeley: Univ. of California Press, 2009) 203. Hereafter Taruskin. Taruskin believes Diaghilev had only a "contingent" relation to the culture of his time and has been "as easily overrated as underrated" (212). The essay originally appeared in 1989. Another useful text is Taruskin's *Defining Russia Musically: Historical and Hermeneutical Essays* (Princeton: Princeton Univ. Press, 1997).

13. W. A. Propert, in *The Russian Ballet in Western Europe, 1909–1920* (London: John Lane, 1921), claims that the cost to produce each issue of the *World of Art* magazine (1899–1904) was approximately six times its selling price (11).

14. Jane Ashton Sharp, *Russian Modernism between East and West: Natal'ia Goncharova and the Moscow Avant-Garde* (Cambridge: Cambridge Univ. Press, 2006, 2018) 145–46. Hereafter Sharp.

15. The Russian tradition of wealthy industrial and commercial magnates participating in and supporting the arts might be epitomized by Sergei Shchukin, a textile manufacturer who assembled one of the greatest modernist art collections in the world. See Natalya Semenova, et al., *The Collector: The Story of Sergei Shchukin and His Lost Masterpieces* (New Haven: Yale Univ. Press, 2018). Shchukin invited Matisse to Moscow. He came in 1911. Another key collector and patron was Ivan Morozov

16. Alfred Edwards at first directed *Le Matin* at its inception in 1884 but then founded his own journal, *Le Matin Français.* He re-acquired *Le Matin* and merged the two papers under the *Le Matin* name.

17. Lopokova in Jennifer Homans, *Apollo's Angels,* 290. In 1925, Lopokova would marry the economist John Maynard Keynes. Hereafter Homans.

18. Diaghilev to Lyadov in Homans, *Apollo's Angels*, 301.

19. Ilyana Karthas, *When Ballet Became French: Modern Ballet and the Cultural Politics of France, 1909–1958* (Montreal: McGill-Queen's Univ. Press, 2015) 78. Hereafter Karthas.

20. On the stylistic distinctions of *The Firebird*, see Taruskin 208–10.

21. On this topic, see Natalia Starostina, "On Nostalgia and Courage: Russian Émigré Experience in Interwar Paris through the Eyes of Nadezhda Teffi," *Diasporas* Vol. 22 (2013). https://journals.openedition.org/diasporas/213.

Also see Ilyana Karthas, "The Émigrés," *When Ballet Became French: Modern Ballet and the Cultural Politics of France, 1909–1958* (Montreal: McGill-Queen's Univ. Press, 2015) 52–59, and Helen Rappaport, *After the Romanovs: Russian Exiles in Paris from the Belle Époque through Revolution and War* (New York: St. Martin's Press, 2022). From Turgenev to Ilya Repin, Paris was home.

22. See Marc Raeff, *Russia Abroad: A Cultural History of the Russian Emigration, 1919–1939* (1990), G. N. Slobin's *Russians Abroad, Literary and Cultural Politics of Diaspora (1919–1939* (Boston: Academic Studies Press, 2013), Daniela Munteanu's "Self and Mission in Russia Abroad," master's thesis, Central European University (2021). file:///C:/Users/Ira/Downloads/munteanu_daniela.pdffile:///C:/Users/Ira/Downloads/munteanu_daniela.pdf.

23. Lynn Garafola, *La Nijinska: Choreographer of the Modern* (New York: Oxford, 2022) 81. Hereafter Garafola, *La Nijinska*.

24. Proust, "Cities of the Plain," *Remembrance of Things Past*, trans. C. K. Scott Moncrieff and Terence Kilmartin, Vol. II (New York: Random House, 1981) 919–20.

25. Louis Énault in Áine Larkin, "Theatre and Dance," *Marcel Proust in Context,* ed. Adam Watt (Cambridge: Cambridge Univ. Press, 2013) 98.

26. Proust in a letter of March 4, 1911. See Modris Eksteins, *Rites of Spring: The Great War and the Birth of the Modern Age* (Toronto: Lester & Orpen Dennys,

1989) 339, n. 10. Also see Ursula Rehn Wolfman, "Misia Sert—Muse and Patron to Poets, Painters and Musicians (II), *Interlude.* July 10, 2016. https://interlude.hk/misia -sert-muse-patron-poets-painters-musicians-ii/. Sert's musical soirees were legendary: Caruso would perform, while Ravel, Satie, Milhaud, Poulenc, and Stravinsky would often play.

27. There was even an element of anti-Semitism. Astruc, Diaghilev's Paris promoter, was the son of a rabbi thought to have too strong an interest in foreign, anti-French culture. Similarly Bakst, also Jewish, and held to account because of his portrayal of sex on stage through his costumes. Gunzburg, the Russian Jewish banker supporting the company, was another figure. And at one point, even the audience for the Ballets Russes was cited as being too Jewish by the critic Maurice Denis. Proust alluded to these matters in a comparison to the Dreyfus Affair in Vol. III of *À la recherche du temps perdu.* See Caddy 136–37.

28. "The Russian Ballet as Presented by Diaghilev," *The World in Vogue*, ed. Bryan Holme and Katherine Tweed (New York: Viking, 1963) 77. Also useful on the influence of the Ballets Russes on style are Davinia Caddy, *The Ballets Russes and Beyond* (Cambridge: Cambridge Univ. Press, 2012) and Juliet Bellow, *Modernism on Stage: The Ballets Russes and the Parisian Avant-garde* (Burlington, VT: Ashgate, 2013).

29. A later expression of such tension is Jerome Robbins' ballet "Afternoon of a Faun" set to Debussy, created in 1953. It is a *pas de deux* set in a rehearsal room with the two figures sexually attracted to, and repelled by, each other.

30. On this topic, see Lynn Garafola, "Reconfiguring the Sexes," *The Ballets Russes and Its World,* ed. Garafola and Baer, 245–68.

31. For a suggestive discussion of the importance of the male dancer, see Sarah Kaufman, "Ballets Russes, and the enduring dancing man," *Washington Post*, May 10, 2013. https://www.washingtonpost.com/entertainment/museums/ballets-russes-and -the-enduring-dancing-man/2013/05/09/0d367e1c-b7ef-11e2-b94c-b684dda07add _story.html.

Rodin's sculpture of Nijinsky, Picasso's 1917 portrait of Massine, Frödman-Cluzel's statue of Bolm as the Polovtsian Chief from *Prince Igor*, Picasso's costume for the Chinese Conjuor from *Parade*, Matisse's costume for a Mandarin from the *Song of the Nightingale*, Cocteau's sketch "Stravinsky at the Piano" are all signs of the masculine impact on art beyond ballet.

32. George B. Stauffer, "Foreword," in Charles M. Joseph, *Stravinsky's Ballets* (New Haven: Yale Univ. Press, 2011) xi.

33. Stephanie Jordan, "Igor Stravinsky and Ballet as Modernism," *Stravinsky in Context*, ed. Graham Griffiths (Cambridge: Cambridge Univ. Press, 2021) 166–67.

34. Fokine quoted in Juliet Bellow, *Modernism on Stage: The Ballets Russes and the Parisian Avant-Garde* (Burlington, VT: Ashgate, 2013) 1.

35. Useful on this point is Valerie Grieg, *Inside Ballet Technique* (Hightstown, NJ: Princeton Book Publishers, 1994).

36. Highlighting these parallels are Renato Poggioli, *The Theory of the Avant-Garde*, trans. Gerald Fitzgerald (Cambridge, MA: Belknap, 1968) and Peter Bürger's *Theory*

of the Avant-Garde, trans. Michael Shaw (Minneapolis: Univ. of Minnesota Press, 1984).

37. Garafola 1989: 261. Garafola even claims that Diaghilev assisted in the birth of "the market for twentieth-century art" (261).

38. In Paris, the Ballets Russes retained an audience of the social elite but in London, the company cut across class lines and had a populist following drawing on the middle, and on occasion, the working classes through performances in music halls. An "economic egalitarianism" replaced private patronage (Garafola 1989: 340).

39. Proust, *Sodom and Gomorrah,* trans. C. Scott Moncrieff and Terence Kilmartin, rev. D. J. Enright (New York: Modern Library, 2003) 420–21. In the complete *À la recherché,* this appears as *The Cities of the Plain.*

40. Not to be outdone, Joyce would allude to the Ballets Russes several times in *Finnegans Wake* (FW 378.29–30).

41. Richard Davenport-Hines, *Proust at the Majestic* (London: Bloomsbury, 2006) 28, 31. Hereafter D-Hines.

42. Proust, "The Captive," *Remembrance of Things Past,* Vol. Two, trans. C. K. Scott Moncrieff (New York: Random House, 1932) 238.

43. Proust, "The Captive," *Remembrance of Things Past,* Vol. Two, 540; D-Haines 167.

44. Joseph Schumpeter, *Capitalism, Socialism and Democracy* (New York: Harper, 1950) 17.

45. Pierre Bourdieu refers to this as the "production of belief" in ch. 2 of *The Field of Cultural Production,* ed. Randal Johnson (New York: Columbia Univ. Press, 1993) 74–111. "The art business," he explains, is "a trade in things that have no price" (74). Hereafter Bourdieu.

46. Stravinsky to Benois, July 24, 1914, in Stephanie Jordan, *Stravinsky Dances: Re-Visions across a Century* (Alton, Hampshire: Dance Books, 2007) 41.

47. Nicoletta Misler, "Dressing Up and Dressing Down: The Body of the Avant-garde," *Amazons of the Avant-garde,* ed. John Bowlt and Matthew Drutt (London: Royal Academy of Arts, 1999) 101.

48. On Rubinstein and Salomé, see Olga Matich, "Gender Trouble in the Amazonian Kingdom: Turn-of-the-Century Representations of Women in Russia," *Amazons of the Avant-garde,* 81–87. To startle, Rubinstein would sometimes disrobe in public to display her long and lithe body (Matich 85). Her most overtly androgynous role was that of St. Sebastian in D'Annunzio's *The Martyrdom of Saint Sebastian* (1911).

49. Brecht's term refers to making contradictions visible to the audience, exposing links between opposites: money and power, injustice and greed. His characters and productions are built on contradictions. See Stephen Unwin, *The Complete Brecht Toolkit* (London: Nick Hern Books, 2014) 67.

In multiple ways, Diaghilev's productions anticipate aspects of Brecht, beginning with dance that is counterintuitive and defined by contrasting perspectives. Brecht's 1937 essay "The Popular and the Realistic" implicitly contains several principles of Diaghilev.

50. Garafola 1989: 311; Taruskin 211. The term referred to the suburbs, areas outside the city, beginning in the 16th century.

51. However, the accompanying staff was all Russian and included a hairdresser, prop man, wardrobe master, and chief machinist.

52. For a sense of his personality and companionship, see Sacheverell Sitwell in John Drummond, *Speaking of Diaghilev* (London: Faber and 1997) 271–78. Sitwell wrote the scenario for Diaghilev's only English ballet, *The Triumph of Neptune.*

53. Scheijen 405. But on Diaghilev's prickly relationship with Cole Porter, see Buckle 458–59, 473.

54. Lydia Lopokova, *Lydia and Maynard Letters*, ed. Polly Hill and Richard Keynes (London: Andre Deutsch, 1989) 266.

55. Constant Lambert, *Music Ho! A study of music in decline* (London: Faber and Faber, 1966) 86.

56. Garafola 372–73, 374; Levinson, "A Crisis in the Ballets Russes," *André Levinson on Dance: Writings from Paris in the Twenties,* ed. Joan Acocella and Lynn Garafola (Hanover, NH: Wesleyan Univ. Press, 1991) 63.

57. Scheijen 440; Garafola 1989: ix. On Lifar attempting to jump into the grave, see Nina Lobanov-Rostovsky, "Diaghilev's Death," *Diaghilev and the Golden Age of the Ballets Russes 1909–1929,* ed. Jane Pritchard, 206.

To pay its debts, the majority of the company's costumes, scores, and sets stored in Paris were sold to a New York impresario who considered reforming the company in the U.S. The 1929 Crash prevented the move.

Chapter 2

Imperial Steps or
Movement and Money

Did the Ballets Russes reach its goals in its search for the total work of art? Did the effort to combine dance with new music, choreography, and set design succeed in shaping a unified vision? Did simplification of movement on stage add complexity to ballet as T. S. Eliot (a fan of the company) described in July 1921 in praise of their latest London season?[1] And did these actions reflect the cultural changes and shifts of modernism? Did the company balance experimental, visionary, and original productions, the source of its reputation, with box office requests for traditional works? In short, did the Ballets Russes sustain itself artistically despite its financial failings?[2]

Diaghilev stated his ideals when he explained that the secret of his company was the renunciation of ideas "in favor of an elemental spontaneity." He sought an art that could convey the complexity of life expressing passions and feelings separate from words and ideas "not rationally but elementally." Nijinsky translated this concept into his movements, the English patron Lady Ottoline Morrell telling him that "when you dance, you are not a man—you are an idea."[3]

Diaghilev's concept of ballet, enacted by his choreographers, incorporated natural movement, irregular positioning, original music, avant-garde set design, and innovative costumes. In addition, he combined temporal juxtapositions, ironic distancing, and stylized, neo-primitivism into a new conception of dance, jettisoning artificiality, formality, and even plot. Sets were no longer just backdrops but integrated with the actual music and action. His aim was to empower new stage and dance techniques to reflect the changing modern world, revoking the moribund and immobile dances of the past. He rejected the formulaic moves, prescribed outfits (mostly tutus and tiaras), and identical turns, whether the ballet was set in the Russian countryside or a baroque ballroom in France. But he also knew that to draw audiences, he had to constantly renew the old as well as the new.

Between 1917 and 1920, Diaghilev abandoned the exoticism and eroticism, with their Russian inflections, that made the name of the Ballets Russes; substituting was an "international modernism: clean, dry and angular."[4] The avant-garde, as he understood it, expanded its hold as new composers and designers began to create: in addition to Stravinsky, there were Poulenc, Auric, Satie, and Milhaud. Matisse, Braque, Utrillo, Miró, de Chirico, Juan Gris, and Max Ernst began to design his sets. But he used these artists only once, suggesting an impatience with any standard style. Only Picasso was a repeat: he designed six ballets for Diaghilev, confirming the shift from dance with Russian characteristics to one more abstract with bold designs and striking colors. Diaghilev allowed Picasso freedom and space, the chance to work on a proscenium-wide scale.

But Diaghilev's renunciation of the avant-garde was not complete: he turned to the vanguard of Russian artists beginning with Natalia Goncharova and Mikhail Larionov, and then to the Russian Constructivists Naum Gabo and Antoine Pevsner. The two designed an unorthodox plastic and metal set for *La Chatte* of 1927. At the time, Diaghilev was also friends with Mayakovsky and Meyerhold, who had his own theater in Moscow from 1920 to 1938; Diaghilev repeatedly and unsuccessfully sought to persuade Meyerhold to direct a ballet for him to enlarge his avant-garde repertoire.[5] Earlier, Meyerhold's stylized dance and theatrical method had influenced Nijinsky's choreography for *L'Après-midi de faune.* Stressing an inner rhythm, Meyerhold sought, in his own words, a "melodious style of delivery and movement in slow motion . . . designed to preserve the implicitness of expression" (in Garafola 1989: 55).

But Diaghilev could be unsympathetic to those who would not follow his conversion to modernism, often eliminating them, Bakst the most notorious example. With his ravishing exotic sets, Bakst made the prewar Ballets Russes a must-see company. But after the war, Diaghilev felt Bakst was *passé*. He promised Bakst the job of designing Stravinsky's opera *Mavra* (1922) but at the last minute, for an unclear reason, replaced Bakst with the Russian modernist Léopold Survage. Bakst took Diaghilev to court; the two men never spoke to each other again.

But to define the evolving visions of the Ballets Russes is first to identity the practice of the company which differed markedly from its predecessors, specifically the Imperial Ballet. In Russia, ballet had a long tradition as a serious art, its formality and elegance duplicating the values of the Court, the Tsar, and the Romanovs.[6] The Court especially venerated the formal and elaborate performances produced for almost sixty years by the ballet master Marius Petipa.

Imperial Steps I

Ironically, despite its being the diametrical opposite in dance and music, the Ballets Russes would *not* have happened without the traditions of the Imperial Ballet and its school. Its performances at the Imperial Theaters set a standard of excellence admired by court members, the aristocracy, choreographers, and the public frequently recorded in nineteenth-century Russian literature. References appear in Dostoevsky's *The Idiot* (part II, ch. 1), ch. 4 of *The Brothers Karamazov*, and Tolstoy's *Anna Karenina* (part 4, chs. 1 and 7).

In *War and Peace*, ballet and dance are present in almost every Book. In Book One, for example, we read that "the count, with playful ceremony somewhat in ballet style, offered his bent arm to Márya Dmítrievna."[7] In Book Four, chapter II: 262, Tolstoy writes that "Natásha rose and went out of the room on tiptoe, like a ballet dancer." Later, just before Natásha sings, Tolstoy remarks that "having lifted her head and let her arms droop lifelessly, as ballet dancers do, Natásha, rising energetically from her heels to her toes, stepped to the middle of the room and stood still" (Book Four, ch. XIV: 298). In Book Seven, ch. VII: 453–54, she dances an impromptu folk dance, while in Book Eight, ch. IX, she attends a European opera with dance in its third act including the French virtuoso Louis Duport who jumped high "and waved his feet very rapidly" (Book Eight, ch. IX: 501).[8]

Earlier, in *Eugene Onegin*, the intense and disciplined director of the ballet at the St. Petersburg opera, Didelot, appears. In Canto I, Stanza XVIII, Onegin attends the ballet but is immediately bored. Letting his glance fall on the stage, he yawns and exclaims,

> "We must change 'em all!"
> I long by ballets have been bored,
> Now Didelot scarce can be endured! (Canto I, XVIII)

Didelot had no patience for turns or jumps, preferring formal arrangements and measured steps. In the preceding verse, however, Pushkin praises the classical dancing of the Russian Avdotia Istomina, the most celebrated ballerina of the 19th century Imperial Ballet.[9]

By the late 1880s, however, the Imperial Ballet had lost most of its energy remounting standardized programs. But at the same time, it was virtually impossible for independent ballet companies to survive: they had neither the resources, dancers, nor connections at court or with the nobility to continue. However, the appearance of the Italian ballerina Virginia Zucchi, who performed in St. Petersburg in 1885, brought change. She introduced Italian techniques with a virtuosity that allowed for freedom from the rigid, if classical, Russian style. Seeing her perform, the Tsar insisted she join the

Mariinsky Theater and then the Bolshoi where she danced until 1888. Her popularity helped to revitalize public interest in ballet. A liaison with a nobleman, however, led to her banishment from the Imperial stages. Nevertheless, her intense and dramatic style partially inspired the "World of Art" movement and the eponymous art magazine created by Diaghilev, Léon Bakst, and Alexandre Benois. The loosely organized program of the movement grew to refract Russian Symbolism which paid attention to aesthetic unity through the simultaneous exploration of multiple media. Bakst, for example, was an artist, fashion designer, and even novelist.[10]

The administration of the Imperial Ballet and Theatres reflected its conservatism. The Tsar appointed the directors of the Imperial Theaters for their aristocratic connections and not artistic talent, knowledge of music, dance, or managerial skill. Their principal task was maintaining good relations with the court, the Imperial family, and St. Petersburg's elite, a holdover from the days of Peter the Great when there was an understanding that the nobility had an obligation to serve the state.

The schedule at the Imperial Ballet was strict. Wednesdays and Sundays in St. Petersburg were set aside for performances of only ballet in the Imperial Theaters, although audiences were limited: mostly children with mothers or governesses and retirees. But evening performances were social occasions, the audience composed of government officials, critics, aristocrats, well-off families with box subscriptions seated alongside Hussars and Horse Guards (Lieven 56, 63). Moral and financial support from the Imperial family and court for the ballet ensured its prestige and traditions.

Diaghilev, who held a managerial position starting in 1900, was soon dismissed by Prince Sergey Volkonsky, managing director of the Imperial Theaters, for challenging the rigid conventions of production. More specifically, Diaghilev wanted artistic control for a production of *Sylvia*. Volkonsky (and others) objected, which led to Diaghilev's departure. On his own, however, he would contest such hierarchies in pursuit of new ways to produce opera and ballet. In response to his firing, he went to Europe but in December 1901, back in St. Petersburg, he followed his love of music, attending the first Contemporary Music Evening with works by Russia's most progressive musicians including a young law student performing at the piano: Igor Stravinsky. This early intersection foretold future connections.

Imperial Steps II

The Imperial Ballet prided itself on traditional forms of advancement: if you were talented, you went to the top, although normal progression followed strict rules and promotion was slow. Rarely were dancers preferred out of rotation. Advancement from the *corps de ballet* to *coryphée* (leading dancer) and then to prima ballerina was lengthy and difficult. The rapid rise of Pavlova and Karsavina in the company was an exception.

The Imperial Ballet Schools were monastic boarding schools where young men and women were trained and educated at the expense of the Tsar. Discipline ruled, with no communication with the greater world beyond; the boys and girls also lived separately. A certain court atmosphere pervaded with formality and rigidity *de rigueur.* Authority was not questioned and a sense of duty pervaded everything, while reverence for tradition dominated. One studied for eight years, two as day pupils and then six as boarding pupils; visitors were not allowed (Lieven, 64–66).

After eight years of intensive training, studying the codified steps of Russian ballet, the students made their debut on the Imperial stage as technically adept dancers. But protocol reigned supreme in the theatre, as well as on stage. Seating followed a strict hierarchy: officers, Imperial Guards, and high officials occupied the front orchestra; lesser officials were relegated to the tiers, while ladies and families occupied the loges. The Imperial Box had a central, commanding view. In the galleries were clerks, valets, artisans, and servant girls. The audience was varied but decorum ruled. Men in the audience stood until the Tsar arrived and sat down in his box; at the end, no one could leave until the Tsar departed. Even curtain calls reflected the regimental aspect of the Imperial Ballet corps: the prima ballerina bowed first to the Tsar's box, then to that of the theater director, and finally to the public (Homans 250; Lieven 62–63).

Sustaining the traditions and security of the Imperial Theaters was its financial stability. The Tsar covered any deficits; profit was not a concern. Job security was assured, as well as pensions for dancers over thirty-five and theatrical staff. There was no need to alter the inherited and unchanging business or artistic practices. Continuity and security were assured. There was a sense of establishment which, translated to the stage, meant a conventional and repeated style of performance. Petipa permitted no deviation from accepted practice. One example: the prima ballerina always came forward for her solo while the *corps* remained waiting and observing up-stage. The choreography did not permit the dancers to mingle. The ballet itself would be divided into distinct parts: *pas seul*, *pas de deux*, or *corps de ballet* with scenery more pompous than artistic. As Prince Lieven explains, there was more attention paid "to producing the illusion of reality than to the artistic purpose of the décor" (Lieven 67).

Perspective dominated in an effort to give the stage depth. A lake or fountain appeared in almost every ballet, while no stage element suggested intimacy or emotion. Backgrounds were only decorative, while costumes were seemingly uniform. Music, itself, was merely an aid for the dancer with ballet masters understanding very little about orchestration.[11] Imperial ballets were also lengthy: *Pharaoh's Daughter*, performed in 1862 and choreographed by Petipa to music by Cesare Pugni, was five hours in length (by contrast, several works of the Ballets Russes would take no more than ten minutes). Pageantry and special effects defined its style: at one point there was a dance for eighteen couples with flower baskets balanced on their heads. It additionally displayed an underwater Nile ballet, an opium dream, and mummies coming to life (Homans 266–67).

Diaghilev made clear his irritation with this style, writing in a 1902 review of the ballets of Léo Delibes that the choreography of Petipa was "clumsy" and the essential inaction of the *corps de ballet* at the Mariinsky "tedious." An earlier critic remarked of Western classical ballet that "our head may be ablaze, but our body hardly lives."[12] Diaghilev and the Ballets Russes would work to change that.

But it is important to acknowledge the association between the early success and reception of the Imperial Ballet and the social atmosphere of Imperial St. Petersburg. The elaborate productions of the Imperial Ballet embodied the social ethos and hierarchies of the Court, sustaining its aristocratic nature and refined, Romanoff behavior. The Court's loyalty to tradition, convention, formality, and conservatism found expression in the performances. The values on stage reflected the values of the aristocracy. There was no need for change largely because dance reasserted the inherited ideals that sustained the Imperial Court. The Minister of the Imperial Court, Baron Vladimir Fredericks, often articulated these values. Politics, or at least court politics, was never very far from the stage of the Imperial Ballet.

By the end of the 19th century, while classical ballet was in Russian hands, Russia itself was about to collapse under the old order which was unable to recognize or accept the new. The ballets of Petipa and his successor Lev Ivanov stood for the aristocratic past. No longer was the form French; it would be Russian but heavily entwined with Imperial Russia. At the same time, cultural and social tensions increased, especially those between Russia and foreign nations like Japan (the Russo-Japanese War of 1904–1905); issues like hierarchy, serfdom, and Eastern folk traditions soon dominated. Ballet became the crossroads where many of these issues collided; one response was the amalgamation of tradition and innovation—in short, the Ballets Russes. But while drawing on avant-garde developments in art as well as music, plus the "anarchic chic of Paris," the underlying inspiration for the Ballets Russes would remain the Imperial Ballet traditions of St. Petersburg, the stimulus always Russian (Homans 290).

Opera

A critical influence on Diaghilev and the formation of the Ballets Russes was the Moscow Russian Private Opera directed by the successful railway magnate Savva Mamontov who believed and practiced the idea of opera as a synthesizing art form. In his effort to turn Russian culture away from Europe and back to Moscow and the East, he poured resources into maintaining the folk traditions of earlier generations. At his estate, he established an artists' colony focused on the study and recreation of peasant arts and crafts. The artisans did not, however, imitate earlier forms but used them to create their own, modern Russian folk-art styles and handicrafts to be sold to the Moscow middle class. Such efforts would strongly influence the vision of the Ballets Russes for both Diaghilev and Stravinsky. Increasingly, Diaghilev's personal dream emerged: to show early Russia to the world, intensified by concern that the old, aristocratic regime was ending.

Importantly, the Moscow Russian Private Opera company established a new sense of stage aesthetics instigating major reforms in acting, directing, and design, all adopted by Diaghilev.[13] In fact, set designers trained at Mamontov's company would soon contribute to Diaghilev's Parisian opera productions, the so-called *Saison russe* in 1907. Beyond a shared repertoire and personnel, Mamontov also mentored Diaghilev, whose first success as a promoter was his "World of Art" exhibition of 1898 displaying Russian painters from the entire country. Many artists were at that time also working for the Moscow Private Opera. Mamontov, himself, would become directly involved with preparing the exhibition and owned a number of the paintings displayed.

From his successes with promoting Russian culture in Paris, Diaghilev was prepared to strike out anew, especially because he believed that Parisian audiences would be receptive to the imaginative, original, and experimental on stage in the form of ballet with a Russian aura. He also knew that financially ballet had a better chance of success than the expensive opera productions requiring large amounts of capital. He also sensed that his career in Russia was tenuous since it lacked the full support of the Tsar and principals of the Imperial Theaters. He would not be able to advance in Russia without their support. Europe would be the answer.

Le Patron (The Boss)

Encouraging greater risks with the music of his new ballets became a hallmark of the Ballets Russes but never without Diaghilev's approval. He always remained in control, even at the beginning. As the artist and then designer for the Ballets Russes, Alexandre Benois wrote in 1907, with a touch of whimsy,

> Generalissimo Diaghilev's staff are beginning to gather here [Hotel Mirabeau].
> Yesterday I found him in real Potemkin style . . . in a loose golden silk
> dressing-gown and horizontally striped pants. It was already about one p.m. but
> his serene highness had only just deigned to roll out of bed. (in Scheijen 156)

The director did not tolerate insubordination and there were frequent conflicts
with dancers and choreographers, in some instances leading to lawsuits.

And challenges persisted: for the Italian production of *Le Pavillon*, the
technical crew did not turn up for the premiere. Benois and Diaghilev had to
operate the machinery themselves. That same season, but in Paris, the dress
rehearsal for *Petrushka* (1911) began twenty minutes late because, as Misia
Sert wrote, a distraught Diaghilev rushed into her box asking for four thousand francs. "Why?" she asked. "The costumier will not leave the costumes
unless he is paid!" was the reply. Sert turned to her chauffeur who departed
and shortly returned with the money. The show went on but the incident
highlights how money controlled and even determined the Ballets Russes's
performances and programs. Only an advance of $45,000 in 1915 from the
Metropolitan Opera, for example, prevented the company's financial ruin
and allowed Diaghilev to restart more adventurous programming (Scheijen
225–26, 309).

These incidents underscore the cost of culture and Diaghilev's at times fran-
tic determination, despite many odds, to see the completion of his projects—
but only by relying on patrons, backers, and occasionally cooperative theater
owners (Scheijen 180). The story of the Ballets Russes is the story of continued setbacks overcome by a strong-minded, if at times callous, Diaghilev. But
sometimes there was good luck. Prince Lvov romantically pursued Nijinsky
in St. Petersburg and wanted to follow him to Paris. Diaghilev told him it
would be impossible and not in Nijinsky's best interests. Surprisingly, Lvov
agreed but to ensure the success of the tour, gave Diaghilev funds to cover
the entire program. The troupe—all 250 dancers, technicians, and singers plus
an eighty-piece orchestra—soon overtook Paris's Théâtre du Châtelet. And it
was a success.

The difficulties Diaghilev encountered with almost every season alternately impeded and encouraged new ballets and renewed his determination
to succeed. He knew he had to make the company financially solvent and
could not always rely on private backers. Inspired, he realized that innovation on stage was one answer to bring in new supporters plus new audiences.
Consequently, he alternately encouraged new music, new designs, and new
choreography, while simultaneously relying on the public's interest in seeing updated versions of the classics. Ballet with an edge, or if not an edge,
controversy, was part of the company's reputation but so were resplendent

productions of *Schéhérazade*. Offsetting the effort to *épater la bourgeoisie* were conservative productions that opened up checkbooks.

Modernist Movement

Almost from the start, the company was perceived as the incarnation of the modern through its choreography and music but this was not always welcomed. In choreography, for example, Diaghilev sought liberation in movement which at first disoriented audiences. The impact of Isadora Duncan, who danced in St. Petersburg in December 1904, contributed dramatically to this shift to the modern, implicitly challenging the artistic ideals of the Imperial Ballet. She rejected classical ballet in favor of improvisation and self-expression, rather than pure technique and fixed choreographic movements. Radically, she *danced* the music, not *to* the music. Her body expressed sound, not simply pure movement. But she scandalously danced in a transparent tunic and barefoot. One could see her body. After one rakish performance, however, and to celebrate her new style, Diaghilev, Fokine, Bakst, and Benois joined Duncan for a memorable dinner at Anna Pavlova's.[14]

The effect of Duncan on Diaghilev's choreographers was profound: his dancers now danced faster and to more difficult tempos with more technical feats such as Nijinsky's leaps. The spacing of the dancers was more modern and complex with attention on structure, stripping away a detailed narrative and heavy theatrical settings characteristic of Imperial Ballet productions. Substituting for the staged movements, pointe work, turn out of the legs, and enforced symmetry of the Imperial Ballet was an erratic, energetic, and vigorous dance style that challenged space and even rhythm.[15] A new, vibrant art appeared on stage replacing the rigid vocabulary of Russian classical ballet. The result was the transposition of ballet from a place of classical stature to a fragmented, avant-garde present and challenging future.

Inspired partly by Isadora Duncan, Fokine initiated a more individualistic style and new, asymmetrical groupings, even placing dancers at different levels. Following Duncan, he also used the works of famous composers; *Les Sylphides* of 1910, for example, was set to Chopin. But some thought this an outrage, which was exactly what Diaghilev wanted. It brought in the crowds, as did the shift that saw the male dancer elevated to a primary role: no longer was he just a prop to carry the ballerina. Nijinsky, Massine, Lifar, Dolin, and Balanchine were among the standouts who literally repositioned the male figure.

Unlike the disciplined, strict regime of the Imperial Ballet, the Ballets Russes was informal, relaxed, and calm—except for the orders from Diaghilev, its director general. His committee of choreographers, composers, designers, aficionados, and professionals, from ballet masters to bankers, all contributed. Decisions were made collectively, although he enforced them individually.[16] One put forward an idea but then corrections, elaborations, and details followed, everyone contributing. A collective discussion on the nature of the music and dance always ensued but the final voice was Diaghilev's.

The relaxed atmosphere of the Ballets Russes found expression in the bodies of the dancers. Unlike the sometimes stout and muscular figures of the Imperial Ballet, those of the Ballets Russes were long and lithe. Their body lines were smooth with muscles evenly developed. This was the result of training largely under the Italian ballet master Enrico Cecchetti who taught most of Diaghilev's future dancers and would soon travel with the company. As the dancer Jennifer Homans notes, instead of focusing on steps and "bravura stunts," the dancers used their technical powers to sculpt their bodies and develop movements that emphasized "flexibility and *plastique*" (Homans 292).

The bodies of the male and female dancers were thin, almost fragile but allowed for a long reach and movement. Pavlova's leg muscles were strong but she looked wispy and gaunt. The combination enthralled audiences, revealing the expressiveness of dance as lyricism replaced an enclosed and rigid story. And remaking the body even found itself in costumes: Nijinsky in *L'Après-midi d'un faune* (1912) wore a skin-tight outfit emphasizing his taut body and stylized use of his hands. He displayed the body not as an over-costumed aristocratic prince but as a sensual creature of nature.

For Diaghilev, publicity and marketing were nonstop; from the start he recognized the merchandizing value of his stars. He publicly feted and praised them, even if backstage there were arguments, disagreements, and bad feelings. His theatricality, on and off the stage, supported the attention he and the press lavished on his principal dancers. But his own ambition and charm made him irresistible to the public—unless money was involved. Then, he was not above deceit, cunning, or even cruelty. But his self-confidence always seemed to triumph, although his hotel bills often remained unpaid and he repeatedly questioned what he felt were overcharges. As Richard Buckle casually but comically remarks in his biography of Diaghilev, the impresario did not "suffer from Proust's snobbery of over-tipping" (Buckle 452, 453).

Artistically, change was taking place on multiple levels initiated not only by choreographers but also by designers. What further added to the uniqueness of the Ballets Russes productions was the integration of the sets and costumes into a unified visual spectacle. The decors, Diaghilev explained, must offer a "symbolic framework that enhances the meaning of the performance."[17] But again, this did not occur overnight. The essentially plotless ballet *Les Sylphides* (1909), for example, had conventional music with dance in the classical style, although it exhibited a more dramatic vocabulary of gesture. The choreographer Fokine, however, contextualized the dance with the space, properly defined by the designs. Soloists had center stage only briefly, Fokine preferring to integrate them into the ensemble. Most importantly, he replaced Petipa's rectilinear masses with smaller, asymmetrical groupings, patterns that constantly shifted. In later productions, this would grow to large, freewheeling crowds moving across the stage.

The integration of design was also crucial. Roger Fry articulated its importance in 1919 noting that before the Ballets Russes, dance and music often outstripped the scenic artists who often designed according to decorative formulas. But now, the work of Mikhail Larionow (or Larionov) offered something new, supporting the choreographic design. For him, the movement of the figure becomes "the fundamental fact of his design."[18] His designs have "a vivid expressive purpose," a purpose adjusted to the *ensemble* of the entire ballet (Fry 291). And his real strength, as that of other designers for the Ballets Russes, is the double meaning of form and color: first as pure design and then as a method to evoke time and place (Fry 293). But an interesting irony is that stage design, rather than the leaps of Nijinsky or music of Stravinsky, astounded, angered, and even puzzled Edwardian audiences. A further irony is that not one of Diaghilev's Russian designers was trained as a set designer or decorator. All came to the stage by way of studio painting and all, including Benois, Bakst, and Larionov, sought to construct rather than paint the sets and costumes of the company.[19] They literally altered the way audiences saw the stage.

Importantly, the Ballets Russes also introduced audiences to modern music through Diaghilev's commission of new pieces by a series of original composers. Debussy, Stravinsky, Ravel, Prokofiev, Massenet, Paul Dukas, Aleksandr Glazunov, Erik Satie, and Nicolas Nabokov were among the key figures. This extended an absolute interest in music during the Russian "Silver Age," supported by special agencies, organizations, and enterprises essential to professional musical life. These works constantly incorporated the new, composers moving to displace musical meter, especially Stravinsky, who relied on repetitive patterns, layered structures, and modal harmonics.[20]

The paradox of Diaghilev was that while the scandals of his more progressive ballets—*L'Après-midi d'un faune, Jeux, Le Sacre du printemps*—created sold-out performances and unprecedented gossip, they alienated important backers leading to his own doubt over their value. And once he fired Nijinsky in 1913, his programs altered, audiences declined, reviews were tepid, and supporters of the new style turned hostile. He appeared to reject, for financial as well as aesthetic reasons, the avant-garde. At the same time, the First World War hindered any touring, while bills mounted: the most famous private dance company in the world faced possible disappearance. A trip to America with a much smaller company seemed its only salvation. Negotiations began early though the trip would not occur until 1916. The undertaking had mixed critical and financial results, the advanced publicity undercut by the company's unexciting performances and absence of several stars.[21]

But if the change to the modern happened gradually and even unwillingly, the events of WWI and the 1917 Revolution accelerated the shift. During WWI, Diaghilev's company temporarily disbanded and when they re-assembled, they provisionally returned to a classical style initiated by a persistent demand for Russian dances in France. At the same time in Russia there was a renewed interest in Imperial classicism expressed in the productions of the Imperial Ballet, a need for classical order amidst the war's destruction. But Diaghilev, under pressure in Paris to attract audiences and fight off competing companies began, with his new choreographer Léonide Massine, to integrate elements of the modernist revolution, leaving the symbolism of Russian folk history behind. *Parade* (1917), with a libretto by Cocteau and music by Satie, plus sets and costumes by Picasso, was one result. Aiding what would become the experimental tradition of the Ballets Russes were the Russian Cubo-Futurists and Constructivists,[22] but to many it seemed that Diaghilev was emphasizing art and décor, not dance, prompting Isadora Duncan to quip that the dancers were no more than moving Picasso pictures and "if that is Art I prefer Aviation" (in Homans 329).

The revolution of 1917 displaced artists in both dance and painting, ironically increasing their availability for Diaghilev, marking an overall sense of artistic disintegration within Russia. Continuity between the Imperial Regime and Russia, including control over the theaters, ended when the Bolsheviks and then the Soviets took power. A new aesthetic of socially realistic ballets emerged which actually enhanced the appeal of the radical Ballets Russes because they were different. Diaghilev's independence from the Soviets allowed him to maintain both his pull to traditional Russian folklore *and* the avant-garde which had been moving towards the abstraction of shape and color before 1917—see Kazimir Malevich's "Red Square" (1915) or his "Dynamic Suprematism Supremus" (ca. 1915). This originated partly in the *World of Art* movement. But soon, there was a new emphasis on "pure feeling" with a focus on dynamic shapes which would soon appear in stagings of the Ballets Russes.[23]

But the immediate aftermath of 1917 meant the collapse of state structures, with law and order in disarray, millions homeless, and artists lost. It is no surprise that many would leave, or try to, from Diaghilev's friends Nouvel and Benois to Kandinsky and Chagall. Rachmaninoff, for example, left from Petrograd for Helsinki on a sled in December 1917. For dancers, work at the Bolshoi or Mariinsky was curtailed: without state support for sets, costumes, salaries, or pensions, the lives of individual dancers were drastically altered. "Should the Bolshoi Exist?" was even the title of one article, while others criticized the use of precious fuel to heat the building even while performances went on. A committee overseeing the theater suggested they buy firewood on the black market since they could no longer rely on the government for supplies.

The Bolshoi ballet troupe met uncertainty with traditional programming, even though resolution of the revolution remained unclear. Outwardly, it may have appeared stable but inwardly there were persistent tensions and disagreements. Artistic inertia, masking fear of crossing Bolshevik/Soviet guidelines, meant a conservative program which soon became a search for a truly socialist ballet. Unsurprisingly, the exodus of dancers began in February 1917, increasing after the October Revolution with various dancers gravitating to Diaghilev in Paris who appeared to offer artistic freedom and the facade of financial stability.[24]

In Russia, the teaching of classical ballet, with its disciplinary emphasis on technique at the expense of drama (the hallmark of the Ballets Russes), was now in jeopardy. Character dancing would become prominent and later, regional dances. But new governing councils proved inept, unable to decide questions of benefits, or performances. Only in 1919 did order return to the Bolshoi with a new director, the stern and stout Elena Malinovskaya who brought earnestly didactic works and direction.

The Ballets Russes was doing no better, especially with money. In 1918, financial challenges increased and in the spring, Diaghilev moved to Madrid and then London where the company would appear at the London Coliseum.[25] But the "Silver Age" was coming to an end, and for those that stayed in St. Petersburg or Moscow, whether ballet masters, dancers, or choreographers, they were soon tasked with creating work that distanced itself from an Imperial past, while celebrating the new industrialized present with its proletarian values and, soon, Stalinist programs.[26] But late in his career in an effort to retrieve lost audiences, Diaghilev returned to experimental productions. After 1922, his ballets became more complex and even intellectual, while turning to mechanical conceptions of ballet and stage design (literally incorporating machines) which in turn meant a new group of artists: Gabo, Pavel, Tchelitchew, and Georgil Yakulov revitalized stage design, while choreographers made their marks: Balanchine for *La Chatte* (1927) and Massine for *Le Pas d'acier* (1927) and *Ode* (1928), all three among Diaghilev's most innovative productions involving new concepts of music and visual expression in an effort to marry nature and technology (Bowlt, "Stage Design" 42).

Choreography: Nijinsky, Nijinska, Balanchine

One might characterize the development of the Ballets Russes as moving from more to less, changes measured by simplified but still complex set design, choreography, and music. Beginning with the visual splendor *of Le Pavillon d'Armide* (1909), *Cléopâtre* (1909), and *Schéhérazade* (1910), the last appearing in the final years of the Belle Époque. But within a decade, productions devolved to the "industrial efficiency" of *La Chatte* (1927) and *Le Pas d'acier* (1927). *La Chatte,* in fact, replaced color with light as the stage aesthetic with startling effects. Anticipating such changes, *Jeux* (1913) projected a sharp geometry matched with a monochromatic stage pallet. This move to simplify, some have suggested, paralleled the shift from Symbolism to the severity of Constructivism with the pictorial triumphing over the aural (Bowlt 242). Audiences came to see, not to hear.

If one could identify periods of artistic change with the Ballets Russes through the music and sets, one could also do so through its choreography. Bronislava Nijinska made the importance of chorography clear, writing that "everything in ballet must be expressed only through choreography."[27] The visual component of ballet actually became the preeminent sign of its modernity, initiated by Nijinsky's choreography for *Le Sacre de printemps* (1913)—erratic, disturbing, and unforgettable. Assisted by new presentations of stage space—divided, framed, or changeable—the movement of dancers was upsetting. Ballet was no longer entertainment for the elite relying on practices of the Imperial Ballet but radical and at times threatening. The point of view was contemporary even if the subject matter was not.

Diaghilev felt it essential that the choreographer work with the composer. There was to be parity between the two, something new, an extension of his belief in collaboration. The music and the dance evolved organically whereas previously the choreographer "ordered" the music, designating the tempos and number of bars in a piece. He or she could also order scenes to be cut or abbreviated. In turn, the composer had to know, or have a profound knowledge of, choreographic structure. But choreographic conventions ruled, especially in the duration of dances. But occasionally composers challenged the conventions. Tchaikovsky, for example, subordinated his music to the needs of narrative unity especially in the so called "white acts or vision scenes" evident in *The Nutcracker* or *Swan Lake* (Garafola 2005: 46). Diaghilev's choreographers—Fokine, Lifar, Massine, Nijinsky and Nijinska (brother and sister), and Balanchine—to cite only a handful, literally took the Ballets Russes into new directions.

Choreographic periods identify the changes of the Ballets Russes: the earlier 1909–1914 period was the era of Mikhail Fokine, chief choreographer and ballet master. Fokine had trained at the Imperial Ballet School and made his debut in *The Talisman*, under the direction of Petipa. In 1902, he began to teach himself how to choreograph at the Imperial Ballet School, at one point directing the young Nijinsky. In 1909, Diaghilev invited him to be the resident choreographer for the first season of the Ballets Russes in Paris, offering a classical undercurrent to the more original productions. His 1910 production of *Schéhérazade* was a hit partly because of its brilliant colors, exoticism, and sexual traces. His 1911 success, *Le Spectre de la Rose*, featured Nijinsky in a sensational *grand jeté* out of a bedroom window at the end that remained a great attraction to audiences.

With *Schéhérazade, The Firebird, Petrushka*, and the *Spectre de la Rose* his main productions, Fokine became a hit. Others with a classical flair were *Le Pavillon d'Armide, Daphnis et Chloë*, and *Le Coq d'Or*. In 1914, he guided the opera ballet *The Golden Cockerel* with sets by Goncharova. Based on a Pushkin story, the ballet is an oblique account of Russian politics and adventurism, one of the few by the company to offer a political critique of the Tsars.

But change, if not choreographic evolution, was inevitable and after a time Diaghilev felt Fokine's picturesque productions were tiresome. There had to be a shift away from the aesthetics of the *World of Art* and traditionalist principles. Diaghilev also quarreled with Benois in 1911 and the following year he allowed Nijinsky to choreograph several works, supplementing Fokine who left the company in 1912. Coincident with these changes was a new aesthetic of composition initially expressed by the Ballets Russes's original, one-act ballets which united dance and pantomime. With the designer and composer, the choreographer created an innovative sense of body movement, establishing visual and emotional intensity expressed physically.

Fokine's work was stylized and heavily aesthetic. Diaghilev wanted something more provocative which Nijinsky offered with his more primitive style relying on a jerky set of movements and sharp body angles, reflecting the tempo and rhythm of Stravinsky in both *L'Après midi* (1912) and *Le Sacre du printemps* (1913). Nijinsky marked the second choreographic period from roughly 1912 until late 1913, overlapping with Fokine. His own animalistic, virile performances, with their astonishing leaps, remained a signature moment in his productions and an image of the company long after his dismissal by Diaghilev. His jumps were repeatedly used as images of the company's exciting performances reprinted on programs and posters.

Nijinsky's work as a choreographer was as startling as it was original, and he found paintings a compelling inspiration (especially Gauguin's) and broke with conventional ideas of dance, allowing more expressionist movement. Public and critical reaction was not kind. In 1913, Diaghilev dismissed Nijinsky but more for personal than artistic reasons (he married), replacing him with Massine, although Fokine also returned in 1914.

Stylistically, however, the company continued in the manner of Nijinsky who returned as a dancer when the company toured the United States in 1916–1917. At the same time, *Parade*, with Léonide Massine as choreographer, was being prepared in Europe, the work soon labeled the "first Cubist ballet." Massine had been a member of the Bolshoi but by 1915 had become Diaghilev's principal choreographer, although he actually began as the company's star male dancer following the departure of Nijinsky. After a short break during the First World War, the reconstituted company now had Russian, British, and Polish dancers and new music by Stravinsky.

Massine marked the third choreographic period, 1915–1921, and turned the company away from the progressive, if not radical style of Nijinsky, back to a modernized ballet tradition highlighted by *Le Soleil de Nuit* (*1915*), *La Boutique fantastique* (1919), and *Le Tricorne* (1919). But he, too, sought independence from Diaghilev and rebelled but still kept ties with the company after Diaghilev's death in 1929, becoming chief choreographer of Colonel de Basil's Ballets Russes, a successor company based in Monte Carlo originating in 1932. He shared the spotlight with Bronislava Nijinska who created *Les Noces* (1923)*, Les Biches* (1924), and *Le Train bleu* (1924)*. Balanchine succeeded both, creating nine ballets including *La Chatte* (1927)*, Le Fils Prodigue* (1929), and *Le Bal* (1929), many starring Serge Lifar.[28]

The addition of Balanchine to the Ballets Russes as a choreographer in 1924, creating nine works before Diaghilev's death, resulted in new dances with new music by Prokofiev, Stravinsky, Satie, and Ravel. His ballet *Apollon musgaète* (1928) combined Greek myth, classical ballet, and jazz but in a plotless work. Content was developed by musical, choreographic images and the movement of the dancers. Working with Stravinsky on *Apollon*, he remarked that it was "the beginning of the direct conversion of sound into visible movement."[29] Balanchine was instrumental in revivifying late Diaghilev and the Ballets Russes as important to the company as it neared its end as Nijinsky was to its beginning. A new excitement and even drama over their productions reappeared.

Balanchine's early career in St. Petersburg was sensational, appearing on stage at the Mariinsky at eleven, creating his first choreography at fifteen. In 1921, he graduated from the Petrograd Theater (Ballet) School and joined the *corps de ballet* of the State Theatre of Opera and Ballet (formerly the Mariinsky) for whom he began to choreograph; the following year (1923) he was named ballet master of the Maly Opera Theater in Petrograd. He simultaneously studied music, which continuously influenced his concept of dance best conceived as a music-based choreography. He studied at the Conservatory of Music and at the age of seven successfully performed a Beethoven sonata. A few years later he could play entire Wagner operas at sight.[30]

Yuri Slonimsky, Soviet dance historian, friend of Balanchine's, and a founder of Balanchine's Young Ballet in 1921, published a lengthy account of Balanchine's youth in Russia in 1976. It begins with his 1913 application by his father to the Imperial Theater School where he would spend the next seven years followed by three with the Mariinsky Theater.[31] The essay is especially strong on Balanchine's early student participation in ballet productions at the Mariinsky.

But the outbreak of World War I and then the Russian Revolution meant the closure of the ballet school and conservatory for a year; Petrograd (the renamed St. Petersburg; the Imperial Theater School became the Petrograd State Theater School) became deserted. His parents retreated to what was Tiflis (current Tbilisi) where his father, a composer and failed businessman, became minister of culture. Balanchine remained in Petrograd living with an aunt but there were hardships from the lack of electricity and gasoline to almost no food. Apartments would suddenly go dark. To survive, Balanchine worked a series of odd jobs from piano player for silent films to messenger boy. Everyone was hungry. Only in 1918, when the People's Commissar of Education convinced Lenin (who resisted spending money on the arts) that ballet was not a decadent art and might benefit the proletariat, did the school and theatre reopen. The lack of fuel, however, meant that audiences sat and dancers performed in freezing theaters. Each morning students had to break the ice formed by the water sprinkled over the wooden floors to prevent skidding the night before. There were still difficulties when he graduated in 1921: one female graduate made a blouse for herself from her grandmother's colored umbrella (Slonimsky 28).

But without teachers, only memory guided the dancers. Many left rather than remain in a country of civil war and then authoritative power where restaged ballets had new productions in more ideologically directed forms. No longer an art for the privileged, nor patronized by the Tsars with their commitment to foreign teachers and dancers, the revolution hastened the democratization of ballet without foreign stars and foreign ballet masters. The director of the Mariinsky Ballet was French, Jean-Bapiste Landé; Marius Petipa, the pre-revolutionary ballet master of the Imperial Theatres of St. Petersburg and principal choreographer of the Imperial Ballet from 1871 to 1903, was also French. But during and shortly after the revolution, all the leading ballerinas, teachers, and even Fokine were outside of Russia. Slonimsky notes that the political/moral reaction to art in Russia after 1905 thwarted the creative potential of ballet. New productions were rarely created (Slonimsky 25). The ballet companies of the Imperial Theaters stood still. Most "of the ballets beginning about 1910 were created abroad" by Diaghilev who attracted the most gifted dancers. Ballets at home in the Imperial Theatres "were obliged to subsist in . . . spiritual poverty" (Slonimsky 25). The sterility of creative art caused many, including Pavlova, to leave. The dismissal of Nijinsky by the court theaters was another sign of decay—all these changes allowing

Diaghilev to assemble a talented, creative, exciting company uninhibited by the moribund outlook and practice of the Imperial Theaters.

However, there were some positive changes: ethnic and religious restrictions for admissions were eliminated after the October Revolution. A set of students shifted the tone; by 1921 there were approximately 200 students. On the eve of the revolution there were somewhere between eighty and one hundred. In March 1919 a new director was selected, Andrei Oblakov, a former dancer, who had seen the triumphs of Diaghilev's Paris seasons and was sensitive to changes at the school (Slonimsky 28–30). He was also an admirer of Stravinsky. The renewal of ballet in Russia was slowly taking shape and Balanchine was at its center. That same year he was accepted into the Conservatory of Music to study piano, practicing in the winter in an unheated theatre sometimes wearing gloves. He also studied harmony, counterpoint, and composition, often writing music for piano, dance, recitation, and voice (Slonimsky 33). He also attempted the violin, French horn, drums, and trumpet.

During his formative years, Balanchine moved between the popular stage, theatrical avant-garde, and his own developing artistic vision shaped by the Imperial values of his schooling and the revolutionary ideals of the Soviet Union. Replacing an early preference for the grand parades of Romanov grandeur, he turned to unsentimental choreography, removing ambiguities. He sought "to purify ballet of its trappings," soon rejecting Diaghilev's bond with Wagner's *Gesamtkunstkwerk* (Christiansen 18). "See the music, hear the dance," he famously stated (Christiansen 18). He also pursued the linear geometry of classical form, the foundation of his radical departures (Homans *Mr. B* 212). Furthermore, he reduced scenery and costume to a minimum while simplifying designs. This turn to formalism met resistance.

New figures began to influence him, notably Fyodor Lopukhov who experimented with the idea of "dancing the music" and Kasyan Goleyzovsky who created radical movements and poses founded on classical precepts. Balanchine began to see dance composition as an "analogue to musical composition beyond literary conjectures [or] subjective interpretations."[32] What Balanchine discovered were bold variations on traditional or classical positions and he learned that "the movement is the feeling."[33] In 1922 he won praise for his solo dance of the jesters from an anniversary performance of *The Nutcracker,* although overall he was only a dancer of the 13th rank in the *corps de ballet* at the Mariinsky in 1923, although eager for new possibilities.

In 1920, Balanchine met and shortly after fell in love with Tamara Geva who was three years younger (she fifteen; he eighteen). But his rival was the poet Mayakovsky (whose work he admired) who was a friend of Tamara's father, a successful and cultured manufacturer of religious objects (Buckle 1988: 22). Mayakovsky's lines from "Mystery-Bouffe," "we are tired of paper passions" and the proclamation "All is new!" became watchwords of a new move for Balanchine and his circle (Slonimsky 34). But his love for Tamara outlasted Mayakovsky's interest and they married in the chapel of the State Theater School. By 1922, he organized a company called Young Ballet performing in Petrograd and Moscow. By 1923 he created a dance for the Queen of Shemakhan in Rimsky-Korsakov's *Le Coq d'or.* He also did chore-ography for Bernard Shaw's *Caesar and Cleopatra* for the Petrograd Drama Theater. He was nineteen.

Authorities, however, became suspicious of his innovative techniques with his Young Ballet company and its attachment to experimental theater. Performing *Pulcinella* with music by Stravinsky bordered on the radical. Could they be counter-revolutionary?[34] The financial collapse of the Young Ballet prevented the mounting of *Pulcinella*. Many of the group's dancers could not rehearse on the side of their full-time responsibilities. Balanchine lacked the very elements that Diaghilev would muster: material and creative support from the theater, scheduled rehearsals, a permanent manager, a direc-tor, and participation by the leading dancers (Slonimsky 77).

In April 1924, Balanchine signed an agreement to travel to the Far East in a newly formed but small company. But within a few weeks, the Asian part was forgotten, a singer and pianist dropped out, and one of the other dancers was mysteriously drowned in a motorboat accident because she apparently knew too much about a certain political secret. The Cheka was involved. Balanchine and his wife were distraught and realized it might be time to leave the Soviet Union for good. They left on their tour in mid-June for Stettin and then Berlin, which was active with White Russians. By the time they arrived in Wiesbaden, they agreed to defect and not return to the Soviet Union. They continued their tour of Germany and received an invitation to perform in London in October at the Empire music hall. They remained for four weeks. They tried Paris after their English work permits expired.[35] After a few days at a cheap hotel near Les Halles, Diaghilev called. The Ballets Russes had been in Germany in September and October and heard about the small Russian troupe. Diaghilev needed a choreographer as well as dancers. Meanwhile, Fokine's choreography incorporating elements of Isadora Duncan and the free style of barefoot dancing was soon superseded by Nijinsky whose radical direction for *L'Après-midi* and then *Le Sacre du printemps* were revolution-ary but his marriage quickly separated him from Diaghilev. Massine replaced him but left in 1921 to then be replaced by Bronislava Nijinska. Then it was Boris Kochno, Diaghilev's young and handsome assistant, principally a librettist, who attempted choreography.

In mid-November, the defectors auditioned for Diaghilev at the studio of Misia Sert where they met Diaghilev and Kochno for the first time. Balanchine displayed his Scriabin *pas de deux*, Danilova danced a few steps of *The*

Firebird. Under pressure and needing dancers for an upcoming Opéra de Monte-Carlo series, he asked Balanchine if he could make ballets for operas and quickly? "Yes" was Balanchine's immediate answer (Buckle 1988: 29). Diaghilev, however, took his time in deciding to hire and returned to London while the group had run out of funds. But at the end of November, Diaghilev made his offer. The dancers accepted in a letter signed by Balanchine on November 23, 1924, not by their titular manager Dmitriev, a former singer who had become a croupier in a government-licensed gambling house, and used his savings to form the original tour. He was not invited to join.

Diaghilev almost immediately simplified Balanchine's name, reversing his practice of Russianizing the names of his English dancers. Diaghilev altered any Russian names he thought Westerners might have trouble pronouncing: Nizinsky became Nijinsky, Miassin became Massine, and Georgi Balanchivadze became George Balanchin to which an "e" would be added for the French.[36] This occurred in December 1924, the same month that Diaghilev asked Balanchine if he could create a new staging of *Le Chant du rossignol*, revising Massine's choreography, a ballet set to music extracted from Stravinsky's opera *Le Rossignol* of 1914. A confident Balanchine immediately said "yes." Alicia Marks, soon to be renamed by Diaghilev Alicia Markova, was to dance the nightingale. At the opening night, Braque, Picasso, and his wife, attended, partly to see the décor by Matisse and observe Balanchine's choreography. It was a success.

But in the winter of 1924, there was unhappiness in the company, particularly Bronislava Nijinska who felt insulted that a second choreographer was needed. Nevertheless, Balanchine's group joined the company in London at a time when Diaghilev was paying off his debts to Sir Oswald Stoll, theatre owner where *The Sleeping Princess* ran over budget. Stoll had earlier rescued Diaghilev in Spain in 1918. Diaghilev was able to repay Stoll because he had a new arrangement to give regular ballet seasons at the Opéra de Monte-Carlo and to provide dancers for its operas. But the Ballets Russes was still not permitted a proper London season: they appeared as a single act at Stoll's Coliseum dancing one ballet every afternoon and evening. No more.

Balanchine's early position was as a character dancer and overall thought the company was in poor shape artistically (see Buckle 1988: 31). But ten days later, meeting Diaghilev's wish to show a more sustained example of his choreographic skills, he demonstrated his movements for Chopin's *March funèbre*. Ninette de Valois and other dancers performed for Diaghilev, who offered no outward response but was inwardly impressed.

In the meantime, Nijinska announced she would be leaving. But Balanchine, at twenty, was too young, so Diaghilev made up with Massine (they had quarrelled) and he returned. And so, the company went to Monte Carlo where

Balanchine made dances for nine operas before the ballet season opened in April. He also provided choreography for the world premiere of Ravel's *L'Enfant et les sortilèges* with Ravel himself playing piano at the rehearsals. It had a text by Colette. But Massine paid no attention to Balanchine and prevented him from attending his rehearsals. Nonetheless, Balanchine's presence brought a new excitement to the company.

Balanchine at first maintained a link with the Imperial Ballet style in productions of *Pastorale* (1925) and *The Triumph of Neptune* (1926). But he soon veered toward the new, the minimal, the precise, with *Apollo* (1928) and *The Prodigal Son* (1929). He was also an admirer of the modernist choreographer Kasyan Goleyzovsky in Leningrad who managed, through an emphasis on the physical, to achieve sculptured effects among the dancers while virtually eliminating their costumes. His presentation of the body matched his presentation of his dances: sleek, refined, and pure. He shared these ideas with Diaghilev who would soon allow them into his programming at Balanchine's suggestion.

Balanchine was also, and importantly, a collaborator despite his reliance on his own vision. One of the most important of his collaborators was Stravinsky. He could visualize Stravinsky's work in terms of correlative physical movement that would serve the composer's score. As he explained, when choreographing Stravinsky's music, he was careful not to hide it. Choreography generally "interferes with the music too much." He rather "subdues" his dances which are always less than the music. "As in modern architecture you rather should do less than more," which became for him a guiding choreographic principle.[37] But Stravinsky was also clear, supporting Balanchine and the independence of choreography which "must realize its own form, one independent of the musical form though measured to the musical unit . . . but it must not seek to duplicate the line and beat of the music." One cannot be a choreographer, he continued, "unless, like Balanchine, one is a musician first" (Stravinsky in Joseph 1).

Both understood dance as the manipulation of time and space framed by an element of theatricality. There was an element of exactitude that matched each other's work. This was evident in *Apollo* where Balanchine revised traditional ballet concepts rooted in Petipa. This meant changes to discrete positionings of the body, the treatment of the ensemble in relation to the soloist, the placement of the arms. One dancer noted that they used angular hands instead of rounded classical hands and that "without any ceremony Apollo lifts Terpsichore onto his back! It was a free movement . . . a completely new vocabulary" (Danilova in Joseph 87–88). This was revolutionary, leading one critic to write that in the lucidity of his themes and their execution, in the incorporation of vernacular movement and gestures, and the return to the fundamental principles of the *danse d'école*, Balanchine's choreography represents a balletic response to acmeist poetics.[38]

Balanchine's contribution to the Ballets Russes from 1924 until 1929 renewed its vitality even if it no longer received the type of praise for its originality it had once earned. A critic in October 1927 complained that for the company, "dance is but a magical decoy" and that the merit of Diaghilev has been to reveal painters and musicians more than dancers yet with the goal he outlined to his stepmother when writing from Venice. There, "all that is real . . . is in constant contact with magic and mystery."[39]

Balanchine flourished creating new ballets with scores by composers as diverse as Ruric, Satie, Handel, and Prokofiev. He had a prodigious talent to create ballets for opera quickly such as a polonaise for *Godunov* or a waltz for *Les Contes d'Hoffmann*. He possessed a "natural ease of invention" which Diaghilev valued and would guide his later, stellar career in Europe and then the U.S. (Buckle 37). But Balanchine brought a new formal clarity and beauty to the company. His *Apollon Musagète* (*Apollo*) of 1928 would become a classic matched by *The Prodigal Son* (1929). Both works featured Lifar. Balanchine learned of the death of Diaghilev in the summer of 1929 in a London film studio, preparing to shoot a dance sequence with Lydia Lopokova and Anton Dolin for England's first sound film, *Dark Red Roses*. He would be on his own but eventually, after a brief appointment with the Paris Opéra, made his way to Copenhagen, London, Monte Carlo, and, finally, America in October 1933 and new success. He was twenty-nine.

Diaghilev still sought the new in music, art, and movement. The search was relentless and composers were soon commissioned to write scores specifically for ballet. Stravinsky was just twenty-seven when he began to compose *The Firebird,* although his collaborators thought his unusual (avant-garde) rhythms were too difficult for dancing. Diaghilev was undeterred and soon employed other new composers: Debussy, Ravel, Satie, and Poulenc. Avant-garde artists also participated, including Goncharova, Picasso, Braque, de Chirico, and even the older Matisse. Changes in costumes, movement, design, and music made everything new, including using the same artist to create both sets and costumes.

This drive for the new absorbed elements of the Russian avant-garde theater, its influence often overlooked in discussions of the Ballets Russes. Statements by the choreographer and mime Alexander Rumnev—"dance must become active and imagistic . . . gesture in dance . . . should assume a concrete meaning"—suggested new directions for the Ballets Russes, while Russian avant-garde theater practice had anticipated much of what Diaghilev initiated in Paris.[40] But London was also a success even if performances at the Coliseum (ca. 1924) meant competing with film. "More ballet" was a familiar audience chant (Christiansen 194).

But for Diaghilev, controversy again took precedent over presentation, a position partly outlined by Marinetti who often proclaimed that the artist always required an enemy.[41] The Futurists, with their emphasis on performance, supported the ideals of the Ballets Russes and Diaghilev who actually spent time with Marinetti in Italy in February and April 1915. A month earlier, Diaghilev had urged Stravinsky to form an alliance with Marinetti. The Futurist sculptor Umberto Boccioni had tea with Stravinsky and wanted to create something with futurist "color, dance and costume."[42] By March, Diaghilev again pressured Stravinsky to work with the Futurist on a new ballet, explaining that although his original idea to have dancers perform without music would not work, action must now be supported not by music but sound, created by noise machines.[43] All of these interventions contributed to shaping the modern vision of the Ballets Russes, one early principle that a change in the movement of the body would result in a change to the dance and the behavior of the actors on the stage. It would also mean a change in costumes to accommodate the more free-flowing action. The body became the primary dramatis personae understood by Diaghilev's early choreographers Massine and Nijinsky.

Transnational Dance

The sources of Diaghilev's vision for the Ballets Russes were multiple: the ongoing radicalism of Russian avant-garde art; Russian and French ballet practices; the eagerness of Parisian audiences for innovation, sometimes equated with novelty. From Russia, new choreographic experiments by Bakst and Massine, plus developments in the theatrical avant-garde, also contributed. In France, the artistic experiments of Cocteau, Picasso, Braque, Gris, and de Chirico influenced the visual aspect of the stage. Contributing to both was music with its essentially Russian foundation (Rimsky-Korsakov, Stravinsky) and French composers like Satie, Poulenc, and Darius Milhaud. Such an international blend of sources resulted in an evolving transnational aesthetic.

The impact of the Ballets Russes on other modern companies, notably the Ballet Suédois with Jean Borlin the principal choreographer, Rolf de Maré director, was profound but always competitive. With music by Ravel, Scriabin, Saint-Saëns, Debussy, and Darius Milhaud, there was an equal draw on audiences seeking the new. Between 1920 and 1924, the Ballet Suédois challenged the hegemony of the Ballets Russes and adopted their vision of modern ballet. But the Ballets Russes still reigned, reasserting its own practices by throwing aside storylines, relying on angular, unexpected moves, using more new music, and making narrative its own performance. Displacement replaced fluidity, partially reflected in new lighting effects.

Diaghilev achieved what he envisioned in his performances through discipline, autocratic behavior, and control over his entire company, including choreographers, dancers, composers, and set designers—but he, paradoxically, encouraged artistic freedom and independence among his contributors. This artistic *laissez-faire* allowed the company to flourish and establish an international presence without a single performance in Russia. This was the ironic fulfillment of Diaghilev's vision to display to the world original ballets that embodied the excellence of Russian art and culture. At the same time, he sought to remake the national consciousness of the country. This is what Diaghilev's dream accomplished—not just a Russian ballet and ballet company but an original, inventive visual Russian culture available to the world.

Branded by the press as revolutionaries and decadents after the death of Grand Duke Vladimir, under Diaghilev's leadership the Ballets Russes nevertheless proved that artistic talent could transcend political prejudice.[44] Grudgingly, Russia accepted the accomplishments of the Ballets Russes. *Petrushka*, with music by Stravinsky and choreography by Fokine, became an instant sensation but it was not performed in Russia until 1921 (and not by the Ballets Russes)—ten years after its Paris premiere. The avant-garde explosion of the early 1910s—Symbolism, Cubo-Futurism, Constructivism, Acmeism—repeated in the 1917–1929 period contributed to shaping the image of the Ballets Russes, which remarkably integrated Russian and European art coalescing under the energy and direction of one man, Serge Diaghilev, who, despite being in constant financial trouble, sought to balance a drive for a stronger nationalism in Russian culture with a determination to incorporate the new. Kazimir Malevich's enthusiastic cry expressed this goal clearly: "I have breached the blue lampshade of color limitations and have passed into the white beyond: follow me, comrade aviators!"[45]

NOTES

1. T. S. Eliot, "London Letter," in Nancy D. Hargrove, "Eliot and Dance," *Journal of Modern Literature* 21.1 (1997) 80. See Hargrove on *Le Sacre du printemps* in the same article. Also useful is Ben J. Richardson, "'A Conversation with Spectres:' Russian Ballet and the Politics of Voice in T.S. Eliot," *Journal of Modern Literature* 37.1 (2013) 158–77.

2. Jane Pritchard, in an essay related to the 2009/10 Victoria & Albert Ballets Russes exhibition, wrote that "there was very little that he [Diaghilev] did not try, from productions without dancers to multimedia works. Diaghilev could be distant

or he could charm, but above all he could radiate extraordinary authority and power, which enabled him to bring together a group of such innovative individuals to create original works of art." Jane Pritchard, "Creating Productions," *Diaghilev and the Golden Age of the Ballets Russes 1909–1929*, ed. Jane Pritchard (London: V&A Publishing, 2010) 88.

3. Diaghilev in Steven G. Marks, *How Russia Shaped the Modern World* (Princeton: Princeton Univ. Press, 2003) 181. Lady Ottoline Morrell in Marks, 184.

4. Joan Acocella, "The Showman: How Diaghilev Came to Dance," *New Yorker* Sept. 13, 2010. https://www.newyorker.com/magazine/2010/09/20/the-showman.

5. On Meyerhold's importance for Nijinsky, Bakst, Diaghilev, and concepts of modernist ballet, see Garafola, 1989: 32–33, 53–56. In 1908, Bakst worked with Meyerhold on Ida Rubenstein's 1908 production of S*alomé.* In 1910, the director attended Diaghilev's *soirees* in his St. Petersburg apartment bringing together artists, musicians, dancers, and composers.

6. André Levinson, "Two Aesthetics," *Ballet Old and New*, trans. Susan Cook Summer (New York: Dance Horizons, 1982) 37–44; Sjeng Scheijen, *Diaghilev* 173.

7. Leo Tolstoy, *War and Peace*, trans. Louise and Aylmer Maude, ed. George Gibian (New York: Norton, 1996). The translation was originally published in 1922. Book One, Ch. 10: 59. Further references are to this edition.

8. The reference on p. 501 is to the popular French ballet star Louis Duport who arrived in St. Petersburg in 1808 and performed at the Mariinsky Theater and was known for the speed of his pirouettes and overall vivacity on stage. In Book Four, ch. 1, Rostov astonishes Natasha when he admits to never having seen Duport dance (Book Four, ch. 1: 261).

When Natasha dances later in the novel, she exhibits an instinctive connection to Russian folk traditions. Dropping her French airs, she breaks into an authentic Russian folk dance which she has never done before but somehow knows its spirit, movements, and "unteachable" Russian gestures. The movements of her shoulder and waist reveal "all that was in . . . every Russian man and woman" (Book Seven, ch. VII: 454). On the dance as a metaphor of Russia's conflicting roots between folk traditions and Europe, see Orlando Figes, *Natasha's Dance: A Cultural History of Russia* (London: Allen Lane, 2002) especially xxv–xxviii.

Earlier, Natasha told Rostov, after demonstrating for a few seconds *en pointe*, that she will never marry "but will be a dancer. Only don't tell anyone" (Book Four, Ch. 1: 262).

9. Pushkin, *Eugene Onegin,* trans. Henry Spalding (London: Macmillan, 1881). Project Gutenberg. http://www.gutenberg.org/files/23997/23997-h/23997-h.htm. Vladimir Nabokov supposedly praised the stanza as the most mellifluous in all Russian poetry.

Istomina became the first Russian dancer *en pointe* and danced in the Imperial Ballet for twenty years. Didelot (1767–1837) became head of the theater school attached to the Imperial Theatres in St. Petersburg in 1802. See Paul Schmidt, "Pushkin and Istomina: Ballet in Nineteenth-Century Russia," *Dance Research Journal* 20.2 (1988): 3–8.

Diaghilev admired Pushkin so strongly that he would make a yearly pilgrimage to the poet's grave and during repairs was supposedly able to kiss the coffin (Homans 296).

10. See John E. Bowlt, "Sergei Diaghilev and Stravinsky: From World of Art to Ballets Russes," *Stravinsky in Context*, ed. Graham Griffiths (Cambridge: Cambridge Univ. Press, 2021) 62–67. Bowlt points out that ballet was initially not the primary example of a synthesizing art for the "World of Art" movement. Book design and architecture took precedence in an effort to reintegrate the arts (Bowlt 66).

11. On the four conventional styles of Russian classical ballet before Diaghilev—the heroic, romantic, eighteenth-century, and national—see Lieven, 68.

12. In John E. Bowlt, *Moscow & St. Petersburg 1900–1920: Art, Life & Culture of the Russian Silver Age* (New York: Vendome Press, 2008) 82.

13. For a full account, see Olga Haldey, "Savva Mamontov, Serge Diaghilev and a Rocky Path to Modernism," *Journal of Musicology* 22.4 (2005): 559–603. Mamontov supported the aesthetic idea of art for art's sake rather than its social relevance or as a representation of reality. He repeatedly shared his perspective with his cousin, the future director of the Moscow Art Theater, Konstantin Stanislavksy. See Haldey 569 and Haldey, *Mamontov's Private Opera: The Search for Modernism in Russian Theater* (Bloomington: Indiana Univ. Press, 2010).

14. There is some debate as to the exact date. See Scheijen 468 n. 7.

15. Nicolas Legat, in *The Story of the Russian School*, trans. Sir Paul Dukes (London: British Continental Press, 1932), offers this description of Petipa's method in producing a ballet: First, he would require absolute silence in the rehearsal hall. Next, consulting his notes, he would methodically work out his groupings based on models like chess pawns, each representing dancers. For separate dance numbers and *pas de deux*, he would compose at rehearsals but only after he had the music played through. Such rigid practice led by a single individual was the antithesis of Diaghilev's technique. See Legat 36–37.

16. Rumors spread by the court did not intimidate the company. Two were that they were dancing in the nude and that the company was actually an anti-Tsarist cabal.

17. Diaghilev in a 1910 interview in Scheijen 185.

18. Roger Fry, "M. Larionow and the Russian Ballet," *A Roger Fry Reader,* ed. Christopher Reed (Chicago: Univ. of Chicago Press, 1996) 291. Hereafter Fry.

For a broader discussion of the Ballets Russes and stage design, see John E. Bowlt, "Stage Design and the Ballets Russes," *Journal of Decorative and Propaganda Arts* 5 (1987): 28–45. Bowlt is especially clear on the design distinctions between Benois, Bakst, and Larionov. Bakst, like Larionov, understood that the dancer, set, choreographer, composer, and costume designer had to work in unison. For example, his stylization and emphasis on the angular nature of the decor of *Petrouchka* visually paralleled the "discordant syncopation of Stravinsky's music" (Bowlt 35). He, like the other designers for the Ballets Russes, understood the stage in three dimensions and not as an extension of the easel.

19. John E. Bowlt, "Stage Design and the Ballets Russes," *Journal of Decorative and Propaganda Arts* 5 (1987): 31. Not all the costume designs were a success,

however. Diaghilev had to threaten dancers with penalties in order to make them dance in Larionov's unwieldy costumes for *Chout* (1921).

20. For a detailed analysis of this development see Pieter C. van den Toorn and John McGinness, *Stravinsky and the Russian Period: Sound and Legacy of a Musical Idiom* (Cambridge: Cambridge Univ. Press, 2012) 20–21.

21. See Hanna Järvinen, "Failed Impressions: Diaghilev's Ballets Russes in America, 1916," *Dance Research Journal* 42.2 (2010) 80–81. For further details outlining the disputes over casting and finances with the second U.S. tour of 1916—a number of dancers in the *corps de ballet* wrote directly to Otto Kahn (chairman of the Metropolitan Opera's board and sponsor of the tour) that their wages did not meet their living expenses—see Lynn Garafola, "The Ballets Russes in America," *The Art of Enchantment: Diaghilev's Ballets Russes 1909–1929*, ed. Nancy Van Norman Baer (San Francisco: Fine Arts Museums of San Francisco, 1988) 122–37. Pages 136–37 give exact financial figures.

22. Homans in *Apollo's Angels* is useful on these changes during and after the war: see 320, 327–28, 330–31.

23. In 1919, El Lissitzky's emblematic "Beat the Whites with the Red Wedge" reduced the complexity of Russia's civil war to a red triangle piercing a white circle. This was a geometric confrontation of good and evil that everyone could comprehend. For an overview, see Martin Sixsmith, "The story of art in the Russian revolution," Royal Academy post, December 20, 2016. https://www.royalacademy.org.uk/article/art-and-the-russian-revolution.

24. For a summary of the situation see Caroline Pouncy, "Dancing Up a Storm: The 1917 Revolution and Russian ballet," *Culture Matters*, March 19, 2017. https://www.culturematters.org.uk/index.php/arts/theatre/item/2484-dancing-up-a-storm-the-1917-revolution-and-russian-ballet.

25. Curiously, Alexandra Balashova left for Paris after the revolution and bought Isadora Duncan's Paris apartment, but in 1921, Duncan arrived in Moscow to open her School of Plastic Dance and curiously stayed at 20 Prechistenka Street, Balashova's former home. Duncan first visited Russia in 1904.

26. On this topic, see Kathryn LeBere, "Red Swans: The Transformation of Ballet after the Russian Cultural Revolution (1924–1937)," Honors thesis, University of Victoria, April 2019. https://www.uvic.ca/humanities/history/assets/docs/honours-thesis---kate-lebere-2019.pdf. Also useful is Douglas M. Priest, "The Bolshoi Meets Bolshevism: Moving Bodies and Body Politics, 1917–1934," PhD thesis, Univ. of Michigan, 2016. file:///C:/Users/Ira/AppData/Local/Temp/Priest_grad.msu_0128D_14463.pdf. Priest at one point claims that "it is not an exaggeration to say the Ballets Russes had more influence on the direction of ballet in the twentieth century than any other single ballet company" (Priest 13).

By the 1930s, there was a return to classicism expressed through the "Vaganova method" which emphasized coordination of the head, hands, arms, and eyes of the dancers moving synchronously with their legs and feet. No less than Gorky in "On Formalism" in *Pravda* argued that the people needed harmonious art forms to make their lives "happier and more beautiful, not complex and depressing." In Le Bere 37;

also see Homans, *Apollo's Angels* 355. Natalia Roslavleva's *Era of Russian Ballet* (1966) is also helpful.

27. Nijinska in Lynn Garafola, "Choreography by Nijinska," *Legacies of Twentieth-Century Dance* (Middletown, CT: Wesleyan Univ. Press, 2005) 195. Hereafter Garafola 2005. In her treatise, "On Movement and the School of Movement," Nijinska began with "movement is the principle of element of dancing," adding that "movement constitutes the material of dance." Nijinska in Garafola, *La Nijinska: Choreographer of the Modern* (New York: Oxford, 2022) 62.

28. Two new works that document the immense contributions of Nijinska and Balanchine are Lynn Garafola, *La Nijinska: Choreographer of the Modern* (2022) and Jennifer Homans, *Mr. B: George Balanchine's 20th Century* (2022).

29. Balanchine in "Great Figures of Russian Ballet," *The Great History of Russian Ballet: Its Art and Choreography,* ed. R. Coalson (Bournemouth: Parkstone Press, 1998) 85.

30. Francis Mason, "Introduction," *I Remember Balanchine: Recollections of the Ballet Master by Those Who Knew Him* (New York: Doubleday, 1991) xi. Hereafter Mason.

31. Yuri Slonimsky, "Balanchine: The Early Years," trans. John Andrews, *Ballet Review* Vol. 5.3 (1976) 1–64; repr. in Mason, ed., *I Remember Balanchine* 19–78. Hereafter Slonimsky.

For a detailed account of Balanchine and the survival of ballets during changes in Soviet cultural life under Lenin's New Economic Plan, see Elizabeth Kendall, *Balanchine and the Lost Muse: Revolution and the Making of a Choreographer* (New York: Oxford Univ. Press, 2013) passim. She especially reveals the importance of cabaret and the Maly Theater for Balanchine, while the Young Ballet group became an experimental, interdisciplinary collective. In addition, she points to Lydia Ivanova as an early muse.

32. Elizabeth Souritz in Robert Gottlieb, *George Balanchine: The Ballet Maker* (New York: Atlas Books, 2004) 23. Also of use is Souritz, *Soviet Choreographers in the 1920s*, trans. Lynn Visson, additional trans. and ed. Sally Banes (Durham, NC: Duke Univ. Press, 1990).

33. Jennifer Homans, "Fluidity," *The New Yorker*, February 20, 2023: 67.

34. One performance required the troupe to dance while students chanted Alexander Blok's poem "The Twelve." The dancers did not illustrate the poem but performed a dance with movements much like Russian folk dances. But the rhythm was difficult. Many rehearsals preceded the performance with Balanchine counting out the steps. Nina Stukolkina in Mason 80.

35. For additional details on these adventures, see Jennifer Homans, *Mr. B* 92–110.

36. Richard Buckle with John Taras, *George Balanchine, Ballet Master: A Biography* (New York: Random House, 1988) 32. Hereafter Buckle 1988.

37. Balanchine in Charles M. Joseph, *Stravinsky & Balanchine: A Journey of Invention* (New Haven: Yale Univ. Press, 2002) 1. Hereafter Joseph.

38. Tim Scholl, *From Petipa to Balanchine: Classical Revival and the Modernization of Ballet* (London: Routledge, 1994) 110.

39. Michel, Georges-Michel, "A New Work by a Great Musician of Today: *Apollon Musagète*," *Excelsior*, October 27, 1927, in Joseph 84. Diaghilev on Venice, in Scheijen 5.

40. Rumnev in Nicoletta Misler, "Precarious Bodies: Performing Constructivism," *Russian Avant-Garde Theatre: War, Revolution & Design* (London: Nick Hern Books, 2014) 53. Hereafter *RAVT*.

Also useful are Misler's *The Russian Art of Movement: 1920–1930* (London: Allemandi & Co., 2017) and the earlier *Russian Art of the Avant-Garde: Theory and Criticism, 1902–1934*, ed. and trans. John E. Bowlt (New York: Viking, 1976).

41. Marinetti in Galina Yelshevskaya, "Russian Avant Garde," https://arzamas .academy/materials/1231. In 1927, the critic and artist Wyndham Lewis began a new journal simply entitled *Enemy.*

42. Marinetti in Lynn Garofola, "The Making of Ballet Modernism," *Dance Research Journal* 20.2 (Winter 1988) 23. This is an important article on the Futurist contribution to the Ballets Russes.

43. Susanna Pasticci, "Futurism," *The Cambridge Stravinsky Encyclopedia*, ed. Edward Campbell and Peter O'Hagan (Cambridge: Cambridge Univ. Press, 2021) 182.

44. See Lieven 84.

45. Kazimir Malevich, "Suprematism," *Russian Art of the Avant-Garde: Theory and Criticism, 1902–1934*, rev. ed., trans. John E. Bowlt (London: Thames and Hudson, 1988) 145.

Chapter 3

Paper Numbers

The Business of Ballet

Serge Diaghilev needed money again. One night at dinner with the Russian banker, balletomane, and devotee of the Ballets Russes, Baron Dmitri Gunzburg, Diaghilev brought up the topic. He had already charmed the Baron into thinking he was an essential partner in the enterprise, appointing him co-director in 1910 and adding his name on posters announcing new programs. Generous but irregular in his accounting methods, the Baron met Diaghilev's request, typically jotting down the advance on his shirt cuffs but often falling "into despair when a shirt with an account had gone to the laundry." Nevertheless, Gunzburg considered his shirt cuff unquestioned proof of money lent, even if his memory was faulty and the cuff cleaned; Diaghilev, in turn, never doubted "the force of such a document."[1]

Shirt cuffs. Not every financial document or exchange was so informal. Initially supported by institutions like the Russian Imperial Theaters, Diaghilev had increasingly to rely on private support from patrons, sponsors, kings, princesses, and the box office. How he did it and re-made the business of ballet is the focus of this chapter which considers the performances of the Ballets Russes within the social and economic conditions of their production, circulation, and consumption.[2]

Diaghilev possessed an uncanny sense of who might financially participate in the company's success and who would not. He understood the desire of the bourgeoise to attach themselves to art and culture (for status as much as enjoyment), transforming such abstract wishes into visible forms on stage and social interactions in the audience. It was a chance to dress, be seen and experience the art; soon *le tout Paris* felt obliged to attend.[3] But only well-supported ballet, as a social commodity, could meet those desires. But Diaghilev's charm could convince even donors to be flexible. He convinced Sir Joseph Beecham, who financed Stravinsky's *Le Rossignol,* to allow the premiere to occur in Paris, not London. But he also knew that he could put advantageous people of standing and wealth at a disadvantage. If he had an appointment at four, he'd appear at six. He would mix his "personal charm and snobbish skill . . . as a weapon to achieve his purpose" (Lieven 247). The service of art must be for beauty at any price but on his terms not others. He constantly sought to impress and astound, seeking sensational effects on and off the stage.

But he often ran into institutional opposition. When he announced to the program committee of the Paris Opéra that he would offer a mixed season of opera and ballet in the Spring of 1909, they objected. He was told ballet was not appropriate for the Opéra, the premiere French National Theater. Incensed, he cancelled the contract. Not everyone welcomed his diverse offerings. But again, Diaghilev recovered, announcing to his company back in St. Petersburg that he had a new contract with the smaller and more modest *Théâtre du Châtelet*. In April 1909, rehearsals began in St. Petersburg with planning for the "Polovtsian Dances" from Borodin's *Prince Igor* with new steps by Fokine. It was the start of an enormously varied *repertoire* but not all of it original. Diaghilev called it *Le Festin* composed of numbers taken from various ballets and operas principally borrowed from the Mariinsky.

Dance is a commodity and ballet is no exception. Diaghilev understood this and the tension between the artistic and the commercial. Despite his focus on aesthetics, often embodying the avant-garde, he was never exempt from the vagaries of the market system. A structure of institutions, whether banks, theatre managers, or impresarios, plus conductors, composers, dancers or choreographers, constantly hindered his ability to produce the imaginative shows he felt should be the hallmark of the Ballets Russes. An obligation to entertain mixed with a desire to imagine met financial obstacles. Nevertheless, he imagined first and thought about budgets second, reversing the typical practice of ballet companies. Although avant-garde experiment showcasing the new and the daring created public excitement, the balance sheet and box office curbed excess and experimentation.[4] Promotion and sales became paramount, new factors in the economics of ballet.

Out of necessity, Diaghilev initiated a new funding model (private donors), while responding, in an *ad hoc* manner, to each situation as needed. Unrestricted in his actions, he could be flexible in his approach and open to every possible source. There was freedom in not being dependent on public or government funded sources. But as Pierre Bourdieu noted, economies jeopardize artistic autonomy as "symbolic goods" become both "a commodity and a symbolic object." Unavoidably, the theater directly experiences "the immediate sanction of the bourgeois public, with its values and conformisms."[5]

Shifting its audience from connoisseurs to consumers, Diaghilev knowingly directed the Ballets Russes into the sphere of business, image making and commodification. By 1913, the company's deluxe programs became collector's items often sold independently of their performances. The ballet consumer valued the programs, props, costumes, and designs, while "performances of the Ballets Russes were transformed from objects d'art to articles whose value was determined by their scarcity in the marketplace" (Garafola, 1989: 298).

Dances only exist when they are public, which unavoidably involves institutionalization: they are part of a company, a school, or a theater program which may ease the matter of financing, promotion, or grants. Occasionally, individual performers, such as Isadora Duncan, were able to promote their art singularly but even that individuality needs to be formed into an organization. The Martha Graham, Alvin Ailey, or Joffrey Ballet companies are but three contemporary examples created to ensure financial and cultural viability, while embodying the work of a single dancer or choreographer.[6] But the public mediation of dance turns it into an item of consumption, an article of artistic commerce.

Diaghilev recognized this and sought to capitalize on its value. But his seeming lack of financial acumen, neglecting proper financial planning, originated not with neglect but with his uncertain and haphazard income sources. He needed to be as original in raising money as he was in commissioning new and experimental works. Non-existent accounting or business practices, with only partial or incomplete financial records, became his standard because of his freewheeling method of funding and unreliable money sources. He could create and prepare in detail a ballet season but overlook or neglect the financial guidance needed for the viability of the productions. With a choreographer or composer, he could outline a nearly complete ballet and program but was unable to do so financially for the company.

Diaghilev's so-called *Black Notebook* of 1910–1911 records the confusion. While attempting to outline plans for a season with entries made in various colors of ink and pencil with frequent deletions, insertions, corrections, and additions, Diaghilev still floundered. Doodles and cartoons supplemented names, figures, and titles. On its large ledger pages are his own sketches for scenes alongside the names of potential dancers and columns of figures often not totalled. Individual figures were added up but then forgotten in what was no more than a gesture toward accounting.[7] In the notebook, items from an irregular expense account vie with the Paris ballet repertoire or notes for the proposed 1912 season in London and Monte Carlo. There are also lists of dancers' names with the number of roles noted for each: Fedorova and Nijinsky each had nine, Karsavina, Nijinska, and Bolm eight, but there is no record of bank deposits, withdrawals, or contracts. Beauty on stage overshadowed numbers on a page.

Nevertheless, there are details on projected ballets, financial records, budgets, and future plans. Almost 50 percent of the entries deal with some aspect of money and although his general expense accounts were unclear, he was specific on individual production costs and the exact sums to be paid each dancer and singer. Contrary to many, he did seem to know his way around balance sheets, although for perhaps tactical reasons, he gave a different impression.[8]

The notebook also shows that Diaghilev was thinking ahead. Among the 1911 jottings in Russian and French, with sketches by the author, are plans for a three-year program with a proposed tour of the U.S. with notes on preliminary casts. There are also notes on how *The Firebird*, *Cléopâtre*, and *Le Carnaval* could be improved. Other items showing his wide-ranging concerns include supplying publicity photos to the theaters he planned to visit in Rome, London, and St. Petersburg. Numerous other ideas and plans for possible ballets appear, many of them later discarded.[9]

Diaghilev chose his irregular financial path not out of neglect or disinterest but the opposite. He likely had a strong sense of what fiscal obligations he would incur if he incorporated or formed a proper business in France, where he principally operated. There, he would be obliged by the French Code to have his main account books inspected and verified by a public official who would certify the accuracy of the information. He would also need to show a journal or daybook of his transactions, only one of many standards in the continental regulation of accounting practices. He would also be required to keep an annual inventory of assets, as well as an annual balance sheet designed to assure every creditor of the solvency of the company. This would be a challenge since his finances fluctuated drastically, every loan a new re-capitalization.

Additionally, the balance sheet must be presented to the stockholders at their annual meeting, the two items an anathema to Diaghilev who preferred, actually insisted on, keeping his finances private. The French Code also required that the annual balance sheet not merely be accessible before the annual meeting but be sent, together with a profit and loss statement, to the shareholders and afterwards published. Diaghilev knew that even the hint of such a publication of record would likely terminate the Ballets Russes because of its persistent record of losses and debts. His objections to keeping proper records, internally or externally, had more to do with avoiding legal obligations than a blasé attitude towards money or financial neglect.[10] If he had become a French business, he would also have had to pay a national income tax levied on the company's net income. Deductions would be permitted but there was constant debate and litigation with the *fisc* (national treasury) on the validity of such deductions. For Diaghilev to enter into the world of deficits, depreciation, inflation, and double entry bookkeeping was a distraction from his developing world of private finance.

Furthermore, contingencies always disrupted plans, often increasing costs; and there was never a surplus which by French law would be necessary if the company was incorporated. And any advantages of increasing capital by issuing stock would be offset by new regulations and responsibilities. Profit was never a possibility especially with the complication that gross profits must equal net sales minus total costs, while profits that have no counterpart in new working capital would be considered fictitious. Allied with the problem of the correct calculation of profits was the need for accounting statements on the costs of production, a guide to pricing policies (namely setting ticket prices), and the requirement to publish under expenses, the salaries and wages of his dancers.

As a French entity, Diaghilev would also have to set aside a proportion of his net surplus in the form of a reserve. For Diaghilev, this was an impossibility. But without a statement of costs (which constantly fluctuated), it was impossible to project his expenses or even debts with any certainty.[11] There was also never any "Depreciation of Capital and Reserve Account" which was to show accumulated losses and gains over a certain period. Cash accounting was a system Diaghilev sought to avoid. His French agent and promoter, Gabriel Astruc, failed in an attempt to form a proper company for the Ballets Russes. Capital was found but the scheme collapsed because there were no legitimate balance sheets or records. There were also no books or ledgers—only scraps of paper with scribbles that only Diaghilev could decipher (Lieven 224–25).

Diaghilev's 1910/11 ledger book also reveals inequities within the company: Pavlova would have received Frs. 25,000 if she participated in the forthcoming Paris season of 1910 but when she became unavailable, he substituted the Moscow ballerina Ekaterina Gelzer at a salary of Frs. 15,000. Members of the ballet corps were to receive Frs. 2,200. Shifting to ballet alone from ballet and opera programs, his initial Paris productions, was a definite savings: there was less scenery and fewer costumes. It made economic sense to concentrate on ballet; opera was simply too expensive. There was no gain in financial transparency, however.

Yet it was to Diaghilev's advantage that he avoided any formal accounting practices which incorporation would entail because he would have to provide details on the nominal value of any working capital, matters of depreciation, expenses, and the existence of a cash reserve. Furthermore, by prolonging his repayments, he repaid with depreciated francs, always worth less than what he borrowed. It made sense, although his own assets also depreciated, while his purchasing power declined. His two business associates other than Dmitri Gunzburg, Grigoriev and Nouvel, had little financial experience and carried out only rudimentary financial actions, mostly paying bills.

But curiously Diaghilev's business practices were in line with the overall economics of France, especially after WWI. The deficit of France generated by the war was met by borrowing: the government could not meet current budgetary expenditures from tax revenues. The Bank of France made large loans to the government, increasing public indebtedness and giving rise to so-called "credit inflation." In some ways, Diaghilev duplicated this practice repeated by businesses attempting to regain their economic footing after the war. Consolidated and floating debt, the *bête noir* of the Ballets Russes, mirrored that of the French economy but both accepted it as common practice. But Diaghilev never issued bonds to be used as collateral to secure his loans either from individuals or banks. His only assets were his sets, costumes, musical scores, reputation, and personality. Yet it was a period of inflation where expenses constantly increased and the franc fell.

If Diaghilev could cut corners, he would, using loaned opera and ballet scenery from the Imperial Theaters and a subsidy of 100,000 rubles from the Tsar's brother, Grand Duke Vladimir, to mount his mixed season of ballet and opera in 1908 Paris. With his new agent, Gabriel Astruc, who would soon handle publicity and ticket sales at half his customary commission, Diaghilev expected a successful 1909 season. He was partially right. It was a critical success but financial disaster. The death of the Grand Duke ended the subsidy, the decision to stop the transfer largely the result of the angered ballerina Kchessinskaya, mistress to the Grand Duke's son, and passed over by Diaghilev as a featured artist of the Paris season.[12] Romance, jealously, money, and dance mixed, with economics playing a devastating role.

The public success of the 1909 season overlooked its financial pitfalls: by June 15, Astruc told Diaghilev they had Frs. 405,000 and to expect Frs. 500,000 or Frs. 510,000 by the end of the season in a few days' time. Expenses, however, were Frs. 600,000. How, Astruc asked, would the bills be paid? Diaghilev was silent on the deficit, showing Astruc a few days later that they were actually Frs. 86,000 in the red. A guarantor (under no obligation to pay any money) generously offered Frs. 10,000. Pressed, Diaghilev found more funds and paid half his total debt of Frs. 76,000 (Frs. 86,000 minus the Frs. 10,000 loan). But as Richard Buckle notes, during the 1908–1909 winter, Diaghilev had only to confront the problem of raising money to subsidize his first season with the company in the West. During the winter of 1909–1910, however, he had to raise money not only for the forthcoming season but to pay off debts of the old (Buckle 158). This would become a repeated pattern and explain why Diaghilev was continuously in debt.

Almost from the start of the Ballets Russes, expenses exceeded box office receipts. In his biography of Diaghilev, Richard Buckle vividly represents the benchmark year of 1909, Diaghilev's so-called *Saison russe* (he did not publicize the name Ballets Russes until 1910). On p. 153, Buckle reproduces the budget (likely prepared by Diaghilev's Paris partner, Astruc, because of issues of negative cash flow), beginning with payment of a tax for the poor (Frs. 50,000), fees for the *corps de ballet* (Frs. 60,000), Frs. 60,000 for the orchestra, Frs. 55,000 for Chaliapin, Frs. 40,000 for ballet soloists, Frs. 65,000 to rent the theater, Frs. 25,000 for stage staff and lighting, Frs. 15,000 for directors and administration, Frs. 25,000 for authors' rights, Frs. 10,000 for tradesmen, and Frs. 30,000 for publicity and posters. Total payments equalled Frs. 590,000. The total receipts were Frs. 522,000. The deficit was actually Frs. 68,000 with Frs. 30,000 already repaid.

But in response, and because of his debts, Astruc seized Diaghilev's sets, costumes, and properties of the Russian season. With these he secured a loan of Frs. 20,000 from Raoul Guinsbourg of the Société de Monaco. The tangible assets would go to the Casino Theater of Monte Carlo if not redeemed by a certain date. There were 668 costumes and 12 decors. Astruc also officially seized Diaghilev's possessions at the Hôtel de Hollande, duplicating the earlier actions of an upholsterer, Belsacq. He then formally applied to bankrupt Diaghilev at the Tribunal de Commerce de la Seine. In response, Diaghilev signed a bill of undertaking to reimburse Astruc Frs. 15,000 within three months, an impossibility.[13] Diaghilev constantly flirted with bankruptcy.

The outstanding debt became Frs. 38,000, which Diaghilev did not have (Buckle 153). Various borrowings began but he often did not honor his obligations, while new problems emerged: he could not find £500 as a down payment for a proposed 1910 visit to London with Karsavina performing. Plans for the London season had to be cancelled. Repeatedly and gallantly, he incurred debts he was unable to pay. Redecorating a theatre for the Paris season was but one example. In retaliation for increasing Paris debts, Astruc worked to permanently damage Diaghilev's reputation at the Imperial Court. One consequence was the refusal of Grand Duke Vladimir's widow to approve a request to grant a Patent of Nobility to a Riga industrialist who offered Diaghilev a sizeable loan. Insulted, Diaghilev announced he would no longer rely on government funds, an explanation that overlooks the collapse of his reputation (Buckle 155–56). Private backers and the box office would have to provide his money, so he thought, or at least hoped.

Renewing his association with Astruc was one solution but it meant entrusting the administration, box office, and publicity to Astruc who would receive 5 percent of the gross receipts of every performance (paid nightly) plus 25 percent of the total profits if any. On the day of the new agreement, Diaghilev paid Astruc Frs. 24,711 owing, plus costs and interest. Their partnership was restarted but necessary if, in the dramatized language of Buckle, "the Russian Ballet [was] to fulfill its destiny" (Buckle 157). Negotiations continued with the two principals constantly exchanging proposals. At one point, after Pavlova announced a London engagement making an appearance with the Ballets Russes impossible, Diaghilev, unwilling to share the news with Astruc, proposed an offer of three performances of the popular *Cléopâtre* at the Châtelet for Frs. 50,000. Astruc countered by saying that for Frs. 45,000 he wanted three performances made up of *Les Sylphies, Cléopâtre*, and *Le Festin*. The following would also have to appear: Kchessinskaya, Pavlova, Karsavina, Rubinstein, Nijinsky, and Fokine; and the works were exclusive to him. Diaghilev found the demands impossible, unable to give up half his repertoire for the Opéra season; and he certainly could not produce Pavlova.

From an associate in Russia, Astruc learned that Diaghilev could not raise any funds, partly because of the scandals surrounding his name because of the debts from the 1909 season. Astruc, infuriated at Diaghilev's financial failures, prepared an eleven-page report to the Russian Court on Diaghilev's malfeasance and how he unofficially signed documents as a personal attaché of the "Chancellerie Personnelle de Sa Majesté l' Empereur de Russie" (Buckle 155). Diaghilev's delinquent payments and deleterious behavior, overlooking deadlines, or neglecting obligations were further indictments.

The new season seemed in jeopardy, yet Diaghilev promised dates to Astruc for the general rehearsal and première without any idea of his principal dancers or the ballets he would present—and without any funds (Buckle 163–64). Such boldness in advancing a plan without any details to overcome financial friction was typical of Diaghilev as well as his habit of promises made but not kept. And only by flattering and honoring the banker Baron Dmitri Gunzburg, who advanced funds, was Diaghilev able to pay Astruc Frs. 5,000 in February 1910 and then, in March 1910, honor a bill for Frs. 17,432. But the 1910 season was still uncertain, although Astruc stepped forward to assist, helping to raise money as a guarantee. Diaghilev accepted all financial responsibility for the season, hiring the Opéra for only a few days and hoping the box office would cover expenses, while assuring Astruc he would receive his percentage (Buckle 165). However, anxiety caused by these money problems led some in his circle to worry over his mental health (Buckle 165).

Limiting the 1910 season to one only of ballet was the remedy. Chaliapin refused to return to Paris and it made no economic sense to produce opera without him. Diaghilev's representatives, however, had to convince the directors of l'Opéra that it was financially sound to offer a season limited only to ballet. It was too risky to transport a large company of singers and mount a cumbersome opera production. Ballet became the answer, a surprising success. Diaghilev's prepackaged programs did not require the massive number of musicians and supernumeraries opera demanded.

What were the reasons for Diaghilev's casual attitude toward money, even when the obligations were contractual and legal? Was it "typical Russian carelessness," as Benois explained, or willful neglect?[14] Overall, it was an optimistic belief that new funds would always, somehow, materialize and that his dancers and his productions would continuously attract patrons and donors, while box office demand would increase. But his seeming indifference to his financial responsibilities, whether to dancers, conductors, composers, choreographers, stagehands, theatre managers, or lenders was also a pose. He was skillful with contracts both for individual dancers and touring. He paid attention to costs but would not approve false economies; he always demanded the best for his productions, whether material for costumes or artists for his sets. But despite a constant quest for money, he disliked dealing with it because of its social stigma: a debt might cause embarrassment, awkwardness, and even accusations of fraud. He avoided all three by avoiding all public displays of need. But he also had to make quick getaways, especially when facing unpaid hotel bills.

Diaghilev endlessly needed funds to operate and cultivated a set of supportive patrons from Baron Gunzburg to Princesse de Polignac (née Winnaretta Singer, heiress of the Singer sewing machine fortune), Misia Sert, Lady Juliet Duff, Coco Chanel, and the British newspaper magnate Lord Rothermere. One more was Sir Joseph Beecham who loaned Diaghilev Frs. 100,000 for his London opera season of 1914—Astruc's empire had by then collapsed (Garafola, 1989: 182). But the terms of repayment to Beecham were steep: installments within forty-eight hours of each performance.[15]

Yet despite the financial obstacles, Diaghilev still planned, encouraging Louis Laloy and Debussy to work on a new ballet as he did with Cocteau and Proust's friend, the composer Reynaldo Hahn. Earlier, in July 1909, he began complicated negotiations with Astruc for the return of his musical scores. Confusing matters were secret discussions with the Paris Opéra without Astruc's knowledge. An infuriated Astruc then worked vigorously to prevent Diaghilev from ever bringing Russian artists to Paris, beginning with an eleven-page report.

Nevertheless, by December 1909, Diaghilev and Astruc, with the assistance of well-placed intermediaries, patched up their differences and renewed a profitable relationship. Part of the new agreement was that Diaghilev would pay Astruc Frs. 24,711 still owing, plus costs and interest. When the 1910 season was finally set, it became a dramatic example of how economics shaped artistic decisions. Ballet was a default choice once Chaliapin refused to sing. And offsetting Diaghilev's cavalier financial behavior was the excitable and idealistic Astruc, trained as a professional theater manager. He was a businessman who carefully organized payments, rents, and salaries, repeatedly taking artistic as well as commercial credit for Diaghilev's successes. He was also a friend of Proust's and helped to edit and published the first edition of *Swann's Way*.[16]

Contracts were always a challenge for Diaghilev who signed only one with Nijinsky, possibly done before the two even met. Preparing for the 1908 Paris season, Diaghilev worked out his list of dancers and gave the details and contracts to Grigoriev to complete. In addition to stage manager, Grigoriev, who would marry one of the ballerinas (Lubov Tchernichva), was responsible for the practical side of the company from the contracts to paydays, cast lists for programs, organization of rehearsals, and even assistance in re-mounting revivals. He even had several walk-on parts, including the Shah's brother in *Schéhérazade.*

Records show that for May and June 1909 in Paris, a contract dated October 10, 1908, was to be signed five times by the neophyte Nijinsky who would receive a fee of Frs. 2,500 and a second-class rail ticket from St. Petersburg to Paris. By contrast, for Fydor Chaliapin to sing in three operas in 1912, he was to receive a fee of Frs. 140,000 of which Frs. 15,000 were to be paid in advance. Furthermore, he was to receive Frs. 4,500 after the first act of each performance until paid in full. Other contracts were for dancers, conductors, designers, and even stagehands. In a collection of such contracts, there is even acknowledgement of a loan of ₽6,000 from Baron Gunzburg to the dancer Adolph Bolm. The many contracts between Diaghilev and his producers and tour promoters, however, had a powerful economic feature: Diaghilev made advance payment of a sum to himself a condition of signing. He then used the advance to pay past debts, provide new personal capital, and with the balance maintain the solvency of the company (Lieven 167).

Diaghilev abhorred competition but often found himself in situations where he had to come up with extra funds to keep his best dancers. Some stars stayed with him even if they could find alternate work and some bargained. Spessivtseva forced Diaghilev to compete for her services; Diaghilev told Nouvel in 1924 that in order to keep her, he would go up to Frs. 100,000 for fifty performances over a two-year period. But before accepting this high offer, she insisted he pay her salary then in arrears. He did. By contrast, Karsavina worked for almost nothing for the privilege of being in his company. New art, not debts, was always his first concern. But he could also shave expenses, eliminating singers called for in the score of *Daphnis et Chloë* over Ravel's objections. A redesigned *Firebird* of 1926 saw economizing with the costumes.

Diaghilev's risky dependency on privately sourced funds, however, was modern, contradicting the Russian tradition of relying on the Imperial Theaters or the Tsar or philanthropic aristocrats for finances. The model for European dance companies had been institutional support, whether the Paris Opéra or the Royal Opera House, London. Diaghilev was largely free from conforming to established tastes or meeting bureaucratic demands as a consequence of his new independence. He did, however, have to rely on the impulses of his individual benefactors, spending excessive time soliciting monies. And his anxiety was constant since he had no idea of the source or amount of his next grant or loan. The uncertainty often led to friction with figures like Nijinsky, Benois, and Stravinsky, all owed money. He gained creative independence but at the cost of financial security and dancers' loyalty.

But his habits did not change. He could be extravagant with other people's money for his personal expenses, while trying to be practical with company funds (Buckle 295). He was not entirely irresponsible and had realized after the debacle of the 1909 that he had to initiate some degree of financial responsibility. This began with his appointment of Baron Gunzburg as the company's co-administrator in 1910, although he had been advising the company since 1909. This was a practical financial as well as social decision. Gunzburg, heir to the largest Jewish banking fortune of the Russian empire, the House of Gunzburg, was one of Europe's leading financiers. He wrote countless checks on the company's behalf and his name soon appeared on all Ballets Russes posters, satisfying his ego. By co-signing contracts, creditors believed that they had a guarantee of repayment for their loans and advances. But by 1913, he became one of the company's principal creditors, owed some Frs. 12,500 (Garafola 1989: 187).[17]

The years 1912–1914 remained a period of great financial turmoil for the Ballets Russes. The box office provided some monies but production capital for new ballets did not materialize. Cash flow problems became acute and short-term bank loans became the only and costly solution, at one point Frs. 300,000 borrowed from Brandeis et Cie.[18] But Diaghilev repeatedly failed to meet the scheduled repayments. A year later, nearly 20 percent of the company's gross income went to pay the previous year's advances. Diaghilev then turned to his principal dancer, Nijinsky, persuading him to lend *him* (Diaghilev) Frs. 100,000 before a South American tour in 1913 to cover the debts from the 1912 and 1913 seasons. But by June 1914, Frs. 176,595 were still outstanding (Garafola 1989: 187). Scenery and costumes were seized from the Paris Opéra. Other creditors included art printers and a theatrical agency which almost prevented the company from presenting its London season of 1913, made possible only because Diaghilev miraculously raised Frs. 188,606, possibly obtained through Sir Joseph Beecham, although Diaghilev's debts were never fully or ever paid off.

America offered one reprieve. It might supply the funds needed to keep the company afloat, although Diaghilev hated sea travel despite crossing to America from Bordeaux in January 1916. Most of the time he spent in his stateroom but when he stepped out, he always wore a lifejacket over his coat. The image is a metaphor of his financial anxiety, the lifejacket a thin, uncertain form of staying afloat (loans) through the irregular and sometimes

volatile support of patrons, protecting him from the larger and more dangerous sea of debt.

"It was one of Diaghilev's characteristics never to mention money."

S. L. Grigoriev, *The Diaghilev Ballet, 1909–1929*

The source of Diaghilev's financial behavior is complex. Paper numbers
meant little to him but also very much. Rather than become a store of value
and standard of deferred payment, he understood money as a down payment
on the future, equally needed and an annoyance. The affective meaning of
funds meant that they became a satisfying set of illusions to be cited, referred
to, and applied but also forgotten. They symbolized control but could be
manipulated and altered, in his case allowing others to analyze and respond
to them. He repeatedly overlooked the accrual principle, which means that
one should record accounting transactions in the period in which they actually
occur, rather than the period in which the cash flows related to them occur.
Properly implemented, the principle allows one to aggregate all revenue and
expense details for an accounting period. But Diaghilev never instituted a
standard accounting period.[19] He preferred the simpler but less accurate cash
method of accounting where you record revenue when cash is received and
expenses when they are paid.

Diaghilev also overlooked the reliability principle in accounting, which is
recording such transactions in an accounting system that can actually be verified objectively. These would include purchase receipts, cancelled checks,
bank statements, and/or promissory notes. Adding to confusion was that
payment or grants occurred in varying currencies: Rubles, Francs, Pounds,
Pesetas, or Dollars. Cash management was almost impossible because he
could not forecast cash flow. He never incorporated a standard reporting
time, whether monthly, quarterly, or annually. His energy went to what is now
labelled "investor relations."

The structure of receipts was itself instructive relating to the finances of the
company. In the prewar period, Diaghilev's agreements stipulated a flat performance fee: £400 in the case of Beecham's initial contract; Frs. 24,000 for
the Champs-Élysées season in 1913. His postwar contracts differed largely
because his stature had begun to diminish: payment was often calculated as
a percentage of box office receipts with a guaranteed performance minimum
(Garafola 1989: 182). This, of course, could never be certain. Nor could the
life of a theatre. Astruc went bankrupt after building the brilliant Théâtre des
Champs-Élysées where the inaugural season included Nijinky's *Le Sacre du
printemps* and Ida Rubinstein's *La Pisanelle*. But with the cost of huge orches-
tras, often seventy or eighty pieces (*Le Sacre* had over ninety instruments),

the expense of armies of extras, the size of opera companies, the cost of costumes, it is no surprise Astruc failed (Garafola 1989: 182). Production costs always exceeded income. Diaghilev challenged these per-production costs by proposing a fixed fee for an entire production. All was prepackaged and theater managers leapt at the proposal. But it did not always work. In 1912, Diaghilev agreed to accept 25 percent of the gross receipts after orchestra, lighting, publicity, and other expenses had been deducted. This was tied in with an advance from Beecham to Diaghilev for £950 (Garafola 1989: 183).

Diaghilev was better adjusted to renege rather than record, turning to others to help finance his debt creating, in turn, new debt. Money was not so much a motivator for Diaghilev as a facilitator. He understood its necessity to produce his ballets but disregarded its obligations. But his *louche* approach towards repayment did not create confidence in lenders.

The origins of this attitude likely reach back to his childhood and his father's bankruptcy in 1890 caused by the loss of his grandfather's distillery business in Perm. The family survived only through a new set of loans, creating new debt. Realistically, bankruptcy meant giving up a twenty-room home with a recital hall, an apartment in St. Petersburg, and a country estate in Bikbarda. The experience set the tone and pattern of his later actions, debt becoming a regular feature of his professional and personal life. Ironically, he could calculate the costs and details concerning scenery or dancers or music, often cutting bars or entire passages, but not those of his company's finances.

He was also artistically ruthless in sabotaging the careers of others, for example, blaming the failure of an American tour on Nijinsky rather than his own mismanagement or suggesting that it was Baron Gunzburg's fault in allowing Nijinsky to marry in September 1913 during the company's South American tour. Gunzburg had been deputized by Diaghilev to manage the company on the trip. This habit of blaming others for his shortcomings became Diaghilev's defense. He also victimized the ballet artists who left the company, frequently trying to block their employment with rivals. And he often undermined company members. Even before Nijinsky was dismissed from the Imperial Theaters, Diaghilev thought he might become his choreographer, negating the position of Fokine who became deeply offended. Page 123 of *The Black Notebook* suggests this change. Stravinsky summarized the situation when he told his wife in 1917 that Fokine "isn't *modern at all* and isn't even trying to be" (in Scheijen 233). Relations between Diaghilev and Fokine had actually been strained as early as 1910 but Nijinsky's new role, thought to bring fresh energy to the company, brought new stress and further divided the impresario and the more established choreographer (Blackwood 355 n. 18).[20] And although he passed off failures as the responsibility of others, everything, nonetheless, had to originate with the master who sought complete control. Compromise was a word little known to him. He always celebrated himself, writing his own (but unsigned) glowing review of his own watercolor show.[21]

Diaghilev understood the power of money as a means not an end, possessing a unique authority both instrumental *and* symbolic. As one economist wrote, money is "probably the most emotionally meaningful object in contemporary life: only food and sex are its close competitors."[22] Diaghilev's emotional relationship with money, like his relationship with love, was both distant and intimate, detailed and abstract, fluid and permanent, parallel to many of his own homosexual love affairs (mostly with men in his company). These became relations where departure or betrayal was often repeated and love lost its value. So, too, with money. Diaghilev found himself divorced from money as he was from permanent love but desiring both. But repayment gained you little; it didn't matter because you could never recapture the initial excitement nor the sense of permanency. Money is ultimately inadequate but its possession extends the self. In addition, money is valuable "because it is the means for the acquisition of values."[23] It is a structuring agent, as Diaghilev came to understand, making possible artistic freedom. Through its use, aesthetic and social values could be established and defined.

Georg Simmel further describes the "double demand upon every moment of life," living as if every moment was final but also that each moment is a transition point to a higher stage. Diaghilev unconsciously understood the "double demand," realizing that each performance was an end in itself, the complete expression of its art, but also a step in the effort to take ballet to higher cultural plateaus, the aim not only the total work of art but pure art unencumbered by money, people, or even time (Simmel 233). So, too, with the purpose of money: it had an immediate purpose, to pay off creditors, but also a higher goal: to permit the formation of new works of expressive movement that might possibly be repeated from one night to the next or from one stage to another. Money was the agent "that brings about the transformations in the sequence of purposes" (Simmel 490). Money brings about freedom.

Money and dance also seemed analogous. Simmel writes that the development of money first

> exhibits certain rhythmic phenomena. . . . From the chaotic fortuitousness that must have characterized its first appearance, money passed through a stage that at least reflects a principle and a meaningful form, until, at a still further stage, money gains a continuity in availability through which it is able to adjust itself to all objective and personal needs, free from the constraint of a rhythmic and, in a deeper sense, still fortuitous framework. (Simmel 497)

This might be a sketch of creation of *Le Sacre du printemps* or, on a larger scale, the acceptance of the avant-garde dances of the Ballets Russes. In a later passage, he adds, as if describing the distinction between the *corps de ballet* and the soloists, the interaction of the "two principles of life" characterized as "the symbols rhythmic—symmetrical and individualistic—spontaneous" (Simmel 498).

Money gained practical meaning for Diaghilev only when threatened with its loss, demonstrating Simmel's view that as money and transactions increase, the independence of an individual decreases (Simmel 509). And for Diaghilev, when another aggrieved party demanded payment, an action that often led to court, his independence was limited. Conflicts with his dancers or suppliers were constant and frequently involved lawyers. Between 1914 and 1916, for example, Nijinsky and his wife pressed a suit against Diaghilev for back wages and won.[24] In America, he had an extended court battle with the Moscow ballerina Xenia Makletzova, a substitute for Karsavina who could not tour. But Makletzova proved to be truculent; he fired her in February 1916 while on tour in the U.S., giving her role in *The Enchanted Princess* to Lydia Lopokova. Makletzova's first response was to have Diaghilev arrested. When that failed, she filed a breach of contract lawsuit; Diaghilev filed a countersuit claiming that her insubordination gave him no choice but to terminate her. It went to trial. Makletzova gave her testimony in court, making a strong impression by wearing an impressive brooch given to her by Czar Nicholas II. After testimonies, the jury found in favor of the dancer, awarding her $4,500.[25] The publicity was intense.

Concerning money, Diaghilev was unreliable, often claiming that financial agreements were opaque or misplaced. And he would often contract to bring star dancers before he even asked them (Ida Rubinstein is one example) and paid old debts with money advanced for new ballets, a form of leveraging which only magnified losses. Any cash flow would be used only to maintain borrowing costs. The equity value of the company only declined because of its increasing cost of credit; assets never exceeded liabilities. Dancers received little and were paid late or not at all. Suppliers were constantly owed funds. Composers often had to sue to get paid. And he often played tricks: when a dancer would call to inquire about his or her salary owing, Diaghilev would answer the phone only to announce he was not in. As a sophisticated grifter, he knew how to hustle.

"I'm a man with a great deal of logic and few principles."

Diaghilev to his stepmother, 1895

Financial numbers were seemingly a blur, paper records a bother, as the operations of the Ballets Russes illustrate. But ironically, instability was the bedrock of the company contributing to its excitement, disruptions, and disagreements. Stravinsky threatened to sue; Fokine actually did. Bakst sent his lawyer to demand an immediate Frs. 10,000 in compensation for lost income, boldly suggesting that Diaghilev take the amount from Stravinsky's fee.

Diaghilev worked hard to avoid financial confrontations but when they occurred, he relied on cajolery, pomposity, belligerency, and artistic presence to combat his antagonists. And he often won. While on one hand he struggled to find benefactors, on the other he berated those to whom he had debts. "Wait, it will come," "don't pressure me" were his often repeated claims while seeking postponements. But his fiscal ground was never solid.

Like his dancers, choreographers, and composers, Diaghilev transformed his career into a commodity. He became an object of gossip, style, fascination, and controversy. His life became his art, his showmanship the source of scandal and celebration. He succeeded, recognized everywhere and admired. His flamboyant manner and behavior guaranteed notoriety. He dressed the part with magnificent topcoats, top hats, and tails matched by elegant suits, a monocle, and when relaxing, colorful silk robes. His creative capital, the work of his choreographers, composers, and dancers, became for him social capital that allowed entrée into the best of European society.

Diaghilev has been presented as a financial buffoon, both negligent and uninformed. But something else emerges when one investigates his apparent aversion to recordkeeping, financial accounting, or planning—a sense of negative success. By avoiding his financial responsibilities, he was able to obtain more support. His early rejection of institutional support became a strategy to encourage private donations and loans; his seemingly blasé attitude towards money displayed an awareness of the positive impact of debt on his reputation and activities. He was disturbed but unflustered by his caricature as a financial neophyte; but he was also a tactician who understood that if, for example, he incorporated, under French law it would force him to be financially accountable and curb his freedom to raise private funds. The law would require him to disclose his donors who often preferred anonymity. Benois believed that Diaghilev was the only member of their early *World of Art* group who truly understood business, although he also complained of Diaghilev's general neglect of details.[26] But the master did not change: he constantly traveled with his Baedeker but never a checkbook (Buckle 284).

For strategic reasons, he may have wanted to give the impression of financial incompetence or confusion and never being fully informed, but he was shrewd and possessed a general understanding of a balance sheet. He may have been thoughtless and sometimes indifferent about the treatment of money and the sources of his funds, but he knew that this very behavior enhanced support. And without this money, he could not realize his creative goals.

Unsurprisingly, the relation between money and the Ballets Russes soon affected aesthetic choices. To be new meant increased amounts of capital for costumes, sets, composers, choreographers, and dancers to sustain a unique style. A concept for a dance was one thing, production costs another, intensified by competition for theatres and public attention. But audiences preferred repetition to innovation. They wanted to see again the Ballets Russes productions of *The Firebird* or *Le Sacre du printemps,* not *Parade,* even if the costumes were by Picasso. The experimental or new found resistance at the box office which soon supported favorites, notably individual dancers and choreographers. But ballet remained a high art form among the French where audiences nostalgically clung to classical ballet, remembering its 18th-century origins, even with a shift in audiences from the aristocrats to the bourgeoisie which began in the mid-19th century (Karthas 71). But a desire to witness the new on and off the stage challenged the traditions of the past reflected in Diaghilev's balanced programming. The challenge was to find ballets innovative enough to arouse audience interest without alienating them.

"Cost Accounting is an essential management tool that can uncover profitability improvements and provide support for key business decisions."

Cost Accounting Fundamentals, 7th ed.

Diaghilev seemingly paid no personal income taxes (despite France instituting such a law in July 1914) and kept virtually no business records, shifting that responsibility to his *régisseur* Serge Grigoriev who managed the company (as best he could) from 1909 to its demise in 1929. His responsibilities included signing contracts with dancers of the lower ranks, while Diaghilev dealt with the composers, painters, and featured soloists whose salaries often reflected their loyalty to him. He, not Grigoriev, negotiated, although on several occasions, he deputized Nouvel to negotiate with someone like Nijinska about her return to the company in 1921.[27]

Grigoriev also organized and conducted rehearsals, supervised numerous aspects of productions, and served as a mediator between Diaghilev and members of the company. In his archive at the Harvard Theater Collection, there are individual and group contracts, salary receipt books, notices, inventories, and company rosters. But even these records are incomplete, since Diaghilev was not entirely compliant with business practices or always honest with money matters, even with Grigoriev. One exception was Nijinsky. A 1917 typed receipt from Nijinsky to Diaghilev confirming payment of the equivalent of $500.00 dollars for performances in the second and fourth ballets at the Theatre Municipal—*Le Spectre de la Rose* and *Les Slyphides*—in

Rio de Janeiro on July 2, 1917, honoring their contract signed in Barcelona that July, represents one of the few honored, official business transactions of the company. It was likely prepared by Grigoriev or Baron Gunzburg and signed by Nijinsky.[28]

General contracts with choruses and groups of singers and dancers provide insight into the organization of the Ballets Russes. Individual contracts with dancers and choreographers in the Grigoriev archive, including such figures as Massine, Bronislava Nijinska, and Balanchine, display the scope of the company's obligations and finances. Despite the company's financial disarray, Diaghilev created a functioning organization with Grigoriev, Nouvel, and later Kochno responsible for general operations, overseeing the dancers, organizing performances, taking care of correspondence, and, at times, even carrying luggage.

In Grigoriev's account, *The Diaghilev Ballet 1909–1929* (1953), one reads a business profile of a company shifting between temporary security and instability with insolvency a monthly if not weekly possibility. Dancers were paid only subsistence allowances, and new funds were always in jeopardy. External forces also had a role: in the postwar period, the cost of living rose continuously, sets were destroyed by fire on a South American tour, stagehands went on strike in Paris, and financial "misunderstandings" were frequent.

For Diaghilev and the company, there was a constant push-and-pull, a tension originating in the company's persistent financial uncertainty. Earlier, stranded in Paris in January 1912 after the St. Petersburg theatre Narodny Dom burned to the ground forcing cancellation of a proposed Russian visit, and without immediate new engagements, financial collapse seemed imminent. But Diaghilev again turned up new performance dates and venues. In 1922, after the failure of *The Sleeping Princess* in London, history seemed to repeat itself with disaster almost imminent. Yet Diaghilev succeeded in organizing several performances at the Paris Opéra but only of familiar favorites: *Schéhérazade, Les Sylphides,* the Polovtsian Dances, and *Le Spectre de la Rose.* New works were not attempted for fear of box office rejection.

The Opéra was important to the Ballets Russes's success but Diaghilev had to balance their attachment to tradition versus his desire to produce the new. Ballet in France had been central in the expression of French identity and cultural preeminence with no institution more significant than the Opéra, created by Louis XIV to house professional dancers, musicians, and singers. Originally founded by the king as the Académie Royale de Danse in 1661 and then renamed and expanded as the Académie Royale de Musique et de Danse in 1669, it had as its original goal the improvement of dance instruction for the training of professional dancers to perform at court. It soon transformed dance into one of spectatorship rather than recreation. The institution, later renamed the Paris Opéra and established in 1671, quickly became the country's preeminent cultural center, well-funded and celebrated. Ballet was seen as an important asset to the state and soon opera and dance were transformed from court entertainments to professional arts (Karthas 107, 150).[29] And knowing how to dance was also vital to a nobleman's success at court; at one point there were reportedly over two hundred dancing schools in Paris in the mid-seventeenth century (Karthas 225).

On one hand, the failure to obtain continuous funding via grants, patrons, sponsors, or the public spurred Diaghilev to be more inventive in his fundraising while, on the other, it restricted his ability to forge new avant-garde works. Creativity was put on hold, becoming subject to direct and indirect financial influence. Nevertheless, Diaghilev was a master campaigner who flattered as much as he cajoled, obtaining financing from impresarios and private patrons *plus* the banks. Amplifying his often desperate situation to potential donors ironically increased their compassion and support. People wanted to help. The myth, as far as the public was concerned, was constant funding from titled patrons but the actuality was short-term capital at high interest rates from private sources and the banks. Yet Diaghilev balanced the ideal (patronage) with the practical (the banks) to keep a privately financed company with high artistic goals functioning. His task was dual: the continuous cultivation of possible backers, while educating public taste for the new.

Capital for new productions was a persistent requirement—premieres were expected at the start of every season—plus working capital to defray or meet operating expenses. But even the intent of the patrons shifted: Princesse de Polignac began by making large donations covering most of a season, but she later funded only specific productions, adjusting her subsidies in kind. And faced with hesitant donors and a questionable box office, he at times chose to liquidate assets, whether props, scores, costumes, or stage curtains. Lack of funds meant that a series of proposed programs failed before they could even begin rehearsal, while others could not go on, even on opening night because in one instance costumers demanded payment or musicians insisted on wages. In 1925, for example, he confronted an unhappy *corps de ballet* who presented a petition and threatened to strike. It went nowhere because he had nothing to offer; there was no reserve. But Diaghilev did take action: he fired the two protest leaders. After a terrible week in Berlin, also in 1925, he did not even have enough money to send the company back to Monte Carlo. His parsimony was notorious: royalties weren't passed on to composers until the very last minute, while his "outbursts of temper and air of entitled hauteur" continued unchecked (Christiansen 197).

Fixed costs played havoc with his budget for new productions because he demanded only materials of the highest quality, the best dancers, the finest choreographers, and the most original music. He had no patience with false economy. It would only ruin his productions. But his reputation worked for and against him, while exceeding budgets became a habit. Operating deficits, beginning with his lavishly illustrated and produced *World of Art* magazine, were nothing new, requiring him from the start of his career to become a financial entrepreneur. And there were always new challenges, from finding proper rehearsal space to preparing costly copies of musical scores and securing permissions. But no cloth could be too expensive to dress his dancers, no fabric too costly to use as a backdrop.

The Ballets Russes had no official headquarters for its first decade and, of course, no securities either in assets or funds. Diaghilev, himself, had no home, living largely in hotels. He also did not delegate: he assumed full creative and financial responsibility for the company rather than divide responsibilities. As his most recent biographer confirms, Diaghilev's money management was erratic at best. Large sums might be extravagantly spent one week with no funds to cover operating expenses the next (Scheijen 42).

Originating with his editorship of the *World of Art*, where debt was inimical, Diaghilev understood it was "better to operate in the red if you were dependent on external backers": it generated sympathy and assured future support (Scheijen 108). And with the journal, he intentionally kept certain sponsors off the books so as not to disclose their roles. By 1906/7, in an effort to establish his Russian season in Paris, he gathered up substantial financial pledges, while his own finances were in tatters. He had to borrow Frs. 500 from Benois to continue (Scheijen 154). This would become his typical pattern: reliance on equivocal patronage, while sustaining persistent company and personal debt. A 1909 letter by Benois summarizes the paradox turning Diaghilev into a financial magician: "In spite of his numerous gaffes, his negligence, and the tricks he has the habit of playing, he also has the habit of success."[30]

But as scandal surrounded him, he constantly had to gesture, at least, toward repayment. But the debts mounted. Following a failed tour of the U.S. in late 1916, he received $75,000 less than agreed and faced more obligations. Three years earlier, a letter from Misia Sert to Stravinsky dated July 11, 1913 confirmed his dire situation:

> Diaghilev is experiencing a terrible time, with financial difficulties that threaten to end in court or in civil war. He has broken with Bakst, perhaps for ever, over *Le Sacre* . . . in spite of the success of *The Firebird* and *Petrushka*, the orchestra made a big scandal at the *Sacre* rehearsal. . . . You must understand that he is risking a great deal, and that, at the moment, *Le Sacre* is the justification of his soul. . . . Be Russian and stay Russian . . . Serge has a Russian soul. (in Scheijen 276)

Part of this plea for patience was the rumor that Diaghilev intended to cut sections of *Le Sacre*. Stravinsky naturally found such a possibility intolerable; Diaghilev reneged.

But what did the absence of a proper financial structure mean for the company and Diaghilev? Constant worry as records remained inaccurate, incomplete, and imperfect. Papers and numbers rarely matched or mattered. No board of directors existed and he had no reserve funds should a backer default or receipts disappoint. He often failed to meet his payroll and failed to give raises in proportion to rises in the cost of living. Yet he assured his dancers he was doing what he could to meet moral and contractual obligations. They acquiesced.

Diaghilev often deflected responsibility, claiming it was the fault of others if he was unable to meet his commitments. In 1911 he told Astruc that delays in staging *Le Dieu bleu* and reviving *The Firebird* were the result of an exhausted Fokine. Astruc and Baskt, he claimed, were responsible for putting extra stress on him. Find a scheme which would be "'less damaging to my reputation and financial prospects'" he implored his French promoter (Buckle 198). This practice of shifting blame was to prevent any accusations that it was he who was guilty of a breach of contract or a default. The importance of paper numbers was now mixed in with protecting one's financial and moral reputation. Yet he miraculously survived and renewed new relationships in love and finance, driven in part by competitiveness, which of course, led to a succession of new crises in-and-out of bed and with the banks. He died penniless in Venice.

Money relates to one's self-concept and identity. Diaghilev had to have it to maintain his image as an impresario and for his individual well-being. It offered him autonomy, time and the freedom to create, or at least produce, plus power. He understood the psychology of money, both its influence and ability to control.[31] It was also a matter of self-esteem. He had social and cultural obligations which could be realized, whether on-or-off the stage, only by money. Pay, however, was not one of those elements.

The reputation of the Ballets Russes was so high that dancers would accept inadequate payment just to be part of the company. Economists call this the "equity equation." Reputation outdid remuneration. But payrolls and salaries never left him alone. Indeed, after the 1910 season, he had to pay at higher rates in order to compensate those who resigned from the Imperial Theater to cover the pensions they lost. Later, enforced economics meant that Stravinsky and Matisse had to split the cost of ospreys for Markova's hat in *Le Chant de Rossignol*. Diaghilev refused to pay for them. On the other hand, when the company arrived in London for the 1918 season at Sir Oswald Stoll's London Coliseum, he insisted on adjustments to the Coliseum's backdrop in order not to distract from the impact of *Les Sylphides*. But survival became more dependent on donations, Coco Chanel contributing Frs. 300,000 for Massine's version of *Le Sacre du printemps.*

Expenses mounted when he began to tour, although it was profitable because his production costs had already been met. In 1913 and 1917, it was South America; in 1916–1917, it was America, although he objected to an American emphasis on schedules, claiming that what he was bringing "was not a 'show' but an 'art exposition.'" If you don't facilitate my needs, I shall cancel, he announced.[32] Stubbornness and resilience may have been his greatest strengths.

The art of ballet propelled Diaghilev into the world of finance but despite its necessity, he did what he could to dismiss its importance publicly, until it trapped him privately. A graph of Diaghilev's finances would alternate between peaks and valleys. The construct of money baffled and yet appealed to Diaghilev simultaneously. Importantly, Diaghilev had no model of funding for an independent ballet. He is a transitional figure seeking ways to balance the commercial and the creative through non-institutional means. He fashioned a system of independent contributions and informal revenue structures that became its own system of insecure (and unsecured) financial sources, without institutional grants from governments, arts councils, or funding agencies.

Despite facing escalating costs, fixed prices, and unexpected charges, his effort at budgeting was *ad hoc* at best with the added problem of ticket prices lagging behind operational expenses. What today is labeled "revenue diversification" was for Diaghilev the very source of his inconsistent support which affected programing, artists, composers, and dancers. Earned revenue was never adequate, while contributed revenue was always uncertain. The bottom line was constantly in conflict with the value-added component of his performances. Financial vulnerability was the watchword of the Ballets Russes from its beginning.[33] Ironically, Diaghilev was the generator of both income and its expenditure; he brought it in and sent it out.

The gap between contributed and earned revenue remained throughout the life of the company. His revenue structure was never fixed, impacting the aesthetic and musical programming of the company. In the beginning, Italian and French ballet of the 16th and 17th centuries enjoyed support from royal households, extended by the founding of the Paris Opéra and then the ballet schools of the Imperial Russian Theaters (notably the Mariinsky). Ballet enjoyed sustained, official support; the public provided roughly only 20 percent of the overall funding. And institutional support continued in the 18th and 19th centuries: most of the world's biggest opera and theater companies, including the Royal Opera in London, the Mariinsky in St. Petersburg, the Paris Opéra in Paris, and La Scala in Milan, had resident ballet troupes, although initially ballet was used decoratively within an opera. With the exception of the Paris Opéra, financed initially by royalty but then, with the rise of the bourgeoisie (re the revolution of 1830), French ballet transformed itself into a private enterprise (Karthas 12).

Government subsidies declined as the role of subscribers—largely government officials, professionals, and businessmen, with a smattering of aristocrats—increased until 1939 when the French state took over.[34] But ballet companies slowly grew independent of opera companies as ballet became expressive, not decorative, and a proper vehicle for narrative and dramatic expression. But independence had a price: the loss of official support resulting in the need for creative funding methods initiated by Diaghilev but with the perennial problem that revenue and expenditures were never in sync.[35]

These shortcomings harmed Diaghilev's relations with his artists and composers, most notably in what was a late scandal, a 1926 production of *Romeo and Juliet*. To save costs, Diaghilev relied on younger and inexperienced artists, beginning with a mediocre score by Constant Lambert and designs by a twenty-five-year-old Christopher Wood. Counting on a revised *Romeo and Juliet* story and a commonplace production, the work seemed to pander to the mainstream.[36] Just before opening, Diaghilev replaced Wood's designs with images by Ernst and Miró and altered the choreography by Nijinska. Lambert was incensed by the changes and sent a letter detailing the horrific result (Garafola, *La Nijinska* 217).

Diaghilev ended up producing the work on a bare stage using front cloths painted by the surrealists who were accused of pandering to the public. It opened in Monte Carlo but at his Paris premiere, left-leaning members of Diaghilev's Paris circle, led by André Breton and Louis Aragon, thought it was a complete sellout to the bourgeoisie and organized a protest. Breton and Aragon's manifesto, strewn about the theatre, declared that "it is intolerable that thought should be at the service of money." Furthermore, the cooperation of Ernst and Miró with Diaghilev put elements of the intellect "into the hands of the most rabid partisans of an equivocal morality. We are incapable of sacrificing our sense of revolutionary reality!"[37]

Catcalls, whistles, and leaflets thrown around the auditorium caused an uproar, partly because the opening scene was of the cast dressed in work clothes taking a class at the *barre*. The shouts and howls prevented the music from being heard; the police, who had warned Diaghilev beforehand that the Surrealists and Communists might demonstrate, had to be called. The only item of interest was the choreography by Nijinska with an *entr'acte* by George Balanchine thrust in between scenes 1 and 2—and that Lady Abdy apparently had her dress torn off her back (Buckle 469). Diaghilev continued to tinker and cut 50 measures from the finale, threatening Lambert that if he didn't make that cut, "I will forbid the dancers from dancing during that time" (Garafola, *La Nijinska* 218). But despite his fiddling, Diaghilev's name was still strong and the company, in London for the summer of 1926, was very much a draw. Attending the London premiere of *Les Noces*, for example, were H. G. Wells, Noël Coward, Lady Diana Cooper, Augustus John, Anthony Asquith, Lord Balfour, and Frederick Ashton whose own first ballet would debut the next night.

Only near the end of his life did Diaghilev exhibit any financial restraint or discipline. While the company was resident in Monte Carlo, he began to moderate his own personal spending. The cause? His sudden desire to acquire rare Russian books and letters, an echo of his early determination to celebrate Russian culture expressed by his successful exhibition of Russian portraits in 1905. A new bibliomania began with the acquisition of several Pushkin letters willed to him by Countess Torby, a direct descendent of Pushkin and the wife of Grand Duke Mikhail Mikhailovich. She tempted Diaghilev to put on a charity gala on the promise that she would leave him one letter. She did. He soon tried to raise additional monies to acquire the remaining ten in her possession. To do so, he sold the original curtain to Picasso's *Three-Cornered Hat* for Frs. 175,000 with the help of Picasso and his dealer Rosenberg. He also had a successful season in London thanks to the assistance of his then agent Eric Wollheim who located new backers and funds since Lord Rothermere had departed. The unexpected financial success of the company permitted a new frenzy of book buying for Diaghilev, purchasing a rare edition of Pushkin for Frs. 3,500. He then paid Frs. 30,000 for the remaining ten Pushkin letters in the Torby estate (Scheijen 423).

Diaghilev assembled a valuable collection of antique Russian titles, a handwritten poem by Pushkin, two mss. of Lermontov and further mss. by Gogol and Turgenev. He kept a catalogue and even rented a Paris apartment for the first time to house his growing library, the collection a fitting expression of his Russian soul which sought to bring Russian dance and culture to Europe despite the cost (Scheijen 424). He was now gathering up that culture to protect it and insure its continuity. But the monies to acquire these treasures remained a mystery. Ironically, at his death, Lifar and others ransacked the apartment and made off with the books and manuscripts which would later be sold at auction, economics again constraining art.[38] But Diaghilev's ability to stay afloat until this moment, while creating a unique modern dance company, exhibits the very alchemy he possessed.

NOTES

1. Peter Lieven, *The Birth of the Ballets Russes* 223. Gunzburg had already invested at least 2,000 rubles in the company's 1909 season but would later be in Diaghilev's bad books. Gunzburg, who accompanied the troupe to South America at Diaghilev's

request, was thought to have masterminded the marriage of Nijinsky and Romola de Pulszky leading to Nijinsky's dismissal by Diaghilev in 1913. The scandal fascinated the public.

Duplicating Diaghilev's dismissal of Nijinsky because of his unsanctioned marriage was Balanchine who, when he learned of Suzanne Farrell's marriage to a company dancer, Paul Mejia, after years as Balanchine's mistress, he fired both of them and rendered her virtually unemployable (Homans, *Mr. B* 489–94).

2. The terminology is Bourdieu's. See *The Field of Cultural Production*, passim.

3. On the shifting taste of Parisian audiences, see Garafola 1989: 344–45.

4. C. S. Bromberg overstated the case when he wrote that "in a society where all art, no matter how daring or reckless, is bought, there can be no avant-garde." Bromberg, "Dance as Commodity," *Dance Scope* Vol. 15. 3 (1981): 9.

5. Bourdieu, *The Field of Cultural Production* 113, 51. Bourdieu goes on to state that the liberty of writers and artists is purely formal. They must submit to "the laws of the market of symbolic goods" (Bourdieu 114). Ironically, the absolute autonomy of the creator is affirmed, although the product itself becomes enfolded in the aura of its production/presentation, in this instance, that of the Ballets Russes.

6. But of course, national and institutional ballet companies still reign as seen in the Royal Ballet (UK), New York City Ballet, the National Ballet of Canada, and the Bolshoi. Similarly, dance schools are generally institutionally affiliated: the Royal Ballet School of London; the Vaganova Academy of Russian Ballet, St. Petersburg (est. 1738); and the School of American Ballet (New York) three examples.

7. See Brian Blackwood, "The Black Notebook of Serge Diaghilev," *Bulletin of the New York Public Library*, 75.8 (October 1971): 345–56. Hereafter Blackwood. Also useful are Diaghilev's business papers at the London Theatre Museum acquired from the estate of Parmenia Migel Ekstrom.

Additional material including contracts plus business and production records are in the S. L. Grigoriev papers at the Harvard Theatre Collection, Houghton Library, Harvard University. Grigoriev was *régisseur* of the Ballets Russes from 1909 to 1929. With Fokine's departure in 1912, Diaghilev appointed Grigoriev "rehearsal-master" (Grigoriev 72). He also served as rehearsal director for Ballets Russes de Col. W. de Basil located in Monte Carlo after Diaghilev's death in 1929.

8. Rupert Christensen overstates the case when he writes that Diaghilev was "never interested in balance sheets," in *Diaghilev's Empire, How the Ballets Russes Enthralled the World* (London: Faber and Faber, 2022) 79.

9. See Blackwood, *Bulletin of the New York Public Library*, 75.8 (October 1971) 345–56 and Jane Pritchard, "Creating Productions," *Diaghilev and the Golden Age of the Ballets Russes*, ed. Pritchard, 72–74.

10. See Henry Rand Hatfield, "Some Variations in Accounting Practice in England, France, Germany and the United States," *Journal of Accounting Research* Vol. 4. 2 (1966): 169–72.

11. See Max J. Wasserman, "Accounting Practice in France during the Period of Monetary Inflation (1919–1927)," *The Accounting Review* Vol. 6. 1 (March 1931): 1–32. This also offers a detailed discussion of inflation.

12. For this often-told story, see Karen Nelson, "How Diaghilev Did It (Without the NEA)," *Dance Scope* Vol. 15. 3 (1981): 34. Hereafter Nelson.

13. For an itemized accounting see Buckle 152–53.

14. Alexandre Benois, *Reminiscences of the Russian Ballet*, trans. Mary Britnieva (London: Putnam, 1941) 312.

15. Garafola, 1989: 184. On Diaghilev's multiple and precise contracts with dancers, see pp. 193, 231. For contracts relating to his first American tour, see Garafola, 1989: 202–6. For the Paris Opéra, see 218–29.

Additional patrons in the late twenties included Lady Juliet Duff, daughter of his prewar patron Lady Ripon. But Lady Juliet's circle would support only the familiar and was not eager to fund eccentric or experimental ballets. Others like Lady Cunard warned Diaghilev not to be too experimental, suggesting *Les Sylphides* not *Les Noces* as a performance for George V (Christiansen 198).

16. Proust returned the favor by assisting Astruc with his autobiography, *Le pavillon des fantômes*. But disputes with Diaghilev over funds were legendary with Diaghilev generally winning.

17. Gunzburg (alternatively Günzburg or Guenzburg) traveled easily between Russia and France; he died in Russia in October 1919 during the revolution. At the time of his death, he had assembled a valuable private library of Jewish texts initially bought by his son-in-law for the Hebrew National Library as it was then known. Partially ransacked by Jewish Communists, it was saved by the Commissar of Education and Maxim Gorky and sent to Moscow. See Solomon Zeitlin, "Dr. Zeitlin Describes Status of Archives," *The Jewish News* (Detroit) July 27, 1956: 1. https://digital.bentley.umich.edu/djnews/djn.1956.07.27.001/1. As of 1998, the catalogued collection of Hebrew manuscripts resides in the Russian State Library, Moscow.

18. This may actually be a typo in Garafola 1989: 187. The bank was likely Bordier & Cie, a Swiss private bank with a Paris office.

19. General examples of the accrual principle in practice Diaghilev did *not* follow:
Record revenue when invoicing the customer, rather than when the customer pays you.
Record an expense when incurred, rather than when you pay for it.
Record the estimated amount of bad debt when invoicing a customer, rather than when it becomes apparent that the customer will not pay.
Record depreciation for a fixed asset over its useful life, rather than charging it to expense in the period purchased.
Record wages in the period earned, rather than in the period paid.

20. Diaghilev continued to behave in this callous manner, renewing a contract with Nijinska under pressure for choreographing *Romeo and Juliet* (Frs. 20,000 plus travel expenses) and rehearsing *Les Noces*. But her presence signaled to Balanchine and Massine that Diaghilev regularly manipulated his choreographers, often pitting them against each other (Garafola, *La Nijinska* 214).

21. Garafola 1989: 264–65. Rupert Christiansen, *Diaghilev's Empire: How the Ballets Russes Enthralled the World* (London: Faber, 2022) 45. Hereafter Christiansen.

22. D. W. Kreuger, "Money, success and success phobia," *The Last Taboo: Money as a symbol and reality in psychotherapy and psychoanalysis* (New York: Brunner/

Mazel, 1986) 3. Also see M. Prince, "Self-concept, money beliefs and values," *Journal of Economic Psychology* 14 (1993): 161–73.

For further thoughts on the meaning of money and its impact on Diaghilev, see Georg Simmel, *The Philosophy of Money*, 3rd ed., ed. David Frisby, trans. Tom Bottomore and David Frisby (London: Routledge, 2005). Hereafter Simmel. The book first appeared in 1900 in German. Ch. 3, "Money in the Sequences of Purposes," including a section on "The psychological growth of means into ends," is particularly valuable (228–33), as is "The possession of money and the self" (327–32).

An earlier discussion of money is Kant, "What Is Money?" a section under "Illustration of Relations of Contract by the Conceptions of Money and a Book," in *The Metaphysical Principles of The Science of Right* (1790) which became the first part of *The Metaphysics of Morals* (1797).

23. Simmel, *The Philosophy of Money* 228, 328. Simmel also writes that "the sense of value has nothing to do with the structure of things . . . [valuation] evolves liberally beyond the objectively justified relation to things" (229). Simmel also considers rhythm and symmetry developed through the possibilities of money and implicitly exhibited by dance (Simmel 494). Rhythm, he writes, is "symmetry in time" while "symmetry is rhythm in space" (494).

24. In a letter to Stravinsky, Nijinsky complained that "Serge owes me a lot of money. I have received nothing for two years, neither for my dancing nor for my staging *Faune, Jeux,* and *Sacre du Printemps.* I worked for the ballet without a contact." In Christiansen, *Diaghilev's Empire* 114.

25. For these and additional details, see Vanessa Banni-Viñas, "Correcting a Ballerina's Story: The Truth Behind Makletzova v. Diaghileff," American Journal of Legal History 53.3 (July 2013): 353–61. Details of the drama underscored the behavior of both parties. In New York, Makletzova did not inform the financial manager of the Met that she would not go on to dance *The Enchanted Princess* until 10 minutes before the performance before a full house. Repeating her New York action, she insisted on the immediate payment of $150 in Boston. Regarding her refusal to perform with the junior dancer Gavriloff, she claimed in court that he was unsuitable because he was an ensemble member, not a featured dancer, although she admitted he had danced *The Enchanted Princess* with Lopokova. She then said she was afraid she would be injured if she had to dance with him but let Diaghilev know she would be willing to do it if he paid her extra. She additionally claimed that she did not have adequate time to rehearse with him, although she is the one who turned down his requests to practice. The evidence suggests that a sympathetic jury reached the wrong verdict.

26. Alexandre Benois, *Reminiscences of the Russian Ballet,* trans. Mary Britnieva (London: Putnam, 1941) 371, 312.

27. The contract for an eleven-month period called for her to be paid Frs. 5,000—she originally demanded Frs. 6,000 and Nouvel initially offered Frs. 3,000. She was also to receive first-class travel expenses; the contract also specified that she had to attend a daily class by the company's teachers, something of an insult (Garafola, *La Nijinska* 82–83).

28. The receipt is in the Ballets Russes archive in the Music Division of the Library of Congress, Washington, DC.

29. Karthas also notes that dancers of Louis XIV's new academy "replicated on the public stage the spectacle of the king and court." Professionalizing ballet made nobility itself a commercial product (Karthas 151).

30. Benois to Misia Sert, December 2, 1909, in Scheijen 197.

31. On the topic, see K. O. Doyle, "Toward a psychology of money," *American Behavioral Scientist* 35 (1992): 708–24 and Adrian Furnham and M. Argyle, *The Psychology of Money* (London: Routledge, 1998) supplemented by V. A. Zelizer, *The Social Meaning of Money* (New York: Basic Books, 1994).

32. *New York Times Magazine*, January 9, 1916: 16.

33. Three recent studies address the issue of the self-funded dance company: Thomas Smith, *Raising the Barre: The Geographic, Financial and Economic Trends of Nonprofit Dance Companies* (Washington, DC: National Endowment for the Arts, 2003), https://www.arts.gov/sites/default/files/RaisingtheBarre.pdf; Deasee Phillips, "Let's get to the Pointe: Ballet and Business," *Business Today*, August 24, 2017, https://journal.businesstoday.org/bt-online/2017/lets-get-to-the-pointe-ballet-and-business; and Daniel J. Wellman, "Ballet Revenue Structures: What's Working and What's Not in Ballet Companies in the USA," master's thesis, Drexel University, 2022, https://drexel.esploro.exlibrisgroup.com/esploro/outputs/graduate/Ballet-Revenue-Structures-Whats-Working-and/991019104705904721?institution=01DRXU_INST.

34. Karthas 8. That same year, the Paris Opéra and the Opéra-Comique joined under the new Réunion des Théâtres Lyriques Nationaux.

35. For contemporary discussions of the importance of revenue diversification for ballet companies, see the following: Karen Nelson, "The Evolution of the Financing of Ballet Companies in the United States," *Journal of Cultural Economics* Vol. 7. 1 (1983): 43–62; Jessica L. Berrett and Bradley S. Holliday, "The Effect of Revenue Diversification on Output Creation in Nonprofit Organizations: A Resource Dependence Perspective," *Voluntas: International Journal of Voluntary and Nonprofit Organizations*, Vol. 29. 6 (2018): 1190–1201; Cyril F. Chang and Howard P. Tuckman, "Revenue Diversification among Non-Profits." *Voluntas*, Vol. 5. 3 (1994): 273–90; Karen A. Froelich, "Diversification of Revenue Strategies: Evolving Resource Dependence in Nonprofit Organizations." *Nonprofit and Voluntary Sector Quarterly*, Vol. 28. 3 (1999): 246–68; Daniel Wellman, "Ballet Revenue Structures: What's Working and What's Not in Ballet Companies in the USA," master's thesis, Drexel University, Dec. 2022, https://drexel.esploro.exlibrisgroup.com/esploro/outputs/graduate/Ballet-Revenue-Structures-Whats-Working-and/991019104705904721?institution=01DRXU_INST.

A further helpful discussion is Terence R. Mitchell and Amy E. Mickel, "The Meaning of Money: An Individual-Difference Perspective," *The Academy of Management Review*, Vol. 24. 3 (1999) 568–78.

What was problematic in Diaghilev's time concerning box office earned revenue for audience-dependent organizations remains true today, making institutional support, plus private and public monies, all the more necessary.

36. For a descriptive summary of the ballet, see Garafola, *La Nijinska* 213–16.

37. Louis Aragon and André Breton, "Surrealist Manifesto," in Serge Lifar, *Serge Diaghilev, His Life, His Work, His Legend: An Intimate Biography* (London: Putnam, 1940) 533.

38. The auction took place at Sotheby Parke-Bernet in Monte Carlo from November 28 to December 1, 1975. The collection was offered as the "Diaghilev-Lifar Library" and comprised 826 lots over four days. See the catalogue with its gilt, ornately printed boards with photographs and facsimiles. The remainder of materials dealing with ballet productions, including work by Picasso, Miró, Stravinsky, Prokofiev, Ravel, and Cocteau, was sold at auction in London in 1984 earning $1.1 million. A working notebook sold for more than $60,000. See Jon Nordheimer, "Diaghilev Memorabilia is sold for $1.1 Million," *New York Times,* May 10, 1984 (section C, 25). https://www.nytimes.com/1984/05/10/arts/diaghilev-memorabilia-is-sold-for-1.1-million.html.

For a partial listing of Diaghilev's books and manuscripts, see Lifar, "Appendix C," *Serge Diaghilev*, 534–35.

Chapter 4

How Much Does a Ballet Cost?

Dance and finance were never apart for the Ballets Russes, and Diaghilev constantly scrambled to keep them united. He tirelessly networked and created a cadre of wealthy supporters. But his use of money was contradictory:

> He was often tight-fisted even over small expenses. I have seen him haggling with a chauffeur in Monte Carlo over two francs, and at times his dinner jacket was sadly frayed. Every penny went into his dreams.[1]

And such dreams were often extravagant. But from the start adjustments were necessary to gain financial viability through new supporters and audiences: introducing the one-act ballet and cultivating an appreciation for new stagings became the first two steps. Persuading donors with honors, flattery, and adulation was the third. The originality of its productions made the Ballets Russes an almost instant hit but with no guarantee of survival from one production to another.

Diaghilev's vision of ballet sometimes offended: as enacted by his choreographers, it incorporated natural movement, irregular positioning, original music, artistic set design, and innovative costumes. In addition, they combined temporal juxtapositions, ironic distancing, and stylized neo-primitivism leading to a new conception of dance jettisoning artificiality, formality, and even plot. Sets were no longer mere backdrops but integrated dramatically with the actual music and action. Instead of "periodic phrasing, rhythmically distinct themes . . . and metrically regular bass-lines," Diaghilev preferred music which constantly changed its phrasing, meter, theme, and key (Caddy 41). Stravinsky would later meet this challenge by putting some music for *Petrushka* (1922) into two keys at once.

Replacing formulaic moves, prescribed outfits (tutus and tiaras), and similar spins, whether the ballet was about the Russian countryside or baroque France, were adventurous productions that challenged the eye and ear. Dance reified action, transforming an abstraction into a physical expression.

Theoretically, it became an unbounded space. Instead of the set dance, often extraneous to the plot, or musical phrasing that emphasized stability, Diaghilev encouraged music that paralleled the unfolding drama on the stage with its "shifting nuances of character and emotion" (Caddy 41). Diaghilev wanted music that would open up the action on the stage, not contain it. His aim was equally to employ new stage and dance techniques that would reflect the changing modern world, rejecting dance practices of the past.

Money, the Marketplace, and France

Enticing donors with honors, appointments, and semi-influence was an on-going activity for Diaghilev. Patrons were suddenly entitled to sit on hastily formed honorary committees, although ethical entanglements between art and money limited their impact. Diaghilev dismissed such concerns: he lauded his donors and encouraged their participation on his committees, although in the end only his artistic ideas and concepts ruled. Money alone did not talk.

But there was never enough, Diaghilev requiring twenty gold pieces to pay off stagehands during rehearsals of *Boris Godunov* to stop the noisy assembly of stage sets to allow the singers to rehearse (Buckle 106). In the beginning, the Tsar's government recognized the value of a triumphal, cultured Russia at international arts venues and overlooked any disputes with Diaghilev and his financial shortcomings. But that quickly changed.

The marketplace, a euphemism for competition, ruled, more so for a company without reliable funding from institutions or government. The marketplace for dance, especially in early 20th-century Paris, was largely governed by established companies affiliated with organizations like the Paris Opéra or the Opéra-Comique. And as with any market economy, supply and demand shaped the production, distribution, and pricing of goods. But a market economy is unplanned, formed in part by what people want and their eagerness to pay for it. One of Diaghilev's accomplishments was to generate demand through the original productions and promotion of the Ballets Russes, often in limited runs. And for the Ballets Russes, the self-regulating market became dependent on publicity, celebrity dancers, promotion, scandal, and general interest. Profit, always elusive in the arts, was a goal but not a necessity, while an irregular funding program only added anxiety for Diaghilev and the company.

In the early 20th century, France was a mixed social market economy, planned and unplanned. But recognizing that creative industries provided jobs had a political as well as cultural purpose which meant agency for opera, theater, and dance. Originally an accompaniment to opera as a *divertissement*, a diversion to the main plot, ballet developed into its own form depicting narrative. Yet at the beginning of the 20th century, ballet had become an art of prescribed moves, still incorporated into opera or the music hall, although new companies were appearing besides the Ballets Russes: Jacques Rouche's revitalized Opéra Ballet and the Ballets Suédois, a breakaway group from the Royal Swedish Ballet under Rolf de Maré and Jean Borlin, were two. Following the Ballets Suédois was another new company organized by Etienne de Beaumont, the "Soirée de Paris" of 1925. To Diaghilev's chagrin, if not anger, Massine joined him, although Stravinsky did not. By 1928, Ida Rubinstein was another new presence. She had previously danced for Diaghilev as Cleopatra and Zobeide in *Schéhérazade* in 1909 and in 1910. She then commissioned Ravel's *Bolero* and Stravinsky's *Le baiser de la fée.*

Ballet was clearly remaking itself during Diaghilev's period of static productions and ever-increasing debts. The well-funded companies of both de Maré and Rubinstein had solid resources. Diaghilev had none and was jealous (Buckle 415). In particular, the Ballets Suédois, which only lasted from 1920 to 1925, also had talent, collaborating with Blaise Cendars, Paul Claudel, and Cocteau and composers such as George Auric, Darius Milhaud, Francis Poulenc, and Satie. Among its designers and artists were de Chirico, Léger, Picabia, and Parr. For a period, it was direct competition to the Ballets Russes (Karthas 124). Not only was the choreography avant-garde but the ballets were often contemporary and catering to Parisian tastes such as *Les mariés de la Tour Eiffel,* a satire on the bourgeoisie with a wedding party on the top of the Eiffel Tower on Bastille Day conceived by Cocteau. *The Skating Ring*, with designs by Léger and music by Arthur Honegger, drew inspiration from apache dances. *Within the Quota*, a piece set to jazz tunes by Cole Porter, had a backdrop which was a blowup of the front page of a Hearst newspaper with improbable headlines (Garafola, 1989: 111). In *Relâche*, designed by Picabia who also wrote the scenario, film was spliced into the dance. The company produced over twenty ballets in five years, receiving wide press coverage with some critics claiming they stood alongside, not behind, the Ballets Russes (Karthas 124).

But during this period, finances continued to hound Diaghilev, with the January 1922 London season a disaster, "the most expensive failure of his career," Buckle writes (397). He owed not only Stoll but other creditors including the Savoy Hotel. He had a spring season planned at the Paris Opéra but was uncertain if any of his dancers would remain with him because he could not pay them. Stoll, as reprisal for unpaid amounts, seized the dresses and scenery for *The Sleeping Princess*, which prevented Diaghilev from moving forward with a Paris production. Spessivtsva, a principal dancer, not paid in full, announced her return to Russia. His valet, fearing imminent financial collapse, took off carrying with him some of Diaghilev's jewelry. Desertion was everywhere.

Escaping to Paris after London but without funds, Diaghilev stayed in a small room at the top of the Hôtel Continental. Boris Kochno, traveling with him, slept in a servant's room; they ate at a cab drivers' restaurant. By February 1922, it appeared as if the company would dissolve as it had temporarily done in 1914 because of World War I. But Kochno and even Stravinsky still believed in Diaghilev, while Prokofiev held out hope as a source of new ballet scores. Diaghilev, dismayed, would still not be defeated, even by the success of new troupes such as the Ballets Suédois. But he was being pursued: Woizikoewski and Sokolova, two dancers from the London production season, tracked him to Paris seeking their wages. Woizikoewski called; Diaghilev himself answered the phone but in a disguised voice telling the caller that Diaghilev was absolutely not in. On their second day, the two dancers waited for him in the entrance hall of the Continental. He slipped out behind their chairs and jumped into a cab. When they finally confronted him, he paid them a small amount claiming poverty and that future plans were uncertain. He then made it clear that Nouvel was in charge of all business matters (Buckle 399). Nonetheless, the overly-confident Diaghilev gave a Paris press conference, reported on February 18, 1922, where he expressed satisfaction with the supposed success of the London *Sleeping Princess* and that he hoped to show it with new costumes in May at the Paris Opéra. Rarely did he let the truth interfere with his plans. But by March, he had surprisingly arranged a short season of twelve performances in Monte Carlo. The principality provided refuge and rescue (Buckle 399–400).

The cultural politics of ballet in France between 1909 and 1929 led to a reshaping of the art. Initially, ballet dancers were seen primarily as workers, not artists (Karthas 4). Degas depicted his ballet figures as working-class professionals, ballet an art form in decline. In Ilyana Karthas' words, ballet became a "space of cross-class sexual exchange, a world of display and male possession" (4). Nevertheless, it revived through its re-creation of past triumphs to become a cultural force only to be challenged and remade again by the originality of the Ballets Russes. Journalism played a major role in this reconfiguring, shaping the public's understanding of the art. It soon mediated between French values and ballet aesthetics. Newspapers, periodicals, and books shaped the discourse of French ballet before, during and after Diaghilev's reign.[2]

Reviews, articles, essays, and even manifestoes repeatedly contributed to the successes and failures of the Ballets Russes. Journalists, critics, intellectuals, artists, musicologists, and dance specialists all contributed to the Diaghilev revolution taking place in traditional and non-traditional venues which ranged from the variety and concert stage to the elegant Opéra

Garnier and the venerable Paris Opéra. Some of the key critics were André Levinson (Russian émigré), Auguste Rodin, Jean Cocteau, and Serge Lifar. Importantly, the arrival of the Ballets Russes encouraged many artistic and intellectual figures to re-examine the artistic potential of ballet. Collectively, they reshaped and cultivated Parisian views of ballet and redefined France's self-image through coherent ideas of national identity, modern aesthetics, and gender norms (Karthas 34–35, 81).

There were, however, no professional dance critics, only literary, opera, or theater critics who also reviewed ballets. They generally misunderstood choreography and its terms, concentrating, instead, on the music, décor, and costumes. Nevertheless, their positive reviews—Henri Ghéon published a fourteen-page article in 1910 on the early ballets of the Ballets Russes in *La Nouvelle Revue Française* and André Gide celebrated the company's collaborative art in various reviews, extending praise of the company's incorporation of symphonic music, décor, and costumes—contributed to the Ballets Russes's success. Jacques Rivère, later to become editor of the *NRF*, wrote an important article, "Of the Ballets Russes and Fokine" (July 1912), proclaiming that it was the dancing, not the music or sets or costumes that established the Ballets Russes as a company apart. Rivère's was the first essay to present this view (Karthas 49). And by relying on Debussy and other French composers in their early performances, the company generated a welcome discourse on French nationalism, music, and aesthetic. The numerous positive reviews also elevated the worth of the company providing credibility which allowed it to tour and establish regular programs in London, Paris, and Monte Carlo.

The arrival of Diaghilev's Ballets Russes confirmed ballet's autonomy as an art form separate from music, pantomime, or even theatrical *divertissements* while simultaneously drawing on them. The contradiction was part of the modernist ethos. The company also marked the beginning of the "celebrity" ballerinas and ballerinos: Pavlova, Karsavina, Nijinsky, Lifar appeared in popular marketing and publicity. This modern use of ballet in advertising reaffirmed its importance as a social *and* cultural institution. The Ballets Russes also confirmed the transnational dimension of ballet, initiated perhaps, when the French choreographer Marius Petipa, thought of as the father of classical ballet, moved to St. Petersburg in 1847 and became choreographer-in-chief of the Imperial Theaters in 1862 and premier ballet master in 1869. He held the post for nearly fifty years as Russia was looking to establish a national style.

Until this point, French ballet had stagnated but the arrival of the Ballets Russes ignited excitement and extensive discussion about the function of ballet in modern society, shaping it as a separate, independent art.[3] There was also a new engagement in reviewing ballet, elevating the reputation of the art form. Diaghilev's innovations altered public perceptions of dance, theater, and drama on stage. Ballet quickly became a way to "construct or contest modern French cultural identities" (Karthas 8).

Modernist Money

In 1909, when the Ballets Russes had its first major successes, critics celebrated how the company embodied Russian nationalism and exotic themes, the virtuosity of the dancers, the company's fusion of the arts, and the origins of ballet in France. What was not discussed was the financial instability of the enterprise as support from official Russia became increasingly unreliable, debts mounted, and Diaghilev searched for credit. Circulars were actually distributed recommending that Russian diplomatic missions abroad were not to fund Diaghilev's projects, although the reason was not clear (Lieven 221): he may have offended influential ballet conservatives or the directorate of the Imperial Theaters led by Prince Sergei Volkonsky, who realized that the popular success of Diaghilev's enterprises was counter to his own plans. Official Russia turned its back on Diaghilev in 1909, before he turned his back on the country.

Expanding his enthusiastic reception in Paris was a public desire for the new and a longing for all things foreign. Stimulating this was the large influx of Russians, especially between 1900 and 1910. Supplementing a new eagerness to experience Russian culture were recent French translations of Russian literary works which carried over to England. Leonard Woolf's gift to Virginia on their honeymoon in 1912 was a French translation of *Crime and Punishment* (*Crime et Châtiment*). She devoured it. Several months later, she read *Un Adolescent.* The unexpected appearance of the Ballets Russes in Paris satisfied such needs. Fashionable at the time were Russian scarves, muffs, and fur hats, appealing as stylistic signs of the exotic or the primitive tamed. As Benois noted, the basic appeal of the Ballets Russes was its primitivism matched by a dramatic, visual sensationalism. It was barbarism under control. The Russians enchant because they excite, wrote the critic Lise-Léon Blum in 1914 (Blum in Karthas 78).

But was Diaghilev really attempting to expand Russian culture in the West or simply inflating his name? The withdrawal of Russian support suggested official displeasure with Diaghilev and reaction against his success but it also meant that he now had the independence to invent, treating his newly cultivated patrons with deference and respect, even when they lacked aesthetic judgment or artistic understanding. But he had the self-confidence to undertake these challenges, often repaying borrowed funds with favors, possibly with the earlier noted Patents of Nobility or a decoration, obtained through government connections. But when there were obstacles, as with a Riga manufacturer when refused an honor, Diaghilev found other means to obtain recognition: reproducing names in programs, placing flattering newspaper stories, offering invitations to exclusive gatherings, and always free tickets or a box. And when the Riga industrialist did finally become a nobleman, the Ballets Russes received the equivalent of £10,000.

But did Diaghilev understand the nature of what might be called "modernist money"? Did he resolve the paradox of disavowing money at the same time he relied on it? Was he a businessman or an aesthete who produced ballets solely for their box office rather than artistic success? The short answer is both. In theoretical terms, Diaghilev understood that money is "not an objective entity whose value is independent of social and political relations" but "a process" whose value "derives from the dynamic, ever-changing and often contested social relations that sustain its circulation."[4] Money does not have a fixed value contained within itself. It is a system whose value alters given conditions.[5] Money for Diaghilev mixed credit (monies advanced for future payment) with capital (paying with currency for immediate expenses). The very sociology of money was the source of its use for him. Credit, capital, and dance were intertwined.

Diaghilev existed in a pluralistic monetary universe where money was unstable as to its source and value but essential. Expenses were fixed whether contracts with dancers, fees for services, rentals for theaters, or salaries for musicians. He knew what he needed but even when the funds were not there, he believed they would turn up. And they often did. The sociology of money, not the idea of money as a system of barter, shaped Diaghilev's monetary practice. When unavoidable, he borrowed from banks, despite their regulations and forms, but more frequently and preferably from individuals with their informal methods of accounting. Shirt cuffs.

Money for Diaghilev was a means, not an end. It permitted creativity and new art forms which he and his choreographers and musicians and dancers transformed into ballets. Diaghilev understood that money "rests on *social relations between its users,*" hence his cultivation of aristocrats, plutocrats, and industrialists, as well as composers, dancers, associates, and friends who often offered money in the form of credit, stock, jewelry, art, and cash (Dodd 8–9). Importantly, "money" was not a fixed entity; it continually reinvented itself (like his ballets) causing Diaghilev and his associates to be flexible in its source and application. A franc was not simply a franc but had value because of its social and political framework. Money, he recognized, was embedded in, and shaped by, its context, which made the Ballets Russes an intriguing site of cultural exchange.

There is a parallel in art where determining value is not based on the actual image but its context.[6] Art exists only in terms of its "frames": art galleries, auctions, collectors, museums, or the art market. These sources determine its worth. The fiscal life of dance, or art, is unseen but generates its material expression on stage through performance or, for the painting, through display. For Diaghilev, what money does was more important than what it is. Dance itself gained authority through its forms of presentation. To see a ballet at the Paris Opéra was itself legitimizing the experience and its credibility. That it was experimental or challenging intensified its authenticity. And where the ballet was performed was as critical as what was being performed. The commercial value validates the cultural. The economic sanction (the space of presentation and cost of attending) reinforces the works' cultural worth (Bourdieu 113). Ballet remained an elite art and carried social weight. To be seen at the ballet at the Opéra validated one's social standing.

The years 1912–1914 were especially difficult financially for Diaghilev. Production costs mounted and required short-term bank loans, necessary for the 1912 season. The amount borrowed from a Paris bank had to be repaid by August 1, 1912. But Diaghilev typically failed to meet the scheduled repayments and they remained unsettled when the Ballets Russes returned to Paris in 1913. Nearly a year later, in June 1914, Frs. 176, 595 was still outstanding (Garafola, 1989: 187). Action had to be taken and scenery and costume trunks were seized at the Paris Opéra. With such debt, could the company survive? Would liabilities always exceed income? Astruc kept careful accounts of monies received and owed.[7] But the question lingered as the Ballets Russes danced through the next several seasons. But time after time Diaghilev managed, almost magically, to resurrect the company from near disaster. He forged an uneasy balance between creativity and the marketplace. Even within the ranks of his company, new divisions of labor occurred determined by money (who had it and who did not), not experience (Garafola, 1989: 189).

But such non-business behavior reflects Diaghilev's belief that as a producer/autocrat he had no need to account to others and certainly not in any organized fashion. The conflict was that Diaghilev modeled the operation of the company on a business but refused to conduct activities in a businesslike manner. Overall, Diaghilev felt money was a nuisance and should be subservient to art; money should only facilitate art. An artistic triumph trumped financial success (or failure) every time. Stravinsky had a different view: he sought money and kept careful accounts and once his concert career began in 1924, received sizeable sums.[8]

Costs

Stabilizing expenses for Diaghilev were the fixed costs of the company starting with the orchestra and dancers. The principal dancers and conductors had secure contracts rather than a per-performance arrangement, although renewals were yearly, usually in the summer (Buckle 462). Technicians and stagehands had similar contracts, production always labor-intensive. Moving sets from city to city and reassembling in a new venue added additional costs. Administration must also be adjusted whether it was the operation of the box office or the tax treatment of income, donations, or sponsorship. Negotiating a schedule for an established theatre also incurred premiums to obtain select dates, while pricing policies had to be altered to suit new performance schedules and hours. Opera tended to be more visible than ballet but also more expensive. But many, and most likely Diaghilev, soon asked if a ballet company made economic sense. The problem in part was the persistent conflict between economic and artistic obligations. The social capital gained by dance was immense but the cost of economic capital was enormous. Picasso's white floor cloth for *Pulcinella*, used to give the effect of moonlight, needed to be repainted for each performance (Buckle 363).

A perennial challenge was salaries. Dancers worked hard and the daily norm was usually three rehearsals or two rehearsals and a performance. A typical day might begin with a morning rehearsal from ten to twelve, possibly beginning with a class by Nijinska, then an afternoon rehearsal from two thirty to five and an evening performance at nine. On Sundays, a matinee at three might have an evening rehearsal from nine to eleven the night before. Fridays were generally devoted entirely to rehearsal. A typical salary for a member of the *corps de ballet* was Frs. 800 a month during performances. During rehearsal periods, only half that amount was paid. To save money, Diaghilev required dancers to provide their own practice clothes including shoes and tights. The company's shoe allowance was penurious: one pair for every twelve performances. Dancers often had to use their own funds for extra shoes.[9] Dancers were also prevented from supplementing their income by performing elsewhere.

At one point during rehearsals for *Les Noces* (1923), they went on strike for higher wages but relented after Diaghilev made an impassioned appeal that no more funds were available followed by an ultimatum: anyone could leave if they desired. None did.[10] Why did the dancers stay? The prestige of dancing with the company, Diaghilev's charisma, and perhaps the irregular legal status of the company's stateless Russians protected by the company's itinerant travels—plus Diaghilev's uncanny ability to acquire Nansen Passports which could be used for travel abroad and to request residency abroad. Importantly, it also protected the holder from deportation. By 1918, less than half the troupe was Russian. Poles, English, Italians, and even French filled the ranks. Stateless, like Diaghilev, they were nevertheless haunted by their separation from their homelands.

After 1914, the working conditions of dancers for the Ballets Russes deteriorated sharply, despite increased social status. While they previously enjoyed a reasonable income, during and after the war salaries fell. In

Switzerland all the dancers received equal pay but by 1916–1917, salaries for the *corps de ballet* seriously declined. A contract from October 1918 for one dancer confirmed Frs. 750 with half pay for the two-month rehearsal period and a four-week annual holiday. In 1919, a new dancer received a monthly salary of Frs. 800 in France but only £4 a week in London, less than that paid to a musical accompanist. Salaries had fallen from the early years when a novice might expect a salary of Frs. 8–10,000 (Garafola 1989: 231–32). Inflation during this period also eroded the real income of the dancers. And the company offered no medical coverage, sick pay, or compensation for injuries. Salaries were also delayed or in some instances not paid at all as at the close of *The Sleeping Princess*. Lawsuits for back pay were common. Job security was non-existent as dancers shifted from being a free artist to a wage earner. Diaghilev's dancers lost their privileges within and beyond the company. The logic of the marketplace ruled.

Diaghilev's stars also did poorly. At the start of his Ballets Russes career in 1909, Nijinsky received only Frs. 2,500. By contrast, Chaliapin received Frs. 5,000. Ninette de Valois, dancing in *Les Noces* in Paris, recorded that she worked all day and every day on a salary of only Frs. 1,500 per month—at the time equal to £5–£6 per week (Buckle 428). When Diaghilev arrived in Paris in 1909, he immediately told Astruc that he had no funds to pay the company; Astruc must pay. "Impossible," Astruc replied, and that it would be dishonest to use subscription and advance booking monies to pay the dancers: if there was a strike, a fire, or a performer's cancellation, he would be obliged to refund monies. Diaghilev's retort was short: "Then there will be no Russian season." Cornered, Astruc pledged his own credit to meet expenses (Buckle 136).

Interestingly, dancers were paid more for dancing at parties than on stage. At a party hosted by a Mme. Ephrussi, Diaghilev arranged for Nijinsky to receive a thousand francs but Karsavina only five hundred. Nijinsky, ill, could not appear; Astruc then told Karsavina that Mme. Ephrussi wanted *her* to have a thousand francs, contrary to Diaghilev's proposal (Buckle 152).

Money and the Princess

Typical of his behavior was his handling of the debacle stemming from the London production of *The Sleeping Princess* (the renamed *Sleeping Beauty*) opening in November 1921 but closing in January 1922. Declining revenue was the cause. Presented in London for the Christmas season of 1921, it was a restaging of Petipa's *Sleeping Beauty* and to play for an estimated six months. The Alhambra Theater Company put up £10,000 for the production to be designed by Bakst, with Stravinsky to arrange Tchaikovsky's music. The choreography was to revive Petipa's staging. But from the start, it was expensive, the enormous number of costumes requiring the finest workshops in Paris and London to work under pressure to meet a deadline. And Diaghilev insisted that only the most expensive materials be used. Mechanically it was also a challenge with various scene changes with difficult stage machinery; a complex rehearsal schedule meant postponement of the premiere for two days at the last minute.

Additional costs beyond the technically complicated sets were inadequate canvas for the painted scenes, a large cast, and breakdowns of scenery on opening night. It was a spectacle but one outdated on a stage too small to contain the dancers, props, curtain, and even a flying machine. The £10,000 budget was spent before the opening; pressed for payment, Diaghilev had to ask for a further £5,000 from the producers but costs still soared and an additional £5,000 was requested, grudgingly granted by the Alhambra Company, doubling their capital investment in the production. The number of seats, however, could not have carried the full financial burden even if the production played to capacity.

If the London revival of *Sleeping Beauty* as *The Sleeping Princess* in November 1921 was to bring financial reprieve, it failed. A full-length ballet was unusual for London audiences which initially responded positively to Tchaikovsky's music, Bakst's scenery and costumes, and two on-stage sets, one in white marble and the other in gold. The leading dancers of the company participated in what was a reproduction of Petipa's choreography. The daily performances meant a rotation of dancers for the title role: Spessivtseva, Lopokova, and Egorova. King George and Queen Mary attended in December. But hopes of a long run faded.

Receipts began to drop after Christmas. Diaghilev and his main backer, Sir Oswald Stoll, tried new publicity efforts but with little success. Diaghilev hoped for a six-month engagement, proceeds allowing him to pay back what he owed Stoll. But long ballet runs did not suit public taste. Stoll suggested transporting scenery and costumes from Paris and alternating between triple bills one night and *The Sleeping Princess* the next. But the threat of the seizure of his French materials because of his debt to Stoll (who had advanced him £20,000), caused Diaghilev to nix the plan. Stoll would have clearly seized the scenery and costumes.

As debts mounted, Diaghilev had to pay the costume makers; otherwise, they would not deliver the items, but he did not pay Bakst, which led to an action in 1923 obtaining an injunction restraining Diaghilev from using his scenery. Their twenty-five-year friendship ended. The delayed opening meant tickets had to be transferred to a new date, upsetting the public and creating a box-office storm. When the ballet did open on November 2, critics admired the splendor of the spectacular sets with the recreation of Petipa's original dances, all with fairy-tale-like pictures ranging over five acts. Some, however, objected to its imitative character, referring to it as the "suicide of the Russian Ballet. It was buried with fitting pomp. . . . The Russian Ballet, as an art force, has ceased to be," wrote a critic in the *Sunday Times*.[11]

Diaghilev managed to pay back a portion of the amount owing partly by selling some of his own possessions, including a black-pearl collar stud presented to him by Lady Ripon (Christiansen 178). But he still owed £13,000. The decision was made to end the London run, with Diaghilev, in typical style, less upset by the debt to Stoll than by the inability to remount the production in Paris (Grigoriev 173–74). And despite Stravinsky's celebration of the work, praising the music of Tchaikovsky—he called the production "the most authentic expression of that period of our Russian life which we call the 'Petersburg Period'"—the ensemble production lost its allure and closed after 105 consecutive performances, audience support for prolonged ballets shrinking.[12]

Even *Vogue* now criticized the older style Diaghilev presented and asked if *The Sleeping Princess* might be a reaction against Futurism and the unpopularity of his earlier, experimental ballet *Chout*. Others noted the literal breakdown of stage machinery: at the end of act two, when trees from an enchanted forest were to rise up from the stage, which worked perfectly in St. Petersburg for Pepita, it became a disaster in London. The machinery, emitting giant cracking sounds, simply stopped operating midway. Diaghilev was in tears (MacDonald 278–79). But not everyone saw disaster. André Levinson believed that the revival of the ballet, with its theme of the monarchy reborn, meant the rebirth of St. Petersburg's aristocratic ballet culture. "The debris of the illustrious Imperial Ballet survived" in the production, representing a "heroic loyalty to the art of dancing" and "ineffectual beauty in the midst of hideous, implacable reality," he wrote (in Garafola, *La Nijinska* 77).

Nevertheless, Diaghilev left a week before the actual close and placed Walter Nouvel, his secretary and business manager, in charge (Buckle 397).[13] He borrowed £300 from the mother of one of his dancers, Hilda Bewicke, and departed for Paris to escape his creditors and recover from the embarrassment. But he treated her shabbily, failing to meet her repayment schedule. Lawyers had to intervene. Back in London, Nouvel faced a possible general strike by dancers who had not been given their full pay, the strike canceled only through the efforts of Grigoriev. But in protest over Diaghilev's retreat, at the concluding performance of *The Sleeping Princess,* a number of the brass players broke into "Ach du Lieber Augustin" during the final mazurka, a musical objection against their poor wages and the decision to close.

Grigoriev was tasked with giving the company (some seventy strong) a month's leave after the close but somehow keep them together despite Diaghilev having no new engagements. Rumors soon spread that the company was dissolving. At the same time, Massine, newly returned to London from a South American tour, began to poach dancers from the idle Ballets Russes. Four key dancers, including Lopokova and Sokolova, left. Grigoriev attempted to stop them. They did not listen.

Stravinsky

Money always framed Diaghilev's star relationships, none more difficult than that with Stravinsky who, after the death of Rimsky-Korsakov, sought a new protector and patron. Diaghilev became that person. By luck, he had attended Stravinsky's February 6, 1909 concert in St. Petersburg where he performed *Scherzo Fantastique* and *Fireworks*; Diaghilev sensed musical possibilities and commissioned *The Firebird* after Tcherepnin dropped out and the dilatory Liadov claimed it would take a year to compose. He settled on the eager twenty-seven-year old Stravinsky who began the work even before he had a formal contract, completing the score in five months (December 1909 to April 1910) with the first performance in Paris on June 25, 1910.

Nonetheless, there was a rush to complete, Stravinsky likely writing the score as he went and handing pages to a copyist "long before" he finished composing (Walsh 137). However, there was an unexpected delay when Stravinsky had a vision in the spring of 1910 of what would become *Le Sacre du printemps*: a group of elders in a circle watching a young girl dance herself to death (Walsh 138). During this time Diaghilev also commissioned Stravinsky to orchestrate a Grieg piano piece for a fee of 75 rubles (Walsh 583 n. 47). But having finished the piano score of *The Firebird,* the entrepreneur Diaghilev set up several sneak previews to gain favorable advance coverage in the press. Stravinsky even performed excerpts at the journal *Apollon.* But the composer's enthusiasm in preparing the work resulted in an exclusive contract with Diaghilev; this meant he could not earn any further money from performances of *The Firebird* by other companies. Stravinsky did earn some extra monies, however, by selling the ms. to a Swiss oil baron, Jean Bartholoni, for Frs. 8,000 just after the war. Money again aided art or at least in this case an artist.

Diaghilev's turbulent relationship with Stravinsky pivoted around money, revealing how Diaghilev dealt with a marquee figure. Temperamentally generous in his praise, he could be cheap in relation to financial support. Publication of Stravinsky's second major work, *Petrushka*, to be published by a new music publishing house founded by Serge Koussevitzky which allowed composers to claim equal royalties with the publisher, created a rift because Diaghilev received not a *centime*.[14] But Diaghilev struck back: when *The Firebird* became an international hit, Stravinsky received almost no royalties because of his earlier contract. Financial friction over commissions and copyright was constant between the impresario and composer.

A 20-minute version of Stravinsky's *La Chant*, written to Diaghilev's specifications, is one example. Commissioned in 1916, Diaghilev had explicitly indicated which extracts Stravinsky was to use and how they were to be altered. The instructions were exact and indicate Diaghilev's authoritarian manner. A letter of November 1916 contained precise directions. Here is a sample:

1. Write a song for the nightingale, reducing a number of bars on p. 49.
2. p. 51 – cut the first three bars in the last line.
3. p. 60 – cut the first five bars.
4. p. 62 – create a transition from the last bar to p. 40. The repeat continues to p. 49.

A final paragraph summarizes the Diaghilev method: pre-emptory, egotistical, controlling:

> In both songs of the nightingale the number of bars must be reduced (*i.e.*, by complete separate bars), otherwise there will be a *deadly longeur* in the choreography. And there's no point in grumbling at me about this! I'm a man of the theatre and, thank God, not yet a composer. (in Scheijen 354)

This is quintessential Diaghilev: knowledgeable, self-assured, exact, and imperial in tone. He was also not above changing the names of his dancers as well as the scores: Alicia Marks, a young girl from London possessed of an almost ethereal serenity on stage he renamed Alicia Markova as he earlier renamed Vera Clark to Vera Savina. The illusion of being Russian was paramount, Slavic names suggesting force mixed with exoticism.[15]

Stravinsky could adjust to musical irreconcilables but not financial contradictions. He once refused to compose a liturgical ballet for Diaghilev because the master wanted him to compose it for the same price as *Les Noces*. Nevertheless, Stravinsky believed that the "more constraints one imposes, the more one frees one's self"; hence, his need to know the dimension of a hall for a work to be performed plus the number of seats and even the direction the orchestra would be facing. In turn, he would respond musically. He believed that the arbitrariness of constraint serves "to obtain precision of execution."[16] He also composed directly at the piano, not at a desk writing musical notations.

But antagonisms increased; at one point, Diaghilev was so upset over Stravinsky's work on *Renard*, largely supported by Princesse de Polignac, that he muttered "with 'our Igor' it's always 'money, money, money.'"[17] But

Stravinsky recognized his own value and approached his compositions like a businessman, always needing to know his deadline, the anticipated length of the work to be composed, how it would be performed, and of course, how much he would be paid. He worked meticulously: his writing desk resembled "a surgeon's instrument case" with bottles of "different coloured inks in their ordered hierarchy," each with a "separate part to play in the ordering of his art."[18] And he had no hesitation in seeking to earn "every penny that my art would enable to extract," writing almost always for commissions (*NYT* April 7, 1971). When he sensed Diaghilev's diminishing fortunes, he began to decline collaborations.

The composer and impresario could also be inflexible, one often accusing the other of moral turpitude and duplicity, Diaghilev repeatedly and harshly criticizing Stravinsky's repeated focus on money. Chastised for this behavior, Stravinsky retaliated by demanding immediate payment for his work, otherwise he would not finish a composition already started.[19] He often felt (correctly) that Diaghilev cheated him from his proper royalties and sensed that Diaghilev was no longer his grand supporter. Yet despite protracted quarrels, the two always managed to reconcile, "a Russian trait," Stephen Walsh suggests:

> Even at the height of mutual recriminations, the deep artistic sympathy and warm personal affection somehow remained intact. . . . Like cartoon Russians, Stravinsky and Diaghilev could hug and get drunk together by night and still wrangle bitterly over money and contracts by day. (Walsh 262, 307)

Furthermore, it was through Diaghilev that Stravinsky would meet his mistress and later second wife, Vera Sudeykina. She was wife of the designer/painter Sergey Sudeykin who worked for Diaghilev. Herself a painter, costume designer, and former actress, Vera captivated Stravinsky, but when her husband found out about their affair, a confrontation with the composer led to a period of strain and struggle. Stravinsky feared damage to his reputation and own family if Sudeykin, intensely possessive, followed through on his threat to kill Vera (Walsh 324–25). But Stravinsky could not give her up and began to consider a double romance: maintain his own marriage and family (he had by then four children), while keeping Vera, something of a Russian habit (Walsh 345).[20] Yet in the midst of this turmoil, he was able to turn back to *Mavra*, a one-act comic opera based on a minor Pushkin work, disassociating his personal and professional life. Vera soon left her husband who then departed for America. A divorce followed, while Stravinsky continued his romance. They would marry in 1940, nineteen years after their affair began.

During this period, Diaghilev was beginning to have misgivings about the reception of Stravinsky's music and padded his performances with ballet stars to attract audiences (Grigoriev 83). But this started earlier: hesitant over the first performance of *Le Sacre de printemps*, for example, Diaghilev balanced the experimental *Le Sacre*, with its changing time signatures and exploding arpeggios and glissandos, causing eruptions in the audience, with other, less explosive works. Complementing the raucous premiere of *Le Sacre* was Nijinsky in a performance of *Le Spectre de la Rose* with his spectacular leap through a large window at the rear of the stage (and caught by four men hidden from the audience) and then *Les Sylphides* and Borodin's *Polovtsian Dances* from *Prince Igor,* all on the same program.[21]

Stravinsky, easily offended, took such actions by Diaghilev—not only in programming but actually interfering with the composition of his work—as a vote of no confidence and on more than one occasion began to secretly negotiate commissions independent of the Ballets Russes. During a meeting in Paris, Diaghilev was so jealous of Stravinsky that he refused to recognize the composer's right to work apart from him. He considered it a breach of faith. But he did express interest in producing Stravinsky's *The Song of the Nightingale* as a ballet with scenery by Matisse. Stravinsky rejected the idea: *The Song* was to be a symphonic poem only for a concert, not stage performance (White 69). Stravinsky believed he was an indispensable component of the company, while simultaneously claiming that he didn't need them. Recognizing that the financing of the company was "something of a conjuring trick," he believed that his financial returns, whether from commissions, fees, the sale of his copyrights, or performing (as both pianist and conductor) were frequently inadequate.[22] In 1911, for example, he sold the rights to *The Firebird* to the Russian music publisher Jurgenson for 1,500 rubles, a considerable sum at the time. When he felt he was treated unfairly, he would turn against Diaghilev; periods of estrangement would follow.

By 1918, Stravinsky's financial position became more precarious. His paltry rights for *The Firebird* expired that June and for *Petrushka* the year before, but despite their repeated performances in Ballets Russes productions in America, Spain, Portugal, and London, he received not a franc. Russia had no international copyright protection so there was no need to pay him. Diaghilev was actually within his legal rights since *The Firebird*, in particular, was then in the public domain. Yet Diaghilev owed Stravinsky thirty thousand francs and had paid him nothing for six months.[23] While expenses mounted, Stravinsky had no dependable or regular income from his music, nor from the Ballets Russes. Sources were erratic. He also had a set of individual loans from Artur Rubinstein, Misia Sert, Sir Joseph Beecham, and the Princesse de Polignac, despite a more or less regular, monthly stipend from Mme. Errazuriz (Walsh 296).[24]

Diaghilev's behavior with Stravinsky was not unique. He was notorious for delaying payments, neglecting payments, or even denying payments. For years he did not make royalty payments to Jurgenson Publishing or RMV (Russischer Musik Verlag) for musical works which he claimed entitlement to perform. Forced to take action, Stravinsky would withhold *Les Noces* until Diaghilev settled his debts. But Diaghilev, himself, had worries, writing to Ernest Ansermet, the Swiss conductor of the Kursaal orchestra at Montreux, in June 1919 that

> I could lose 120,000 francs a season in London [but] I knew I [could] always find resources in Russia. Some merchant would be ennobled and I would get the consideration, out of which I could create art. Now there are no Excellencies or Grand Dukes left; a year ago I had debts of a million; London has saved me; but I'm not rich; I've only been able to pay my debts; and as I've now only myself to count on, if I want [to] survive I must be careful. (Walsh 302)

The letter sets the tone and behavior of Diaghilev, who dealt almost daily with the tenuous finances of his company. To Ansermet, in fact, he suggested that he might transfer the Ballets Russes to a syndicate and either stay on as a director or take over a theater in Russia (Walsh 303). The involvement of Misia Sert, however, solved the immediate crisis, although it meant further complicated negotiations with Stravinsky over nonexclusive rights for *Les Noces* and the *Le Sacre du printemps* for the 1919 season in Paris. Stravinsky received ten thousand francs a year but only after haggling over the terms (Walsh 303). But payment was always unreliable: at one point, Ansermet had to hand Stravinsky Diaghilev's check through the window of a train at Morges on August 8, 1919. The impresario refused to deal with Stravinsky directly (Walsh 304).

But despite their bickering, feuding, and disagreements, Diaghilev's death in 1929 at age fifty-seven shook Stravinsky, who would regularly visit the grave on the Venetian island of San Michele. He, himself, would be buried there in 1971 only a few yards from the impresario.

Programming and Patrons

New works and mixed programs generated less revenue than the classics, but in the case of the Ballets Russes excitement over their varied and often controversial ballets contributed to their reputation as *provocateurs* and made new productions more appealing. Pricing, however, remained a constant issue, Diaghilev having to choose between maximizing profit and filling seats with lower-priced tickets. Increasing profit (and larger loans), however, made it possible for the company to spend more on commercially risky productions, although one had to be sensitive to the charge of elitism—so prices varied, especially between the orchestra and the upper balcony. But the goal always remained maximum attendance, although demand depended on the specific work to be danced, the time of day, day of the week, and season. Promoters, aware of the shaky audiences for the Ballets Russes, tended to allow them to lease theatrical space in the spring or summer when there was less demand for the theaters. This suited Diaghilev because many of his dancers at the start of his company were on summer leave from the Mariinsky or Bolshoi until he was able to form his own company.

Diaghilev constantly flattered his patrons and supporters with invitations to dress rehearsals and behind-the-scenes events, opportunities to meet the dancers and possibly view a class.[25] He understood that in economic terms every ballet has an option value and an existence value; the first is the additional value attached to the experience for the patron, donor, or ticket holder. It is a benefit beyond the existence value, the actual attendance at a performance.[26] Option value is the knowledge and benefit of an experience that continues after the theater. It is the value of the resource outside or beyond the theater, something Diaghilev expanded through exchanges within his network of donors and admirers. These socio-cultural factors add importance to the option value which becomes a potential source of benefit in the future: from a patron's point of view, supporting the Ballets Russes allowed future opportunities for further cultural experiences, new social connections, and chances to explore further art forms. Existence value is the immediate benefit and satisfaction or pleasure people receive from the actual present use value: a night at the ballet or meeting dancers and other patrons.

Diaghilev's confidence in his organizing ability never faltered as he managed to locate funds when they were desperately needed. For the most part, he succeeded, although his habit of undertaking projects without knowing if he could raise the money was legendary (Lieven 225). Risk became the defining feature of his collaborations. But his vision was so powerful and self-confidence so strong that artists would take a chance in the belief that they would be paid. There was also the reputation of the Ballets Russes which expanded because of its innovative and progressive productions.

But searching for capital was always problematic. Needing money to launch his London season of 1910, Diaghilev met George Edwardes, a relative of Benois and a prominent figure in the London theatrical world. Edwardes agreed to underwrite and organize the season but when Diaghilev returned to Paris and received a detailed letter from Edwardes requesting information on costs and anticipated fees, Diaghilev chose not to answer. Losing patience, Edwardes cancelled his participation with so unbusinesslike a partner. The likelihood of a London season seemed impossible.

But what explains Diaghilev's behavior? Laziness, neglect? On one hand, he had extreme energy but, on the other, lethargy. He rarely answered letters, never read books, opposed rising before eleven, and preferred taking his coffee and newspapers in bed. He hated walking, always opting for a closed carriage. But in Paris during the season, he sometimes made over thirty calls a day to ensure his stage success, spending hours with donors as well as carpenters, workmen, and stagehands. He, himself, was never a systematic worker but a sporadic, explosive figure. Working for, or with him was never dull. And his informal attitude to debt may have been a ruse, a maneuver allowing him to pursue even more funds because he owed so much.

But challenges constantly appeared, beginning with the Théâtre Châtelet, site of the company's first Paris season. The space was rundown and new carpets in the foyer and corridors had to be laid, lighting had to be improved, and flowers and plants had to be set in the entrance. To accommodate his large orchestra, Diaghilev had several rows of stalls removed, improving the look but reducing the number of seats for sale. Much of the space had to be painted, while the stage had to be overhauled, replacing its uneven floor. While rehearsals were underway, the stage was shared with carpenters, stage scenery, and packing cases recently arrived from Russia. Friends came to witness the preparations and often chat with the dancers, which distracted them and angered Fokine who one day threw out Robert Brussel not realizing he was the music critic of *Le Figaro* and a special friend of Diaghilev's. But all of these improvements legitimized the art of the company in its refurbished theatrical space, validating its effort, reshaping the field of its cultural production emanating outward from the stage to the audience and beyond.

At the *répétition générale* of May 1909, a dress rehearsal the night before the opening, he carefully screened his audience: journalists, writers, musicians, artists, donors, and aristocrats filled the theatre (Grigoriev 19). The next day, May 19, 1909, was historic: the opening night of the Ballets Russes. Just before the curtain went up, Diaghilev went on stage to encourage his dancers and confirm that all was ready. He ordered the house lights to be dimmed and the curtain up. Nijinsky, Pavlova, and Fokine worked their magic. The evening was an immense success, especially the Polovtsian dances from *Prince Igor* which showed a primitive but powerful folk Russia. Diaghilev demonstrated to Paris the resurrection of ballet into something modern, dramatic, mesmerizing—spectacular. Jennifer Homans, in fact, credits Diaghilev for turning ballet "into an image of Russia." But not imperial Russia which he saw as dying but as an "imagined Slavic ur-Russia, exotic, primitive, modern" and styled for export to the West. He constantly sought "new fronts for the avant-garde using old Russian forms" (Homans *Mr. B* 113–14).

But spectacle was impractical for a touring company, although his quest for special effects did not diminish. He also sought historical accuracy but acknowledged that an impressionistic approach was more effective. In his first Paris season with Russian stage machinist Carl Waltz, for example, he had fountains that shot up onto the stage in *Le Pavillon d'Armide*. In the first production of *The Firebird* (1910), the bird flew on wires and the Knights of Night and Day rode on horseback, although bold *jetés* soon replaced both. Such elaborate devices, however, were found to be distracting and were dropped from a remounting of the ballet eighteen months later in a more modernized performance. Diaghilev also soon streamlined other productions (to reduce costs) with fewer crowds of on-stage performers, although he maintained large operatic choruses for *Godunov* and selections from additional Russian operas.

The integrated visual spectacles remained. The decors, Diaghilev explained, must offer a "'symbolic framework that enhances the meaning of the performance.'"[27] But again, this did not occur overnight. The essentially plotless ballet *Les Sylphides* (1909), for example, had conventional music with dance in the classical style, although it exhibited a more dramatic vocabulary of gesture. The choreographer Fokine contextualized the dance with the space defined by the designs. Soloists had center stage only briefly, Fokine preferring to integrate them into the ensemble. Most importantly, he replaced Petipa's rectilinear masses with smaller, asymmetrical groupings, patterns that constantly shifted. In later productions, this would grow to large, freewheeling crowds moving across the stage. Artistically, change was taking place on multiple levels initiated not only by choreographers but designers.

But all this took sponsorship, patrons, donations, and financial goodwill and Diaghilev constantly brokered and exploited contacts to keep the company operating in a competitive commercial world. He continually searched for capital and when it was available, spent time managing it. Without a permanent home or government support, he repeatedly coaxed, flattered, enticed, and wooed donors wherever they lived. No single entity underwrote the company, requiring committees in various cities to endorse and even guarantee productions, often with financial advances. In theoretical terms, this modernized "the practical means of cultural production."[28] Individuals, not institutional policy, shaped the creative economy of ballet; in these terms, and given his need to be independent, Diaghilev was a rebel—or innovator. Artistically, Diaghilev carefully managed the ballet company's evolving aesthetic, although economically, all was amorphous.

Financially, Diaghilev was on his own, and the tenuous financial conditions made every step perilous. He had obligations but also creative freedom, at least on the surface. Patrons and banks expected a return, at least of the monies borrowed, while suggesting more temperate programs to ensure attendance. Without any formal requirements or restrictions, his ensemble could invent and create but an eye (even half closed) had to be kept on the ledgers or accounts. Financial autonomy and its inherent uncertainty permitted independence but at a cost. Such freedom was deceptive. Substituting for institutional dependence were individual patrons, donors, or even banks. The "vulgar demands of economics" still ruled alongside the pressures of an anonymous market. Diaghilev sought art as a symbolic good of singular importance but could not escape its existence as a commodity (Bourdieu 113–14). Theater managers, dancers, composers, choreographers, artists, and stagehands reminded him of the vulgar demands of economics.

Dancing the Avant-garde

Aesthetically, the freedom of the Ballets Russes from established ballet frameworks allowed it to remake the cultural field of dance. This change occurred as its popularity as a "radical form" increased, encouraging newer works via younger avant-garde artists and composers who were cheaper than more well-known figures, an often forgotten aspect when celebrating early works by Stravinsky or even Picasso. To commission a work from one of these new artists made economic sense to Diaghilev. They were a bargain. In turn, these often scandalous new productions generated box office sales, initially reshaping the market structure of dance. And the more public the scandals or disputes between Diaghilev and his designers, composers, or critics, the greater the public interest in the productions, which always had limited performances which increased demand because of minimal supply.

But while Diaghilev promoted the avant-garde work of new and established artists, it is important to consider the reverse: Diaghilev's impact on the avant-garde. Whether it was the avant-garde Russian theater, painting, or certainly music, Diaghilev's promotion of new artists and composers stimulated their realization that their art had agency.[29] But the evolution of his modernist aesthetic depended on his appropriation of their avant-garde work which, in turn, encouraged the artists to further their own experiments, revisions, and imaginations. By example, he showed them that new, formalist approaches could exceed the limitations of their original medium. Art itself became an end, not a means, fulfilling ideals of the Russian avant-garde.[30]

Art went on stage in the backdrops of Goncharova, the art of Larionov, the costumes of Picasso, and the musical experiments of Stravinsky. And it impacted the work of others. Diaghilev remade the company in the image of the avant-garde itself (especially between 1914 and 1917) which, in turn, directly affected the avant-garde artists themselves, generating a new self-confidence to push form and color further. They not only united the visual and the verbal, but became more intense and committed to finding new fields of expression, which meant new experimentation.[31] "Any work of art that lacks a sense of aggression can never be a masterpiece," Marinetti proclaimed, Diaghilev pronouncing something similar to his followers. Aiding

Diaghilev was his belief in the Futurists' trinity of "courage, boldness and rebellion."[32]

An example of avant-garde change: Diaghilev's *Le Bal* (1929) designed by de Chirico, which presented the stage as a ruin, the space littered with eroded arches, empty pedestals, and overgrown temples. The costumes of the dancers possessed a similar set of debris including marble hair, thighs made of Doric columns, and terracotta necks. The dancers became ancient statues that jerkily moved. Balanchine choreographed and emphasized grotesque foxtrots, jigs, military marches, and acrobatic, angular steps at a ball. Balanchine, meeting the wishes of de Chirico and Diaghilev, showed the human form reduced to columns, bricks, and bones.[33] De Chirico was to receive Frs. 15,000 for his work, half payable on receipt of the sketches, the other half the day after the premiere. The draft agreement written by Diaghilev was signed November 29, 1928. De Chirico later wrote that he had been paid in full by May 9, 1929 (Buckle 583 n. 189).

The avant-garde experiments of France, Italy, and Russia coalesced in the synergistic work of the painters, composers, choreographers, and dancers of the Ballets Russes. A 1917 photo highlights the new cross-fertilization: Goncharova, Cocteau, Larionov, and Picasso smile at each other on a Roman street corner.[34] Diaghilev likely orchestrated their union since the company was there in residence. Picasso, on his first visit to Italy, and Diaghilev soon began work on *Parade* to premiere that May in Paris. Cocteau had invited Picasso to join him and Diaghilev on the production. Appropriately, Cocteau and Picasso stayed at the Hotel de Russie. In Rome, Picasso also met the ballerina Olga Khokhlova whom he would marry the following year. He also met Massine and Stravinsky.

A later photo by Cocteau shows Picasso and Massine at Pompeii; in Naples, they witnessed the *commedia dell'arte*. Inspired, three years later Picasso, Stravinsky, and Massine premiered *Pulcinella,* with its roots in the *commedia,* for the Ballets Russes. Additionally, on April 10, 1917 in Rome, there was an exhibition of works from Massine's private collection in the foyer of the Teatro Costanzi, home of the Rome Opera. The night before, the Ballets Russes had performed Stravinsky's *Firebird* and *Feux d'artifice.* The composer conducted, while many of the avant-garde artists in the show were present: Bakst, Balla, Depero, Prampolini.[35]

Larionov, with whom Goncharova had been working on sets and costumes for Diaghilev's productions since 1915, set out the new aesthetic that unites the Ballets Russes and the avant-garde. Writing of Picasso, he said that Picasso doesn't look but finds.[36] This is precisely what Diaghilev accomplished. In the avant-garde artists he found there was confirmation of his own vision which, in turn, promoted and expanded those of the very artists and composers he employed. In his knowledge of a vast musical repertoire, he found works to be reinterpreted by the Ballets Russes. The reception of his imaginative ballets encouraged new efforts by avant-garde artists to work in fresh mediums, not only from the studio to the stage, but the reverse.

Allied with this new exchange was the idea of superposition, the overlay of artistic elements, a variation of Wagner's total work of art. The temporal (dance) and spatial (choreography) integrated simultaneously, partially linked to Cubism where moving around an object allowed one to view it from "several successive appearances which, fused into a single image, reconstitute it in time."[37] This, in other words, was ballet, a form of synthetic theater where the arts unite through the eye and the ear at the same time. Experiments in form on stage meant original, avant-garde experiments in music, movement, and the canvas. The interdependence was clear, supported by artistic, critical, and public support.

The impact of Diaghilev and the Ballets Russes on Cocteau, Apollinaire, and the Futurists, Constructivists, and Acmeists was profound, licensing them to go further in their own artistic explorations. Goncharova's designs for *Le Coq d'or* and its use of superposition is one illustration, one where on-stage design affected artists and designers. Similarly, with *Parade* and later *La Chatte* (1927), avant-garde in form and presentation with so-called kinetic constructions. It proved to be popular, even touring regionally. Designed by Naum Gabo and Antoine Pevsner, the *mise-en-scène* was a stylized kitchen of geometric shapes with transparent mica furniture and "angles and planes that suggested Euclid's propositions," wrote an anonymous critic (in Pritchard 225). Balanchine contributed "biomechanical-like dances of interlocking limbs" (Homans 132).

Jane Pritchard writes that

> the backcloth was black American cloth, the floor was made up of three distinct surfaces and Pevsner's contribution was the raised figure of Aphrodite. Side-lighting on the reflective surfaces gave a wholly new look to the futuristic set and costumes. The dancers' costumes included plastic headdresses which may have been inspired by the Soviet science fiction film *Aelita* (1924) designed by [Alexandra] Exter, a plastic tutu for the ballerina and plastic shin pads and single epaulettes for the men. Over their grey shorts and vests, the all-male corps wore curiously structured tunics reminiscent of circles of orange peel. (Pritchard 225)

The impact on Balanchine was to liberate him to create more experimental choreography. This, however, did not always meet with Diaghilev's approval.

In 1928, for example, at the end of the London season, Grigoriev mentioned to Diaghilev that his contract with Balanchine had expired and should be renewed. Diaghilev said it will happen when Balanchine visits him in

Venice. But when they met again in Paris after the holidays, Grigoriev asked if Diaghilev had in fact renewed Balanchine's contract. Diaghilev flew into a rage, abusing the young choreographer. Only reluctantly did he approve the renewal after Grigoriev pressed him. In reality, with Massine gone only Balanchine was a suitable replacement (Grigoriev 248–49).

Le Pas d'acier (*The Steel Step*) went further, an attempt to create a Russian Constructivist work set in a factory with wheels, platforms, and ladders incorporated into the dance. Prokofiev said it was

> to be a ballet of construction, with hammers big and small being wielded, transmission belts and flywheels revolving, light signals flashing, all leading to a general creative upsurge with dance groups operating machines and at the same time depicting the work of the machines choreographically. (in Pritchard 226)

The costumes were asymmetrically cut work clothes in plain colors with caps and jackets made of simulated cowhide. The rapid movement of the dancers and the sensation of machinery and noise was realistic, although critics were unsympathetic: "Le Pas d'acier is a remarkably clever tour de force that should be seen and then—forgotten."[38]

Interestingly, exhibitions of the Russian avant-garde artists were short-lived, largely because of Soviet objections to their formalist art, a style counter to the approved socialist realism. The *First Russian Art Exhibition* of 1922 was held in Berlin, the show the first overview in the West of the Russian avant-garde. The Russian pavilion of the XIV Venice Biennale in 1924 was the last. One of Diaghilev's accomplishment was displaying the work of these artists to a Europe which had little knowledge of such work.[39] And an interesting feature is the preponderance of women artists. The conceptual and historical context is crucial, which John Bowlt addresses in his essay "Women of Genius," showing that by 1910 women were a critical part of the Russian avant-garde art world and that "without them, future avant-garde trajectories would have been impossible."[40]

In sum, the exchange between the avant-garde of Russia and Europe and that of Diaghilev was reciprocal. One enhanced the other in remaking the idea of performance, incorporating avant-garde elements of design, color, form, and movement. And for the Russian avant-garde, it meant exposure to the West. Diaghilev continued as a curator of art as well as dance.

The Committee and the Master

The committee method both inhibited and facilitated programming for the Ballets Russes—but as artistic director, every detail needed Diaghilev's approval. Sometimes, his revisions were minute and other times grand. He consulted friends and patrons when planning a ballet but at stage rehearsals, he dictatorially directed technicians, musicians, dancers, and composers. He was also aware of the geographical responsibilities: if the company was to present Russian ballets, they had to be inclusive: the Russian steppes appear in *Prince Igor*, shaman sites of Mongolia in the *Le Sacre du printemps* and the Caucuses in *Thamar*, while the Orient of Samarkand appears in *Schéhérazade*. *The Firebird* showed kremlins (walled cities) with onion- domed churches. Before 1917, the company emphasized the diversity of Russia, although by the 1920s, it looked back on that world with nostalgia. It was by then responding to new artistic cues such as Constructivism in *Le Pas d'acier.*

But the committee or cabinet remained instrumental, ranging from Benois and Bakst to the critic and later business manager Valerian Svetlov and Walter Nouvel, augmented by Fokine and Grigoriev. This Russian group focused on artistic matters; a Parisian group, led by Misia Sert and Comtesse de Greffulhe, formed a committee of wealthy supporters and dealt with fundraising and promotion. During World War I, Diaghilev formed a new advisory committee which actually travelled with him to Switzerland, Spain, and Italy.

But operating the company was haphazard. As noted, there was no board of trustees or regularized budgets, which were creatively remade for each production often relying on yet-to-be confirmed subsidies and donations. He commissioned new works without financial backing, prepared to take on financial risk through his belief that art would triumph over all circumstances. Credit was his survival method, but he often failed to repay or meet deadlines. At one point, owing the British theater manager Oswald Stoll £11,000 he did not have, he had to sell personal items. Royalties to composers were regularly overlooked and his personal expenditures were inextricably tied up with those of the company. Nevertheless, he seemed to recover miraculously from such disasters.[41]

After the war, patrons had an even greater role, the composition of these committees a gauge of the Ballets Russes's fortunes as its evolving performance vision shifted from the Russia of folk traditions to a modernist, avant-garde environment with the occasional conventional piece to satisfy a conservative box office. These were presented to maintain connections with an audience they could not afford to lose. Not every performance should create, as happened in 1913 with *Le Sacre du printemps*, a riot.[42] Every performance should be a box office success.

Wealth entitled one to join Diaghilev's committees: for Princesse de Polignac, it was as heiress to the Singer sewing machine company; for Lord Rothermere, the *Daily Mail*; for Coco Chanel, *haute couture*. But every new artist, dancer, composer, or choreographer joining the company had to meet with the committee's approval and accept a list of people the committee advised the new figure *not* to see. They included anyone Diaghilev ever quarreled with or his rivals who might join or set up their own competing company.[43]

As productions took shape, Diaghilev kept busy supervising scene painting, costume selection, and musical changes. He would visit studios and workrooms almost daily to review colors and fabrics and where arguments took place over the color of a costume or the placement of props. But he knew what and who he wanted. In September 1919, he and Stravinsky made an unannounced visit to Matisse at his home outside of Paris. Diaghilev wanted him involved in one of his projects. When previously asked, Matisse always declined. He did not want to compete with Picasso. Diaghilev specifically sought Matisse for *Le Chant du rossignol*, a ballet version of Stravinsky's opera.

Diaghilev outlined a marvelous gold and black décor to Matisse, while Stravinsky played extracts on a piano. Matisse envisioned simple shapes in clear light with color but he was hesitant. For the next few weeks, there was silence from the impresario, a strategy to make Matisse worry. But in October 1919, Diaghilev imperiously summoned Matisse from across the channel to meet. He came, he stayed, he worked on costumes and sets under Diaghilev's command. Matisse compared him to Louis XIV, adding that "at bottom the only thing that counts is himself and his affairs" (in Scheijen 352). Diaghilev's creative will remained obstinate and independent, while his work ethic overwhelmed. But Matisse completed his designs and the materials were successfully tested under stage lights by the time he returned to France at the beginning of November disenchanted by Diaghilev's preemptory manner.

Others also found Diaghilev intrusive, notably Prokofiev. Diaghilev micromanaged his scores, whether it was *Chout* (1921), *Le Pas d'acier* (1927), or *Le fils prodigue* (1929). Each required adjustment. Diaghilev exerted strong influence on the young composer's compositions beyond declaring the subject and style of each score. He outlined revisions in detail explaining which section had to be developed and which had to be cut. The minor key of *Chout*, for example, had to go and Diaghilev wanted to extend orchestral interludes to allow for scene changes. Prokofiev complied. But such interference soon became intervention, while the variety of the three works, the first derived from Russian folktales, the second set in a factory, and the third a biblical parable, reflected a revolving aesthetic caused by the company's precarious financial conditions necessitating selections that suited audience taste and box office demands.[44] Works had to suit audience preferences. But Prokofiev also knew the exposure of his work through the Ballets Russes was unparalleled.

Publicity and Programs

Publicity was Diaghilev's most effective tool for keeping the Ballets Russes in the news and attracting donors. Early books and articles, supplementing the reviews, provided credibility and importance to the company beyond its fashionableness. Even art galleries got into the act, the Knoedler Gallery in New York exhibiting designs of Bakst in 1920. The work of the artists and designers drew attention, whether Baskt and his magnificent, original costumes or Natalia Goncharova, designer, illustrator, painter, and printmaker.

Baskt's sensational work on *Schéhérazade* of 1910 was memorable with its contrasting colors—scarlet, orange, purple, rose, and blue—set against the brown and gold and silver of the slaves with green background curtains, and was yet a harmonious whole.[45] His aesthetic was internationalist, rejecting the idea of costume as an ornamental disguise. He made mobility and framing the body the key, designing twelve stage productions between 1909 and 1914, culminating in his grandiose ideas for *The Sleeping Princess* produced in 1921. He had a new passion for Hollywood glamour and even film design, cultivated during visits to the U.S. between 1922 and 1924.

Goncharaova's sensational curtain of onion-domed Russian Orthodox churches for the 1926 version of *The Firebird* startled and dazzled. As early as 1921, W. A. Propert's *The Russian Ballet in Western Europe* appeared with sixty-three illustrations and a cover page by Goncharova whose work was nationalist, drawing from folklore and fabrics from her youth, reflecting a neo-primitivism which had found its way into *Le Coq d'or, Les Noces,* and *Aurora's Wedding.* Her art evoked traditional Russian folk patterns. Earlier, she had illustrated Pushkin's medieval tale "Conte de Tsar Saltan."

Preceding Propert's book and reflecting a growing public curiosity if not fascination with ballet, was a collection of ninety-four caricatures by brothers and Imperial Ballet dancers at the Mariinsky, Nikolai and Sergei Legat: *Russian Ballet in Caricatures* (St. Petersburg, 1902–1905). Originally printed individually, the caricatures were eventually collected and sold in sets. The fashion of visualizing ballet off the stage—possibly initiated by Degas in the 1860s with his backstage drawings and paintings of ballerinas at the Paris Opéra—became increasingly popular.[46] Tamara Karsavina and Mikhail Fokine were often subjects.

Soon, souvenir programs, advertisements, interviews, posters, magazine photos, postcards, radio, film, and other early forms of social media created a presence for the company whether in Paris, London, or Monte Carlo. Gossip columns and profiles further enhanced popular awareness. Later, it would be perfume, musical compositions, and a 30-kopek Russian stamp printed in 2000.

One of the most sustained forms of publicity was the company's souvenir programs. They not only offered commentary and introductions to the ballets of a particular season, accompanied by carefully rendered illustrations of the costumes, but flattered donors by listing their names. Advertisements from the most elegant Parisian stores accompanied remarks on the state of the company and even its future. Often more than sixty pages, these booklets showed how Diaghilev appropriated society's own artistic values, especially consumption, for the ballet. Women's taste and an identity with fashionable culture, visually and textually, dominated. These souvenir programs became printed records of a world that lasted long after the performances. They also reproduced important works of art such as the May 1917 program for performances at the Théâtre du Châtelet which contained a drawing of Picasso by Leon Bakst.

This particular sixty-four-page program is a remarkable mini-history of the company exhibiting a powerful awareness of its audience. The title alone situates the company and its pedigree:

Mai 1917
LES BALLETS RUSSES
A PARIS
Représentations Exceptionnelles
avec le gracious Concours des
Artistes de M. Serge De Diaghilev

Following an image of a coquettish ballerina seemingly floating in air resting on her right foot with her left leg flung out to the left and her shoulders turned but her face confronting the viewer, we read "AU BENEFICE DES OEUVRES" and then a list of the four organizations benefitting from the performances: "Oeuvre du Soldat Blessé ou Malade," "Pour les Ardennais," "Les Cantines au Front," and "Pour les Prisonners Polonais."[47] The message is immediate: others will gain from the performance of the Ballets Russes.

The next page is an advertisement from the couturier Paul Poiret, explaining that he had to close because of the war but that he will reopen when possible. The third page repeats the honorees of this benefit performance under the heading "COMITÉ DE PATRONAGE." Another advertisement follows from Callot Soeurs and then a full-page, two-column list of the women patrons of the season. Eight pages of women photographed in the latest styles follow, each an advertisement for a different couturier. Only at that point does the program appear with a full-page image of a Chinese figure from *Parade* under the heading of "Programme des ballets Russes." The meta-textual elements preceding this page situate the performances and company within the fashionable context of Paris. But one more advertisement—for furs—appears before the list of dances that comprise the season running from May 11 to 23. Among the twelve works (four each evening) are *L'Oiseau de feu, Les Contes Russes, Les Sylphides, Parade, Petrouchka*, and *Soleil de Nuit*.

Interspersed in the program are short introductions to each ballet and essays on such topics as "Les ballets Russes depuis la Guerre" by Michel Georges-Michel; "Choregraphie et Decors des Nouveaux Ballets Russes" by Léon Bakst; and commentary on each ballet. The most fascinating item is Apollinaire's two-page essay, "'Parade' et l'Esprit nouveau" where he describes the work as a "poem scénique" transferred by the new musician Erik Satie to an expressive but clear and simple form. One will immediately recognize the lucid spirt of France itself. Picasso and Massine have also united in the work to create an alliance of painting and dance suggesting a more complete art. Through Cubism there is a new harmony. *Parade* is a form of surrealism which, according to Apollinaire, is the starting point of a new modernism. Confidently, Apollinaire writes that the new spirit will seduce the elite and, with Massine's choreography, go beyond pantomime. The truth in the piece, Apollinaire writes, is "so lyrical, so human, so joyful that it would be quite capable of illuminating . . . the dreadful black sun of Durer's Melancholy" (Apollinaire, "Parade," n.p.).

Picasso's Cubist sets and costumes testify to the strength of his art, Apollinaire continues, but such originality has agitated the art world in the effort to return art to its strictest, most fundamental elements. Apollinaire then celebrates Picasso's art in *Parade* and his translation of reality, although representation overtakes pure content. The spectacle of a Chinese music hall will enthrall, as will an acrobat in a white swimsuit. Agility will mix with exquisite taste, he concludes. But advertisements again commodify the experience with ads for perfume, as well as dresses, lingerie, stylish hats, *objets d'art*, furniture, art books, raincoats (*Les Vêtements Imperméables*), champagne, and even aspirin, as well as toothpaste. Movie theaters advertise on the back cover.

In the souvenir program, Diaghilev has taken care to educate his audience, presenting the ballets in a sophisticated, intellectual manner. The program is a keepsake that mixes education, material culture, a sense of status, and a record of what would be much more than entertainment, offering critiques and guides to the dances. A portrait of Picasso by Bakst appears on p. 38; Picasso's own sketch of the riders in *Parade* appears on p. 41, as well as his image of Bakst. And new ideas are noted: at the end of the "Argument" for *Les femmes de Bonne Humeur*, the text reads, "*le peintre Bakst a réalise avec son décor le premier essai de déformation de perspective au théatre.*" Viewers should be aware.

Reflecting his use of publicity in an effort to reach a wide audience was the company's name. In early advertisements, the company was first known as *Les Ballets Russes de Serge Diaghilev* emphasizing his personal role. In English, it was simplified to "The Russian Ballet" or "Diaghilev's Russian Ballet" or more casually, "Diaghilev's Ballet," but with his name always prominent. Occasionally, publicity referred to the name in the singular: "The Ballet Russian." But Diaghilev decided to apply the plural "Ballets Russes" to emphasize the plurality of Russian dances they performed following his first successful season in Paris labelled simply "Saison russe." Capitalizing on the fascination with all things Russian and adding some mystery, he pluralized the name for the 1910 season: it had intrigue, variety, and curiosity for the eager public.

But publicity could work for and against the company. First, it was the success and celebration of Nijinsky, not only the company's most captivating dancer but successor to Fokine as a choreographer and Diaghilev's lover. But fame and notoriety were soon in conflict as the press revealed when Nijinsky left his mentor to marry fellow dancer Romola de Pulszky in 1913 while on tour in South America. An angry Diaghilev immediately dismissed him from the company, making more headlines. The Golden Slave in *Schéhérazade,* the masturbatory faun *in L'Après-midi d'un faune,* the puppet in *Petrushka,* and the "Specter of the Rose" was gone. His termination and marriage made international news.[48]

More importantly, perhaps, is that all these changes were symptomatic of the complicated, contradictory, and often confusing aspects of running a company while touring, facing debts, and losing dancers. Diaghilev's intransigence, determination, and resistance to accommodating his equally determined, self-willed dancers did not make things easy. He had similar flare-ups with his composers, designers, and even a panther. Visiting the acclaimed dancer Ida Rubinstein in her Paris apartment, Diaghilev excited her pet panther who lunged at him, causing the not-so-agile impresario to leap upon a tabletop. Several days later, the panther was removed.[49]

But despite the international reputation of the company, money crises continued, matched by unexpected setbacks. Leaving London in December 1919 to begin forty performances at the Paris Opéra, a boon financially and professionally, there was an unplanned-for surprise: the orchestra had gone on strike. But Diaghilev was sanguine: as he repeated often, "there is no interest in achieving the possible, but it is exceedingly interesting to perform the impossible" (Buckle 351). Alternate plans were quickly improvised.

Diaghilev Redux

Despite being known as a confidence man, charlatan, and dissembler, Diaghilev always seemed to recover. Every season presented new challenges which alternately impeded and encouraged new ballets and theatrical experiences. He knew he could not always rely on private backers nor innovative productions. Consequently, while he encouraged new music, new designs, and new choreography, he simultaneously relied on the public's interest in seeing updated versions of the classics. Ballet with an edge, or if not an edge, controversy, was part of the company's reputation but so were resplendent productions of *Schéhérazade*. Offsetting the effort to *Épater la bourgeoisie* were conservative productions that opened up checkbooks. But critics suggested that in the post-Armistice period, none of Diaghilev's ballets reached new esthetic ground. More recently, Lynn Garafola observed that from *Parade* to *Chout*, almost all of the Ballets Russes's new productions "coasted on the breakthroughs of the war years." Money might be the reason, she adds: a "paucity of means" kept Diaghilev from venturing into new artistic territory but audience preferences also played a role: the avant-garde no longer attracted (Garafola, 1989: 221).

But for Diaghilev, publicity and marketing were nonstop; from the start he recognized the merchandising value of his stars. He publicly feted and praised them, even if backstage there were arguments, disagreements, and bad feelings. His theatricality, on and off the stage, supported the attention he and the press lavished on his principal dancers. His own ambition and charm also made him irresistible to the public—unless money was involved. Then, he was not above deceit, cunning, or even ruthlessness. But his self-confidence always seemed to triumph, although his hotel bills often remained unpaid and he repeatedly questioned what he felt were overcharges.

The complicated question of whether Diaghilev's private expenditures were part of the Ballets Russes's costs remains unclear. He paid himself no salary but stayed at the best hotels and lived extremely well, charging expenses to the company. And there were discrepancies: Lifar, at the time his lover, was paid; Kochno was not, yet Diaghilev paid for their clothes and lodgings. Some ballet money also went to Diaghilev's library of rare first editions which he began to collect. Most dramatically, to raise money for the ballet and his library, in 1928 he sold off, with Picasso's permission, the curtain for *Le Tricorne* and a few additional items. Diaghilev himself cut up the curtain for one of Picasso's dealers, Paul Rosenberg. By early May, he had Frs. 175,000. At the time, he had only Frs. 16,700 in the bank (Buckle 496).

Diaghliev in general did not like to discuss money but by 1926 he was again in a difficult financial situation because of the failure of a Berlin season—receipts so small at the *Deutsches Künstlertheater* that Diaghilev could not pay his dancers, nor transportation for the company to their next stop, Monte Carlo. Diaghilev was indignant and departed for Paris in hopes of raising funds, handing over what little cash he had to Grigoriev and Nouvel. Banks would no longer offer credit and dancers became despondent, performing to a nearly empty Berlin house (Grigoriev 213). Explanations for the poor attendance had to do with showing too many French, not Russian, works or that Diaghilev's talents were not appreciated in Germany. But then, unexpectedly, the day before their departure, monies arrived but no one could explain the change.

But when Rothermere ended support, Diaghilev became desperate. He needed an English backer and theater. Wollheim, his agent, sought remedies but obstacles continued, notably the loss of various dancers including his ballerina Vera Nemtchinova, as well as Nicolas Zverev and Nicolas Efimov who suffered from the Tolstoy complex and added a twist to the business of ballet. As Tolstoyans, they followed Tolstoy's doctrine forbidding the signing of contracts, a form of indenture. Diaghilev had consented to a "Gentleman's Agreement" with them and they had been with the company some ten years. But they suddenly left in 1926 when they received an offer from Charles Cochran's new revue in London. This put Diaghilev in a difficult situation since *his* contract for the season in Monte Carlo made Nemtchinova's appearance obligatory. But she left, forcing Diaghilev to find a substitute, Danilova (Grigoriev 214).

By 1926 to meet his debts, Diaghilev told Grigoriev that he might have to sell the curtain Picasso did for *Le Tricorne* and his figure paintings on the *décor* for *Cuadro Flamenco,* all of them signed (Grigoriev 219). He instructed Grigoriev to produce them and he would do the cutting himself, despite the fear of public censure. The cutting out of the *Tricorne* curtain referred to a small panel in the large curtain. He also expressed interest in selling the curtain for *Parade* but could not because the design covered the entire piece of large canvas (Grigoriev 219).

Rescue initially took the form of Lord Rothermere, who one day accompanied Diaghilev to a rehearsal. Diaghilev followed his practice of entering the room, bowing to the company, shaking hands with the *regisseur*, the choreographer, and leading dancers, and then sitting down. But on this occasion, Diaghilev introduced the visitor, saying Lord Rothermere was an ardent admirer. The two then sat and observed with Rothermere becoming a regular visitor, partly because he was infatuated with the dancer Sokolova often used by Diaghilev to "wheedle" more finds from Rothermere (Grigoriev 218; Scheijen 405).

But money's effect on the company's programing became acute. In 1927, he sought to celebrate the twentieth anniversary of his theatrical activities in Europe with a Russian season. Works by Stravinsky, Prokofiev, and Dukelsky were to be featured. But funds were unavailable, telling Prokofiev if he could find him eight hundred francs, he would start rehearsing his ballet tomorrow (Scheijen 405). But throughout 1927, finances plagued him and he continued to cut expenses by economizing on materials for sets and costumes, already cutting costs on composers and engaging cheaper conductors, although he, nevertheless, sought to maintain quality (Scheijen 405). But even with conductors, there were still walkouts and resignations, as there had been with such figures as the choreographer Fokine; the ballet master Legat; and the two Tolstoyans, the dancers Nemtchinova and Zverev; the dancer and choreographer Massine; and later, the marvelous choreographer Nijinska. In most instances, the principals were offended by Diaghilev's actions or inactions: with Nijinska it was Diaghilev's decision to rehearse secretly with someone else, Serge Lifar, who had once been Nijinska's pupil.

The paradox of Diaghilev was that while the scandals of his more progressive ballets—*L'Après-midi d'un faune*, *Jeux*, *Le Sacre du printemps*—created sold-out performances and unprecedented gossip, they alienated important backers and the public, leading to his own doubt over the value of his experimental works. And once he fired Nijinsky in 1913, his programs altered, audiences declined, reviews were tepid, and supporters of the new style turned hostile. He appeared to reject or at least grow skeptical of the avant-garde. The First World War hindered any touring, while bills mounted and the most famous private dance company in the world faced possible disappearance. A trip to America with a much smaller company seemed its only salvation. Negotiations began early though the trip would not occur until 1916. The undertaking had mixed critical and financial results, the advanced publicity undercut by the company's unexciting performances and absence of several stars.[50]

But for Diaghilev, controversy took precedence over presentation, a position partly outlined by Marinetti and the Futurists who often proclaimed that the artist always required an enemy.[51] The Futurists, with their emphasis on performance, supported the ideals of the Ballets Russes and Diaghilev, who had spent time with Marinetti in Italy in 1915. A month earlier, Diaghilev had urged Stravinsky to form an alliance with the Futurist founder. Stravinsky had actually attended a Futurist puppet show in Milan which he found mesmerizing, although he later admitted that the Futurists "were absurd, but sympathetically so."[52]

But Diaghilev went further, moving from innovation to experimentation indirectly extending the avant-garde presence. His 1928 production of *Ode* at the Théâtre Sarah Bernhardt in Paris with Lifar and Beliankina incorporated neon lighting by Pavel Tchelitchew and cinematic projections by Pierre Charbonnier. It was a choreographic interpretation by Massine of a neoclassical hymn to nature by the 18th-century polymath and court poet Mikhail Lomonosov. A statue of Nature comes to life and reveals some of the wonders of nature. The student is eager to participate but the frightened statue returns to its petrified state. Lifar was to dance the part of the student. The scenario was by Boris Kochno who had become Diaghilev's secretary in 1921. Music was by Nicolas Nabokov.

The conjunction of forms, neon lights, and a hymn to nature revealed Diaghilev's late-career effort to cling to the new, mixing pinwheels of neon light with film of men in fencing masks diving in slow motion—all of this an effort to remain current (Buckle, 497–98). The staging also incorporated white body tights for the dancers, a radical visual departure. Unhappy with the progress and preparations for *Ode*, Diaghilev took over, from supervising the sewing of costumes to painting props and dominating orchestral and dance rehearsals.[53] The lighting, gauze transparencies, projections, and patterns of white rope used by the dancers to create original geometrical diagrams was revolutionary. In the second tableaux, "faceless men appeared as the Constellations in blue all-over bodytights decorated by Tchelitchev in luminous paint" (Pritchard 227). The dancers of the Aurora Borealis became part of an abstracted background.

But the effort was not a commercial success, partly because other companies were offering even more experimental ballets which undermined this new direction.[54] Lord Rothermere, who had funded the last two seasons of the ballet in London, suddenly withdrew support for the current year's programming despite it being half planned. The cause was at first mysterious but Grigoriev explained that Diaghilev was desperate for funds (Grigoriev 243). Lady Juliet Duff stepped in and set up a committee of patrons who each paid a hundred pounds to fund the season.

Transformation was one of Diaghilev's talents and Nicolas Nabokov recorded that very act on the opening day of *Ode* when he witnessed a dejected Diaghilev leave the theater an hour before the performance:

> He looked worn, grey and sallow as he crossed the stage covered with a two-day growth of beard. . . . Fifteen minutes before the curtain went up, I saw Diaghilev come in through this backstage door in full evening dress . . . calm, confident and resplendent. (in Buckle 500)

Diaghilev achieved what he envisioned in his performances through discipline, autocratic behavior, and control over his entire company, including choreographers, dancers, composers, and set designers—while paradoxically encouraging artistic freedom and independence among his contributors. This artistic laissez-faire (in contrast with a managerial manner) allowed the company to flourish and establish an international presence without a single performance in Russia. Ironically, this was what Diaghilev envisioned: to display to the world original ballets that embodied the excellence of Russian art and culture. At the same time, he sought to remake the national consciousness of the country. This is what Diaghilev's dream accomplished—not just a Russian ballet and ballet company but an original, inventive visual Russian culture available to the world.

NOTES

1. Arnold Haskell, *Balletomania Then & Now* (New York: Knopf, 1977) 75.

2. For a detailed analysis of this development, see Karthas, *When Ballet Became French* 6–9. Karthas reads ballet as the nexus for various anxieties of French cultural life and adds that intellectuals in particular "used ballet as a platform upon which to work out definitions of French modern identity" (Karthas 25).

3. On the synergy of a French choreographer going to Russia and a Russian ballet company establishing itself in France, see Karthas 16–17.

4. Nigel Dodd, *The Social Life of Money* (Princeton: Princeton Univ. Press, 2014) 386. Hereafter Dodd.

5. Dodd, "Introduction," *Social Life of Money* (rev. 2016) ix.

6. See Ernst Gombrich, *The Sense of Order* (1979; New York: Phaidon Press, 1984).

7. See the papers of Gabriel Astruc at the Dance Collection of the NYPL for the Performing Arts, Lincoln Center, New York. Call number is (S) *MGZMC-Res. 1. The collection number is *ZBD-161.

8. For details see "Money" in Stephen Walsh, *Stravinsky: A Creative Spring: Russia and France, 1882–1934* (New York: Knopf, 1999) 540–41. For the amount of Stravinsky's commission for *The Firebird*, his first major work and estimated to be ₽2,000 or just under Frs. 5,000, see Walsh 592 n.40.

9. On matters financial and the company, especially in relation to preparations for *Les Noces*, see Drue Ferguson, "Bringing *Les Noces* to the Stage," *The Ballets Russes and Its World*, ed. Lynn Garafola and Nancy Van Norman Baer (London: British Library, 1999) 167–87, plus Lifar, *Serge Diaghilev* (London: Putnam, 1945) 258 and *Ma Vie, From Kiev to Kiev, An Autobiography*, trans. James Homan Mason (London: Hutchinson 1970), 31–32.

Payroll sheets kept by Grigoriev are at the Harvard Theatre Collection accompanied by many of the contracts for dancers. Vera Rosenstein, a Russian raised in Paris and daughter of the company's physician, was another source on salaries for Ferguson (see 372 n. 14).

10. Serge Lifar, *Diaghilev* 258–59.

11. Ernest Newman in *Sunday Times* Nov. 6, 1921, in *Diaghilev Observed*, ed. Nesta MacDonald (New York: Dance Horizons, 1975) 276. Hereafter MacDonald.

12. For Stravinsky on *The Sleeping Princess*, see Lynn Garafola, *La Nijinska* 81.

13. He had earlier been on the editorial board of Diaghilev's *World of Art* journal responsible for its music criticism. Until 1911, with Alfred Nourok, he organized the popular Contemporary Music Evenings in St. Petersburg where new Russian and foreign music was performed. After Diaghilev's death, Nouvel moved to France and became a close friend of Stravinsky whose autobiography he co-wrote.

For further details on the financial dealings of the company, from expenditures to income, management fees, and administrative costs, see the "Ekstrom Collection," Diaghilev and Stravinsky Foundation, Victoria and Albert Museum, London. Of particular importance is the correspondence between Diaghilev and his agents relating to business and finance. https://archiveshub.jisc.ac.uk/search/archives/c446cbf1-8ec3-3183-9464-60a32727c9e4.

14. Eric Walter White, *Stravinsky: The Composer and His Works*, 2nd ed. (Berkeley: Univ. of California Press, 1979) 37. Hereafter White. During this period, Stravinsky began to negotiate with a Milanese publishing house, although they found his demands too exaggerated and cancelled discussions (White 54). For more detail, see Stephen Walsh 159.

15. Philip Richardson's short, satirical play *No English Need Apply* satirizes this topic. It exposes a series of dancers with exotic names that are actually really John or Janet. See *Dancing Times* (December 1923) 347–49. Richardson edited *Dancing Times* from 1910 to 1957.

Further examples from Diaghilev: Margot Luck became Astafieva II and Patrick Healy-Kay became Anton Dolin. Hilda Munnings became Lydia Sokolova and Edris Stannus became Ninette de Valois. See Buckle 389; Christiansen 227.

16. Stravinsky in "Igor Stravinsky: An 'Inirentor of Music' Whose Works Created a Revolution," *New York Times* April 7, 1971, https://www.nytimes.com/1971/04/07/archives/igor-stravinsky-an-inventor-of-music-whose-works-created-a.html. Hereafter *NYT* 1971.

17. Stravinsky in Sylvia Kahan, *Music's Modern Muse: A Life of Winnaretta Singer, Princess de Polignac* (Rochester, NY: University of Rochester Press, 2009) 203. Also see Stella Di Virgilio, "Igor Stravinsky and the Salon of Winnaretta Singer," https://parisianmusicsalon.wordpress.com/igor-stravinsky-and-the-salon-of-winnaretta-singer/. Singer was the daughter of the inventor of the Singer sewing machine.

18. C. F. Ramuz, *Souvenirs sur Igor Strawinsky* (Paris: NRF, 1929) in White 57.

19. Charles M. Joseph, "Diaghilev and Stravinsky," *The Ballets Russes and Its World*, ed. Lynn Garafola and Nancy Van Norman Baer (New Haven: Yale Univ. Press, 1999) 190.

20. On parallels between Stravinsky's affair and Russian writing, see Ira Nadel, *Love and Russian Literature* (London: Bloomsbury, 2023). Vera Sudeykin had been married twice by age twenty-three, but ran away from her second husband to take up with Sudeykin who was, himself, already married to a cabaret dancer, Olga Glebova. Anna Akhmatova was one of Sudeykin's earlier lovers (Walsh 335–36). Stravinsky's affair apparently began in the summer of 1920.

21. Thomas Kelly, *First Nights: Five Musical Premieres* (New Haven: Yale Univ. Press, 2000) 305, 315.

22. White 50. For further details on Stravinsky's publishing ventures, copyright problems, and lawsuits, see White 70 and Stephen Walsh, *Stravinsky: A Creative Spring: Russia and France 1882–1934* (New York: Knopf, 1999) 296–302. For a further financial survey, see "Financial Situation," *The Cambridge Stravinsky* 158–59.

23. For a vivid account of the challenges in raising funds, see Stephen Walsh, *Stravinsky: A Creative Spring* 285–87.

24. Needing funds, in 1928 he signed a contract with Ida Rubinstein for *The Fairy's Kiss*, an allegorical ballet, aware of a potential conflict with Diaghilev. He received $6,000 and conducted the premiere at the Paris Opéra on November 27, 1928. Diaghilev wrote a scathing review in a letter to Lifar and then publicly in an émigré paper, *Vozrozhdenije*, in mid-December 1928. Diaghilev was jealous of Rubinstein. See "The Fairy's Kiss," *The Cambridge Stravinsky* 152.

25. For a copy of one of Diaghilev's invitations to attend a "Final Rehearsal" of Stravinsky's *Renard* see Buckle 530.

26. Useful on this subject is Jörg Schimmelpfenning, "Ballet," *A Handbook of Cultural Economics*, ed. Roth Towse (Northampton, MA: Elgar Publishing, 2003), https://core.ac.uk/download/pdf/18507441.pdf.

27. Diaghilev in a 1910 interview in Scheijen 185.

28. Sarah Sonner, "Sponsorship and Funding for the Ballets Russes," *Diaghilev and the Golden Age of the Ballets Russes 1909–1929,* ed. Jane Pritchard (London: V&A Publishing, 2010) 95. Also useful is Pierre Bourdieu, "The Field of Cultural Production," *The Field of Cultural Production* 29–73.

29. Bellow suggests some of this interaction in *Modernism on Stage*, 2–5.

30. See David Burliuk, "Cubism (Surface-Plane), 1912," *The Russian Avant-garde and Radical Modernism: An Introductory Reader,* ed. Dennis G. Ioffe and Frederic H. White (Boston: Academic Studies Press, 2012) 95.

31. Especially useful on this topic is Jane Pritchard, "From the Russian avant-garde to Serge Diaghilev's Ballets Russes," *Studies in Theater and Performance* 36.3 (2016): 219–29. Hereafter Pritchard.

Another helpful source is Elena Strutinskaia, "Paris 1925: The European Premiere of the Russian Theatrical Avant-Garde," *Russian Avant-garde Theatre: War, Revolution and Design,* edited by John Bowlt (London: Nick Hern Books, 2014) 71–91.

32. F. T. Marinetti, "The Futurist Manifesto," *Critical Writings*, ed. Günter Berghaus, trans. Doug Thompson (New York: Farrar, Straus and Giroux, 2006) 14, 13.

33. An earlier, equally dramatic staging was *Relâche* (cancelled, 1924) by Picabia with music by Satie and performed by the Ballets Suédois. This was a multimedia production uniting blinding klieg lights and a cinematic interlude by René Clair. As part of the performance, a fireman wandered around the stage pouring water from one bucket into another.

34. The photo appears in Sharp, *Russian Modernism* 9.

35. Graham Spicer, "Picasso in Rome . . . The Ballets Russes and Parade," Gramilano, March 22, 2017, https://www.gramilano.com/2017/03/picasso-in-rome-with-diaghilev-cocteau-and-massine-the-ballets-russes-and-parade/. Picasso painted the Cubist "The Italian Woman" (1917) at this time.

36. Larionov in Sharp, *Russian Modernism* 9. Sharp provides a useful chronology of the development of the Russian avant-garde, its East-West orientation, and how it created a new national self-fashioning on pp. 10–14.

In 1916/17, Larionov's 1912 manifesto on Rayonism, an abstract movement derived from the Impressionists, appeared in Italian as "Radiantismo." In English it appears as "Rayonist Paintings," along with "Rayonists and Futurists: A Manifesto, 1913," in *Russian Art of the Avant-garde: Theory and Criticism, 1902–1934*, ed.

John E. Bowlt (New York: Viking, 1976) 91–100, 87–91. Both Larionov and Goncharova were involved with the nationalistic, neo-primitive group known as the Jack of Diamonds which united Russian folk art with Western modernist ideas, something Diaghilev was developing with the Ballets Russes at the same time. A key Rayonist concept was its concern with "spatial forms that can arise from the intersection of the reflected rays of different objects, forms chosen by the artist's will" (Larionov, "Rayonist Painting, 1913" in Bowlt 93).

Useful on the subject is *The Russian Avant-Garde and Radical Modernism: An Introductory Reader*, ed. Dennis G. Ioffe and Frederick H. White (Boston: Academic Studies Press, 2012).

37. Albert Gleizes and Jean Metzinger, "Du Cubisme" (1912) in Caddy 170. One unusual example of simultaneity was the Eiffel Tower, at once an object of gaze and a "panoramic vantage point." It also established synchronized time, sending out the first time signal around the world at 10 a.m. on July 13, 1913 (Caddy 170 n. 29).

38. Anon, "The Sitter Out," *Dancing Times* (August 1927) 296.

39. Three important texts on the topic are Rowell Margit, *Art of the Avant-garde in Russia: Selections from the George Costakis Collection* (1981); Schirn Kunstalle Frankfurt, *The Great Utopia: The Russian and Soviet Avant-Garde, 1915–1932* (1992); and *Amazons of the Avant-garde*, ed. John E. Bowlt and Matthew Drutt (2000), all three works published by the Guggenheim Museum, New York.

40. Matthew Drutt, "Introduction," *Amazons of the Avant-garde*, ed. John Bowlt and Matthew Drutt (New York: Guggenheim Museum, 2000), 14. Also important in the same volume are essays on Russia's modern women, noting that fashion trends made women appear more masculine long before the Russian Revolution proclaimed the sexes equal. See Nicoletta Misler, "Dressing Up and Dressing Down: The Body of the Avant-garde," *Amazons* 95–108.

Misler and others noted that the new styles were arrangements of horizontal and vertical lines and that a puritanism and asceticism perforated post-Revolutionary avant-garde ideology, leading Misler to write that "the female body seemed to disappear within the spacious, if clumsy geometric volumes of the new style, at least in the case of Exter, Popova, and Stepanova" (*Amazons* 97).

41. Rupert Christiansen, *Diaghilev's Empire* 53, 197.

42. Reaction to *Le Sacre du printemps*'s first performance on May 29, 1913 has been well-documented. On the first-night brouhaha, with shouts from the audience drowning out the orchestra, see Gillian Moore, *The Rite of Spring: The Music of Modernity* (2019, 92–123), Lynn Garafola, *Diaghilev's Ballets Russes* (1989, 63–65), Charles Joseph's *Stravinsky's Ballets* (2011, 95–98), and Modris Eksteins' *Rites of Spring* (1989, 10–16). Additional and often contrasting accounts are found in Grigoriev, *The Diaghilev Ballet* (1953; 1990, 82–84), André Levinson, "Stravinsky and the Dance," *André Levinson on Dance,* ed. Joan Acocella and Lynn Garafola (1991, 38–41), and Richard Buckle, *Diaghilev* 25–56. Cocteau, Gertrude Stein, and Carl Van Vechten also left accounts.

43. On the nature of Diaghilev's committees, see Jane Pritchard, "Creating Productions," *Diaghilev and the Golden Age of the Ballets Russes*, 72–74.

44. For a discussion of the fraught collaboration between the impresario and com-poser and the issue of musical changes, see Stephen D. Press, *Prokofiev's Ballets for Diaghilev* (Burlington, VT: Ashgate, 2006). Also see David Nice, *Prokofiev: From Russia to the West, 1891–1935* (New Haven: Yale Univ. Press, 2003) 170–71.

45. W. A. Propert, *The Russian Ballet in Western Europe, 1909–1920* (New York: John Lane, 1921) 17. Propert is useful on the color schemes and decors of Diaghilev's major ballets. His interest is the visual artistry of the Ballets Russes, less so the music and dancing. On pp. 43–45, for example, he skeptically outlines the prin-ciples of Cubist-Rayonnist theory. On pp. 47–48, he offers his reading of the Russian aesthetic, both its origin and practice.

46. On Degas and ballet, see Manon Garrigues, "Edgar Degas and the dancer: The artist's most beautiful representations," *Vogue* (French) March 7, 2021, https://www.vogue.fr/fashion-culture/article/edgar-degas-and-the-dancer-the-artists-most-beautiful-representations. Degas' favorite location was the foyer of the Palais Garnier.

47. *Les Ballets Russes à Paris, Representations exceptionnelles* (Program), Library of Congress, Washington, DC, 35, https://tile.loc.gov/storage-services/service/music/vaultscan.2/200181871/200181871.pdf. No page numbers.

48. But Nijinsky and scandal should not have been a surprise. In 1911 at the Mariinsky in St. Petersburg at a gala performance of *Giselle* for the Imperial Court, the dancer went on stage in a black velvet vest and close-fitting white silk tights but without the obligatory small slip required to cover the genitalia of all male dancers. The dowager empress took one look and fled from her box, followed by the Czar's young daughters. This event preceded Nijinsky's time with the Ballets Russes but precipitated his departure from the Mariinsky.

49. In Judith Chazin-Bennahum, *René Blum and The Ballets Russes* (New York: Oxford, 2011) 98.

50. See Hanna Järvinen, "Failed Impressions: Diaghilev's Ballets Russes in America, 1916," *Dance Research Journal* 42.2 (2010): 80–81. For further details outlining the disputes over casting and finances with the second U.S. tour of 1916—a number of dancers in the *corps de ballet* wrote directly to Otto Kahn (chairman of the Metropolitan Opera's board and sponsor of the tour) that their wages did not meet their living expenses—see Lynn Garafola, "The Ballets Russes in America," *The Art of Enchantment: Diaghilev's Ballets Russes 1909–1929*, ed. Nancy Van Norman Baer (San Francisco: Fine Arts Museums of San Francisco, 1988) 122–37. Pages 136–37 give exact financial figures.

51. Marinetti in Galina Yelshevskaya, "Russian Avant Garde," https://arzamas.academy/materials/1231. In 1927, the critic and artist Wyndham Lewis began a new journal simply titled *Enemy.*

52. Stravinsky to Robert Craft in Stravinsky and Craft, "Some Painters of the Russian Ballet," *The Atlantic* (August 1958). https://www.theatlantic.com/magazine/archive/1958/08/some-painters-of-the-russian-ballet/641640/.

53. Joy Melville, *Diaghilev and Friends* (London: Haus Publishing, 2009) 238–39.

54. For a fuller description, see Bellow, *The Modernist Stage* 237–38.

Chapter 5

The Ballets

Riot and Revolution

It was on stage where the fireworks of the Ballets Russes ignited, lighting up the Parisian and European skies. The prelude was *The Firebird* which lit the flame of controversy and debate to be followed by *Petruska, L'Apres-midi d'un faune, Le Sacre du printemps, Parade*, and then late works like *Le Train bleu* and *Apollo*. Each was revolutionary in its way and embodied originality, inventiveness, and even chaos identified by Stravinsky's biographer as "controlled disorganization."[1] This was the result of uniting musical originality, with unusual designs and expressive physical action; each ballet startled as they presented new sounds and movements by composers, choreographies, designers, and dancers. Picasso's large front curtain for *Le Train bleu* of two gigantic women partially undressed running with arms extended vertically and horizontally was as dominating as it was captivating. This metaphorically represents the impact of the Ballets Russes, rushing off the stage into the social and cultural life of the early 20th century.

However, it is important to recognize that while works like *Le Sacre du printemps* promoted the image of the Ballets Russes as the hotbed of experimentation and the new, it did little to alter the overall aesthetic of the company. That remained rooted in the exoticism of Russia and the symbolist inheritance of the *fin-de-siècle*. Only after World War I and the encounter with the futurist avant-garde would the Ballets Russes jettison the past for the new, although not entirely. Neither the box office, nor the competition could be forgotten (Garafola 1989: 75). Traditional ballets still had a place in a repertoire that ranged from the radical *Parade* to the conservative *Le Pavillon d'Armide*. This was especially important for the success of the company in France.

Of course, there were other outstanding ballets by the Ballets Russes in its twenty-year career under Diaghilev in addition to the seven represented in this chapter. They include Stravinsky's *Les Noces* (1923), in final form

143

created with four pianos, percussion, and the human voice, with costumes and décor by Natalie Gontcharova. Another is *La Chatte* (1927), an experimental and important short work of one act and ten minutes in length with the production emphasizing Constructivist sets and costumes by the avant-garde artists Naum Gabo and Antoine Pevsner with Balanchine doing the choreography. But the seven works selected for this chapter were groundbreaking in multiple ways and had a lasting impact on dance.

The change begins with the appearance of the stage. No longer were there a series of scene painters—there were five for Petipa's *Sleeping Beauty* of 1890—but only one for Diaghilev's *Parade* (essentially Picasso). Diaghilev's approach differed, seeking one artist to provide designs for the scenery and costumes. Visual coherence was now possible, even if the action was fragmented, establishing a new tension on stage. Bakst and Benois inaugurated this practice for Diaghilev. The one-act ballet was another mark of his breaking with the past.

Stravinsky, for whom all but two of his ballet scores were for Diaghilev between 1910 and 1929, worked with all the company's major choreographers, although it was only in 1926 that Diaghilev asked him for new work, the first time since the war. Money was one obstacle: Stravinsky was famous and commanded important sums. Another was their prolonged disagreements, although in an exchange of letters in April 1926 they confessed their faults to each other (Scheijen 406–7). He attended a revamped *Firebird* in Paris in May that year and presented Diaghilev with an opera-oratorio; *Oedipus Rex* previewed in late May at the home of Princesse de Polignac with a premiere the next night. It was not a success but the gesture renewed their admiration for each other.

Stravinsky found the greatest synergy with Fokine who sought to reform the formulaic classical style, with its set pieces for the *corps de ballet*. He preferred a naturalistic style directly reflecting the context and narrative of the ballet. But Stravinsky's music was a challenge and it was Nijinsky who choreographed the *Le Sacre de printemps*, reflecting his own bodily experiments, beginning with a reversal of the classical turnout giving the impression of "pigeon toes" for the dancers. He also eliminated the long body line and lightness in favor of inward bodily shapes, stamping and flat-footed jumps to reflect Stravinsky's intentionally barbaric music. Stravinsky's later work with Massine favored the dynamic use of movement; in 1920, he reset *Le Sacre*, working in counterpoint to Stravinsky's music, unlike Nijinsky who set every beat. Working with Bronislava Nijinska meant further adjustments between the music and movement as seen in her austere choreography for *Les Noces*. Stravinsky later developed a neo-classical manner when he worked with Diaghilev's last chief choreographer, Balanchine.[2]

The Firebird, June 25, 1910. With music by Stravinsky, choreography by Fokine, costumes by Léon Bakst, and sets by Aleksandr Golovin, this work established a new, unsettling tone, musically and balletically, for the Ballets Russes. A 45-minute, one-act ballet first performed at the Théâtre National de l'Opéra, Paris, the official program read, "Les ballets russes de Serge Diaghilev," making it clear who was in charge. The conductor was Gabriel Pierné. Bakst designed the costumes for the Firebird and the beautiful Tsarevna.

The Firebird became one of the most regularly performed works of the company. Anna Pavlova was expected to dance the leading role, but Tamara Karsavina took her place. The work made Stravinsky an overnight sensation and immediately expanded the reputation of the Ballets Russes for several reasons, not the least its blend of Orientalist and Russian exoticism. In the work, Fokine's choreography and Stravinsky's music united the two strands in a search for a new national identity originating in a mixed Eurasian heritage.[3] But there was also a market: European audiences were eager to discover this mysterious world with its Asiatic thread countering the graceful and symmetrical world of 19th-century Imperial Russian ballet. In the world of the Ballets Russes, an Islamic Orient joined a pre-Christian Russia along with a folkloric tradition. Audiences were equally bewildered and mesmerized, while the export/commodity aspect of the ballet was not lost on Diaghilev or his inner circle in an effort to expand attendance.

Diaghilev, of course, should get credit for his discovery, development, and promotion of Stravinsky, a young and untested composer when the maestro selected him for the chance to compose a ballet (although he was his third choice after Tcherepnin and Lyadov). In turn, despite disputes, disagreements and, dissatisfactions, Stravinsky said of Diaghilev that he "had a wonderful flair, a marvelous faculty for seizing at a glance the novelty and freshness of an idea, surrendering himself to it without pausing to reason it out."[4] Diaghilev's force and focus were almost unstoppable and his attention to visual effects, unleashed by his multiple and original designers, found echo in Stravinsky's own liberating scores, although he was "acclaimed as a genius and denounced as an anarchist" (Propert 101).

It was in 1909 St. Petersburg where Diaghilev discovered Stravinsky's early work. At the time, Diaghilev was generating notable interest in Russian art, opera, and music in Paris, drawing on work from Mussorgsky, Borodin, and Rimsky-Korsakov. But music for ballet employing Russian themes had yet to be written. Fokine had also just taken over as choreographer and believed that expressive forms for the body should be adjusted to the theme of each ballet. He believed that classical ballets promoted meaningless, fixed patterns of lines moving across the stage unrelated to the music. "Ballet must be drama, only plastic drama," he wrote in his memoir, while seeking to break up the horizontal line of groupings on stage (Schouvaloff 18). He also declared the he wanted "neither to suggest situations or emotions, but simply to manifest, to express them. . . . I always aim at straightforward expression in its simplest form" (Propert 102–3).

The birth of *The Firebird* occurred in an effort to present a new work based on Russian folk themes for the 1909 summer season in Paris which was to consist of both opera and ballet. The story, or dance libretto, was created by a group of artists including Benois, Fokine, and the painters Steletzky and Golovin. But realizing their vision was difficult to enact musically, many on Diaghilev's artistic committee began to lose interest. A score was first suggested to Nicolai Tcherepnin but he never started it; the request then went to Anatoly Lyadov but he procrastinated. Diaghilev then proposed to give the commission to the twenty-seven-year-old Stravinsky who would go on to present eight ballets and two operas for the company.[5]

Stravinsky was new and untested and cheap. Grigoriev refers to him as a "promising beginner" in his account. Later, when the composer began to play passages for Diaghilev's artistic committee, they were greeted by silence and thought unsuitable for dancing (Grigoriev 29, 31). At rehearsals, the company became dismayed by the absence of a melody. Stravinsky was often present to indicate the tempo and rhythms. The original music, however, led Fokine to invent a set of original steps.

Fokine outlined the method he and Stravinsky followed to create *The Firebird*: Stravinsky played musical sketches for Fokine who demonstrated the scenes but urged him to break up the folk themes "into short phrases corresponding to the separate moments of a scene, separate gestures and poses." For example, when Stravinsky presented a Russian melody for the entrance of Ivan Tsarevich to Fokine, the choreographer suggested presenting only hints of the complete melody by means of separate notes. This "de-construction" or "de-composition" of the melody to its parts initiated some of the most original passages by Stravinsky in the work. As Diaghilev told Tamara Karsavina, "omission is the essence of art"; suggest don't declare, he emphasized.[6] Diaghilev paid Stravinsky 1,500 rubles for the one-act *Firebird* which was revived in 1926 in London with new scenery and costumes by Natalia Gontcharova.

Fokine had actually presented Stravinsky with a general scenario for *The Firebird* agreed upon by Diaghilev's artistic committee. He gave strict instructions as to its construction. There were also to be no applause breaks, while the ballet vocabulary was to be realistic, while framed within a folk style. Prince Ivan in the ballet was to appear more rustic than noble. Fokine also gave strict instructions as to the construction of the score, the music created as a kind of accompaniment to the choreography. To Parisian audiences, the visual exoticism made it seem avant-garde (Jordan 29). To others, the expanded orchestra—a monumental ninety-nine members squeezed into the orchestra pit—suggested a colossal production. There were seventeen orchestral rehearsals and five with the dancers before the premiere, further inflating expenses. But Diaghilev approved every expenditure, sensing the revolutionary nature of the work. Financial encouragement came from Astruc who wanted to fill his new theatre, the Théâtre des Champs-Élysées, and host the 1913 Ballets Russes season. He paid Diaghilev Frs. 25,000 per performance, twice as much has he paid the previous year.[7] Money made the avant-garde production possible, francs encouraging the possibilities of art.

The plot was rooted in myth: Prince Ivan Tsarevich wanders into Kashchei's garden at night enticed by a tree with golden apples. He sees and catches the Firebird who begs for her freedom, obtained only after she gives him a magic feather. He then meets thirteen princesses captive under the spell of Kashchei. Ivan falls in love with one. But at dawn, they must return to the palace. Ivan follows but is taken prisoner by monster guards. He waves his magic feather and the Firebird appears and makes Kashchei and his monsters dance until they fall exhausted. The Firebird shows Ivan an egg which contains the life and death of Kashchei. Ivan breaks the egg on the ground and Kashchei dies and the princesses are freed. The two lovers reunite.

But incongruities emerged between movement and the completed music, Bronislava Nijinska noting that at the first orchestral rehearsal the sounds were so unexpected that many dancers missed their entrances (Walsh 141). The day before the premiere, Fokine produced a new crew of extras for a coronation scene but they had nothing to wear; Diaghilev had to ransack the wardrobe of *Boris Godunov* (produced two years earlier) for costumes. Adding to the confusion was Diaghilev's decision to direct the complex lighting scenario himself. However, word quickly got around that the premiere would be a momentous event and it took place on June 25, 1910 with *tout le gratin parisien* (the upper crust of Paris) present. Additionally, all the writers and artists who mattered, from Proust to Debussy, from Claudel to Sarah Bernhardt, attended (Walsh 142). Reviewers admired the integration of the music with the dance and design but were also confused. However, it was new and original and vastly different from the classical *Giselle* which preceded it but found an indifferent reception. It was not, as Diaghilev anticipated, what Parisian audiences wished to see danced by Russians. And disagreements within the company persisted, from dancers who could not understand the choreography to musicians who in rehearsal repeatedly interrupted the conductor, Pierre Monteux, to correct what they believed to be mistakes.

Benois thought *The Firebird* too short; Stravinsky thought it was too long. Diaghilev and Stravinsky both disliked story ballets of three to five acts, Diaghilev in particular preferring something compressed, something more in step with the revolutionary times (Buckle 175). But the work proved popular, Diaghilev adding two additional performances.

The impact of the ballet had much to do with the way the music captured or even echoed the movement outlined by Fokine, who believed in drama. He introduced the mime, action where precise, economic but poetic gestures took over, supported by the natural movement of the body united with a certain stylistic conception dictated by the music. The result was an original treatment of the Russian theme in ballet with new symbols presenting the fairy-tale Russian past. Importantly, the choreographic images emanated from the musical images. The well-known Parisian conductor Gabriel Pierné took charge of the orchestra. Stravinsky attended the orchestra rehearsals partly to explain the music. But they, like the dancers, were bewildered. Adding to the expense was the need for two dress rehearsals because of the complicated sets and lighting and the music. Difficulty in securing the stage, however, meant only one dress rehearsal and that occurred on the day of the first night. It did not go well and Diaghilev, himself, took over control of the lighting, operating the electrician's switchboard himself at the opening, preventing him from seeing the first night (Grigoriev 38).

The production was expensive, involving the entire company and various extras including two horses and Karsavina, the Firebird, flying in twice on a wire. This was physically challenging as was Stravinsky's music which treated rhythm irregularly with mutable beats and themes. There were also sudden changes of accent that somehow had to be united but these very musical irregularities, incorporated into the ballet, changed and reshaped modern choreography and possibly the concept of modernism itself. Stravinsky managed to give harmonious tonal music to the moral characters such as Ivan Tsarevich, while chromatic, non-tonal music relates to the supernatural figures. He also introduced the "ladder of thirds," alternating patterns of thirds generating the supernatural music of the Firebird's chromatic action.

The goal was a contrapuntal correspondence between music and movement. It was no longer necessary to count the beats to the musical accompaniment but to achieve a mutually dependent freedom of musical and physical exchange. No coinciding of dance rhythms and beats would occur, but these new forms of expression meant new ways of revealing character (Schouvaloff 21). As a critic for the *Nouvelle Revue française* wrote, the work was "a danced symphony," distinct from other ballets where the movement merely illustrated the music (Walsh 143). Audiences remained enthusiastic and eager to see it.

Petrushka, June 13, 1911. The second ballet by Fokine and Stravinsky premiered at the Théâtre Châtelet on June 13, 1911 and consolidated Diaghilev's early success, while setting a new standard for the Russian season.

Stravinsky, himself, described the process of composition, noting that he wanted the piano to play an important role and had in mind a puppet endowed with life, exasperating the orchestra with a series of cascading *arpeggios*. The orchestra retaliates with trumpet blasts. The outcome is noise which ends with the collapse of the puppet. After showing his musical sketches to Diaghilev (who loved them), they needed someone to create the scenarios and turned to Benois who created the ballet in response to Stravinsky's music as personal memories and artistic purpose united through the ubiquitous harlequin theme in Russian art.

Importantly, the ballet score started out not as music to be danced but as an unnamed abstract symphonic score. But with the input of others, it moved from a sketch to the stage; the narrative and title came later, although Stravinsky admitted that while composing the music he had in mind a distinct picture of a puppet suddenly endowed with life.

When he began to sketch *Petrushka*, Stravinsky imagined a musician rolling two objects over the black and white keys of the piano. He translated this into sound, creating a bitonal effect made by combining the white-note C major *arpeggio* with the black-note F-sharp major *arpeggio*. This double-sided sonority dominates Petrushka's scene (the first music Stravinsky wrote). As the work progressed, it came to represent the conflicting sides of his character—the human versus the puppet.

Fokine became involved only after the scenario and music had been composed but he understood the sense of tragedy, Petrushka portraying solitude and impotence. Nijinsky's dancing lent further pathos and energy to the character, conveying unspoken feelings through movement.[8] The completed work contained dramatic, figurative, and stylistic methods that Stravinsky would expand in later works. But Stravinsky's ballet highlights the eternal triangle just as Pierrot, Columbine, and the Harlequin define the *commedia dell'arte*. Yet, the work was a unified piece fusing music, dance, and design.

The production did not, however, go smoothly. Fokine delayed completion, Benois argued with Diaghilev over the design, and the large stage crowd of "supers" did not follow directions. Monteux, the thirty-six-year-old conductor, had to break up his orchestra into groups of instruments to master Stravinsky's music. The stage at the Théâtre du Châtelet was littered with props making rehearsals distracting, made more challenging because the sets arrived from Russia damaged. The elements of the fair, from merry-go-rounds to swings and booths, limited stage movement. Diaghilev and Benois then quarreled over a portrait of the magician, owner of the puppet show, appearing in the second tableau. Benois refused to alter it so Diaghilev had it repainted by Bakst who reported the change to Benois who, furious, left the theater at the *répétition générale*, never to return. And the dress rehearsal was chaotic, partly because of the unusual music and necessity of changing the scenery in complete darkness with large numbers of people on the stage. Dancers complained that the items for the fair made movement difficult, and that four huge drums in the prompt corner ordered by Stravinsky further interfered with entrances and exits. Furthermore, Stravinsky and Fokine could not agree on the tempo of the music (Grigoriev 53–54). And yet, the opening night was a success, despite a twenty-minute delay before the curtain went up while Misia Sert wrote a check for four thousand francs to allow Diaghilev to pay off the costumer (Walsh 162).

The ballet became something of a turning point in the careers of all three, the critic André Levinson writing that the ballet "saved Diaghilev's enterprise from the inevitable accusation of monotony," becoming an "artistic victory."[9] The score was less in the Russian folk tradition than *The Firebird*, more musically lucid, marking a certain maturity and independence for Stravinsky. In *The Firebird*, the aim was inventiveness; in *Petrushka* it was expressiveness, according to the composer Boris Asafiev who suggested that "it was as if Russian intonations had been turned into living musical speech" (Schouvaloff 22). It was also more expensive with crowds of spectators, unusual props—puppets—and an unusual staging moving from realism to symbolism as the ballet shifted from the fair to Petrushka's spare, almost surreal room.

Nijinsky had the title role and enthralled the audience when he mysteriously reappeared on the roof of a booth at the fair, magically escaping the Moor's attempts to kill him. The opening tableau in St. Petersburg's Admiralty Square during a Shrovetide Fair, a carnival preceding Lent, stresses crowds with a group of drunken revelers emerging from the gathering. Visually stirring, but it added to the expense. The second tableau is in Petrushka's room where the clown's admired ballerina unexpectedly visits. The third tableau is the Moor's room, as the ballet moves from the many to the few and then to the singular, triumphant clown.

The four scenes of the ballet comprise 43 minutes with Nijinsky's role of Petrushka the centerpiece. Tamara Karsavina was the Ballerina, the object of Petrushka's love; the ballet teacher and master Enrico Ceccehetti was the Showman, with Alexander Orlov the Moor. In more detail, following the opening in Admiralty Square, the Showman appears with three puppets: a Moor, a Ballerina, and Petrushka. The puppets then dance on orders from the Showman with the Moor and Petrushka in love with the Ballerina who prefers the Moor, soon attacked by Petrushka. Scene 2 is Petrushka's room, kicked into his space by the Showman. Petrushka tries to escape when the Ballerina unexpectedly emerges. Petrushka expresses his love for her but she does not respond and leaves him.

Scene 3 is the room of the Moor visited by the ballerina who dances to excite him. He embraces her as Petrushka enters but is chased away by the

Moor. The final scene is back in Admiralty Square with another dancing crowd but Petrushka suddenly rushes out of his booth, chased by the Moor who stabs him. A policeman arrives but the Showman picks up the body to show all it is only a puppet. The crowd is relieved but as the Showman returns to the booth, the ghost of Petrushka appears above it and threatens the Showman and the crowd for refusing to believe that he is more than a puppet; he is a man. On the program at its premiere was *Schéhérazade* and *Le Spectre de la Rose*, forming a set of three box office hits.

Reaction was at first mixed, with the public finding the music dissonant and confusing. By contrast, Parisian critics applauded, Louis Vuillemin declaring in the arts daily *Comœida* that there is "not an indifferent bar [of music]. And what boldness in the orchestral layout! What fluency! What life! What youth!" (in Walsh 163). Stravinsky, himself, was somewhat skeptical, writing in a letter that the ballet was a success with the critics, adding that this time the press was *not* bought off by Diaghilev (often by invitations to dress rehearsals and other favors), adding that "this year the press took absolutely no interest" and those who persistently hurled abuse at the Russian dances did so again (Walsh 163).

Audiences in London, where it was performed on February 4, 1913 at the Royal Opera House, were equally enthusiastic: the music was engaging although the plot mystifying, the work "inaccessible to judgment by old or ordinary standards. It is supremely clever, supremely modern and supremely baroque," wrote the *Observer*. The imagination must rise to the occasion to understand it, the critic concluded.[10]

Sir Thomas Beecham conducted to Stravinsky's satisfaction, noting that an earlier performance with a European orchestra gave endless trouble: "Oboists and trumpeters declared their parts to be unplayable, and, indeed, performed them as if they really were," Stravinsky said in a *Daily Mail* interview (Macdonald 76). In Vienna, where the opera orchestra was to perform the score, the violinists threw down their bows in disgust at a rehearsal. Diaghilev stepped in and chastised them. But even at the first performance, the musicians tried to sabotage the score in response to the erratic notes and sounds (Buckle 241). The public, however, loved it, or if they did not love it, wanted to be part of the musical adventure. And until the *Le Sacre du printemps* two years later, *Petrushka* was considered the latest word in modern music displaying, through sound and movement, the inner emotion and expressiveness of its characters.

L'Après-midi d'un faune, May 29, 1912. This twelve-minute work with music by Debussy, choreography by Nijinsky, and costumes by Bakst created international headlines, one declaring, "Wicked Paris Shocked at Last" when it debuted at the Théâtre du Châtelet. Inspired by a poem by Mallarmé, the ballet was instantly controversial because of its erotic imagery.

A letter to the press by Auguste Rodin defending the work only intensified the debate and led some to question Rodin's stature as a national artist. Nijinsky fashioned the elusive music into a fantasy without any actual dancing supplemented by "a new plastic art." Movement was largely large groups of dancers passing each other in parallel lines, moving in profile as if a frieze had come to life. Graceful poses were absent as were *jetés*. Replacing fluid body stretches were quasi-robotic jerks. Diaghilev's choice of Nijinsky to choreograph led to Fokine's decision to leave the company.

The accompanying music by Debussy became less prominent as the action dominated; it provided only an atmospheric background, not a series of beats for individual steps. Mallarmé's poem, from which the music takes its title, is not a key to its understanding, nor four critical words written by Horace: "*Faune nympharum fugientum amator*" ("Faun, you have a passion for fleeing nymphs"; Macdonald 80). The actions of Nijinsky determined the reaction of the crowd: his crouching movements, stiff poses, single leap, and final caress of the scarf in a masturbatory manner was seen by many as scandalously erotic, extremely expressive, and not to be missed. Meyerhold was an influence with his emphasis on two dimensionality and angled, planed gestures which controlled Nijinsky's movements. Rehearsals were frequent and strenuous with odd movements by the dancers as Nijinsky aimed "to set in motion an archaic Greek bas-relief" (Grigoriev 65–66).

The ballet itself, an experiment by Nijinsky, created uncertainty for Diaghilev until he saw it dressed, lit, and performed on stage. Only then did he feel comfortable with its premiere on May 29, 1912. The score was well-known, but the movements were shocking, Nijinsky telling his dancers to "land like a goat!" Even the company was divided: Bakst, who had done the designs, admired it; Fokine was unsympathetic; Stravinsky thought it magnificent. To confirm his confidence in the production, Diaghilev invited the press and friends to a midday rehearsal on May 28—he actually began to shape critical opinion by inviting friends to attend all of Nijinsky's rehearsals hoping "word of mouth" would publicize the work, although he only walked through his part. But at the end of the May rehearsal day, the audience supposedly sat in silence shocked by the action and astonished by its beauty but disturbed by the faun's seemingly indecent action with the nymph's scarf. After a private, behind-the-curtain conference, the promoter Astruc appeared and suggested that understanding the piece required a second viewing; the ballet was repeated. At its conclusion, scattered applause could be heard (Buckle 223–24).

The action is simple: an idle Faun observes seven Nymphs, his desire aroused by one who undresses in a stream. When he approaches her, she flees; he consoles himself only with the scarf she has dropped. The faun then begins on-stage lovemaking with the scarf which he carries back to his rock culminating "in a stylized jerk of the pelvis" suggesting orgasm (Buckle 224). But the movements and the music often ignore each other, although certain surges of sound mimic the actions of the Faun. The first-night Parisian audience was surprised but not shocked, although boos could intermittently be heard.

At the end, the audience divided into applause and protests which shocked Diaghilev who then appeared on stage to appease and instruct the crowd, announcing that the work would be repeated at that very moment. This "encore" was to persuade the public of the work's beauty and encourage Nijinsky in his choreographic undertaking, although the ballet had very little dancing with only one small jump by Nijinsky. The *Comœdia*, the daily paper that covered all theatrical events, contained a three-column front-page celebration of the work. By contrast, the editor of *Le Figaro* denounced the ballet, also on its front page, with the headline "UN FAUX PAS." The objections were moral: the "true public will never accept such animal realism," Gaston Calmette wrote. Immoral was the general reaction. More suitable and expressing proper charm, good taste, and *l'esprit français* was *Le Spectre de la Rose*, staged fifteen minutes later (Buckle 225–26). Nevertheless, the scandal brought out the public.

Within twenty-four hours, Diaghilev registered a letter of protest with support from Rodin and Odilon Redon, a friend of Mallarmé's. Diaghilev's letter appeared on May 31. Rodin's own essay on the ballet appeared in *Le Matin*. Rodin, who sought to sculpt Nijinsky and started a piece, explained that Nijinsky had

> a most extraordinary power to bend his body so as to interpret the most diverse sentiments. . . . The harmony between his mimicry and his plasticity is perfect. His whole body expresses what his mind dictates. He possesses the beauty of the antique frescoes and statues. He is the ideal model for whom every painter and sculptor has longed.[11]

Public interest heightened and there was a clamor for tickets. In later performances, however, Nijinsky adjusted his hand movements, keeping them at his sides instead of under his body, and simply lowered himself onto the scarf with no jerking. The police attended the second performance of *L'Après* and approved; the ballet had its third and fourth performances on June 1 and 2. Attention shifted to Rodin and whether or not he should be removed from his state-supported apartment.

In 1916 while on tour, the company performed the dance in Los Angeles with Charlie Chaplin in the audience; he found Nijinsky's dancing memorable. The entire company actually visited Chaplin on the set of *Easy Street*. In his 1919 film *Sunnyside*, he includes a parody of the movements as the

Little Tramp encounters a group of young nymphs in the countryside. He met Nijinsky in 1917 and twenty years later made notes for a possible film about the dancer.

Before its London premiere nine years later, Diaghliev asked for the "moral support of London artists and art-lovers" because the work offers "no concessions whatever to the Philistines."[12] In an interview in the *Pall Mall Gazette*, Nijinsky emphasized that nothing in the ballet is immodest: "It has no story really: it is simply a fragment drawn from a classic bas-relief" (Macdonald 78). Not all agreed and it had to be withdrawn after three performances in London in the summer of 1921. T. S. Eliot disapprovingly wrote that while the spirit of the music was modern, that of the ballet itself was "primitive ceremony."[13] He may have been reacting to the two-dimensional movements of the dancers and Nijinsky's fondling of the scarf dropped by the nymph at the end suggesting everything from masturbation to bestiality. But there was little doubt that in both Paris and London the work was a sensation despite its lack of narrative coherence and erasure of the line separating fantasy and reality. Performances were sold-out.

Le Sacre du printemps, May 29, 1913. This thirty-eight-minute tableau of pagan Russia in two acts remains the most revolutionary ballet in the Ballets Russes repertoire and perhaps the most revolutionary dance score of the modernist period. Choreographed by Nijinsky, the work was expensive with numerous dancers and a huge number of settings, yet it possessed what some called a "frenzied pagan fire" (Schouvaloff 65). Nicolai Roerich, a painter, designed the first production which, between May 29 and July 23, saw three performances in Paris (and two later performances) and then three in London. Propert's opinion was that the "world was baffled by it, but the active hostility of the French was at least more intelligent than the polite indifference of the English" (Propert 31).

Stravinsky had been thinking about such a story after *The Firebird*, dreaming of a scene of pagan ritual where a sacrificial virgin dances herself to death, but he had been distracted by *Petrushka*. The early sketches were based on five folk-like melodies, associated with the very festivals on which Roerich based the scenario. But musically, he introduced dissonance, especially in the so-called "Augurs of Spring" chord repeated with an insistence unprecedented in art-music before *Le Sacre*, according to Peter Hill.[14] It mesmerized critics and obliterated any sense of harmony in the piece. One of the anomalies of the music and performance was that even after it was completed, the dancers had to rehearse only to piano scores; they seldom heard the full orchestrated music of the ballet until a day or two before the first public performance. It was shocking. Their choreographed movements were radical, stomping and kicking rather than dancing. In the words of one dancer, they fought against "the habits of the body" as they often moved against the beat,

3 against 4 or 4 against 5.[15] The production also stressed weight, heaviness, rather than aerialism or grace. Nevertheless, its controversy helped market the Ballets Russes and expand its audience. Its primitivism, coupled with the dissonant music, startled audiences with its pre-human content, the work composed primarily as a dance, not musical, score.

But the process of bringing *Le Sacre* to the stage was long and expensive. Months were spent on the movements, while Stravinsky spent hours on the complicated score, unaware of the challenges for the dancers unaccustomed to his irregular rhythms. Other expenses were the enormous amount of orchestral rehearsals required: twenty-six, five with the dancers, mostly within the two weeks before the premiere. The technical crew, administrative obligations, costumers, and others had to be paid. And all this for only eight performances (five in Paris, three in London).[16] Diaghilev was again caught between his desire to offer to the public a radically new art form and the need to achieve a commercial success. At the same time, he was pressuring Nijinsky to complete *Jeux* which opened on May 15, 1913, followed two weeks later by *Le Sacre,* the date chosen by the superstitious Diaghilev because it was the anniversary of *L'Après-midi.* In between was a revival of *Boris Godunov* on the hundredth anniversary of Wagner's birth, May 22, 1913.

Nijinsky experimented with movement, arresting and containing action, the body no longer a means of escape but internalizing the soul, wrote the critic Jacques Rivière (in Garafola 1989: 69). The dancers, as masses, become a society of seemingly programmed, twisted figures with only the Chosen Virgin dancing alone. Collectivity dominated the depersonalized mass, the center of the work's primitivism which looked back but also forward, since it visualized the world of the machine with assembly lines and mass production. The movements paralleled those of Meyerhold who treated the group similarly in a controversial 1911 production of *Boris Godunov* which took its cue from Diaghilev's Paris production in 1908. Chaliapin starred. Meyerhold did not individualize the crowd but treated them as groups. The ensemble became a group of "generic figures mortared with violence" (Garafola 1989: 70). Stravinsky, in a note to the conductor Serge Koussevitzky in February 1914, explained that *Le Sacre* was "a musical-choreographic work [representing] pagan Russia" unified by "the mystery and great surge of the creative power of Spring" (in Van den Toorn, 26). The music, however, was a combination of unusual orchestral sounds interrupted by arpeggios, shrieks, and glissandos supposedly to represent spurts of growth and convulsions of nature (Buckle 252–53). But the publicity value of the scandal of its first night was immense.

Part I of the ballet is the adoration of the earth with ritual dances celebrating the return of spring. In Russian, the title (*Vesna svyashchennaya*) means "Holy Spring." Part II is the sacrifice with a victim chosen and then her death sanctified by priests. The ritual of primeval mysticism set in Moscow antiquity is a workable description which begins with the worship of light on the return of spring and then the sacrifice that symbolize and exalt the fertility of the earth. Nature and the mystery of existence confront each other. After various ritual dances partly guided by venerable priests led by the Sage, the sacrificial maiden is selected and honored in dance, while the elders conduct a pious ceremony. The bride has been lying rigid in a trance until she awakens and begins a dance of religious frenzy; exhausted, she dies.

The Paris premiere was to take place at Astruc's new theatre, the Théâtre des Champs-Élysées, but the conductor Pierre Monteux had concerns about the space and its ability to project the music. He had no idea how the music would actually sound. He then specified individual measures in section 28 which should be altered because the horns were not loud enough; "at bar 37, measures 3 and 4, it is impossible to hear a single note of the flute accompanied by four horns and four trumpets," he claimed. Stravinsky listened and implemented all of the conductor's suggestions, although the composer strangely avoided the musical rehearsals but attended those for the ballet (Hill 29).

The dress rehearsal on the 28th was largely a specialist one with a smattering of society plus music critics, artists, and musicians, somewhat disappointed they were not invited to the premiere (Walsh 203). The performance on the 29th, the official premiere, was a subscription event with a full program which included *Les Sylphides, Le Sacre, Spectre de la Rose,* and *Prince Igor.* To insure attendance and again take advantage of the physical space, Diaghilev generously gave away tickets. Because of the theater design, there was an ambulatory (walking space) between the boxes of the dress circle and it was here that Diaghilev's supporters gathered. Cocteau, in attendance at the premiere, noted that among those in tails and tulle, diamonds and ospreys, were "the suits and *bandeaux* of the aesthetic crowed. The latter would applaud novelty simply to show their contempt for the people in the boxes. . . . The audience played the role that was written for it" (in Hill 30). In short order, the detractors and supporters made their views vocal drowning out the orchestra. "The theater seemed to be shaken by an earthquake," wrote the critic and artist Valentine Gross (Karthas 63). The dancers had trouble following and only Nijinsky, shouting out the numbers of their counting schemes from the wings, provided direction. Another witness reported that people shouted insults, howled, and whistled. Meanwhile, the dancers jumped up and down in a ritual dance, incomprehensible to the audience. They were also knock-kneed and had long braided hair which startled the audience as the curtain went up.

The police were called at the end of Part I. At the start of Part II, the protests continued, now with Diaghilev, who had been shouting instructions from his box, moving to the gallery, imploring calm. He headed backstage to flick the house lights on-and-off to distract the audience, shortly joined by an unnerved Stravinsky; both found Nijinsky standing on a chair yelling out numbers to guide the moves of the dancers. Only Monteux seemed calm, focusing on the score, not the dancers, concentrating on rendering the exact tempo as Stravinsky outlined. Gertrude Stein recalled from attending the second performance that it was "all incredibly fierce" and supposedly witnessed a man smash another's top hat with his cane. She wrote a poem about the performance, "The One."[17] But the publicity value of the evening was incalculable and Stravinsky recalled the mix of emotions from anger and disgust to happiness. Diaghilev's only comment was, "exactly what I wanted" (Hill 31).[18] A riot at a ballet seemed to be the epitome of sensationalism inaugurating the modern.

What caused the uproar? The music with its dissonance, critics proudly proclaiming that *Le Sacre* is no more than noise. Stravinsky doesn't attempt to argue or connect sounds logically, he just makes a racket, argued the critic Edward J. Dent. Responding to the central "Augurs" section, he referred to its odd harmony made up of tonal chords in "dissonant conjunction," a useful phrase for the musicality of the entire piece. Technically speaking, other dissonances in *Le Sacre* occur either from a triad plus a dissonant note or from a superimposition of a dominant seventh and triad. The root of the music may be the use of the octatonic scale (eight steps of alternating semitones and tones), something that fascinated Stravinsky's teacher, Rimsky-Korsakov. The diatonic scale, by contrast, was used largely for folk-derived music, octatonic possessing a more symbolic function, associated with the magical or fantastic.

But most listeners and critics did not understand this, one writer in *Le Temps* announcing that the cult of the wrong note has never been better served: from the first bar to the last, the note you expect is never heard. The sharp and powerful rhythms animate an inner energy, while the hard, loud, and dense harmonies excite disgust and enthusiasm. In response, Stravinsky explained that he wanted to express "the sublime uprising of Nature renewing herself—the whole pantheistic uprising of the universal harvest" (in Hall 93).

The dancing, with its orgiastic elements and dynamic ending, received equal criticism and praise, from its uncontrollable movements to action in radical conjunction with the music. The *Times of London* praised the rhythmical counterpoint in the choral sections, intensified by the close of scene 1 "where figures in scarlet run wildly round the stage in a great circle, while the shifting masses within are ceaselessly splitting up into tiny groups revolving on eccentric axes" (Hill 96). But the music? More intentionally bizarre than sincere, with the asymmetry of the dancing matching the irregularities of the sounds, critics concluded. But others felt like the poet Siegfried Sassoon who satirically wrote, "Lynch the conductor! Jugulate the drums! Butch the brass!

Ensanguinate the strings!" lines from his "Concert-Interpretation (*Le Sacre du printemps*)" (Hill 100).

Summing up the unsympathetic response might be Henri Quittard's review in *Le Figaro* for May 31, 1913:

> Here is a strange spectacle, of a laborious and puerile barbarity, which the audience of the Théâtre des Champs-Élysées received without respect. And we are sorry to see an artist such as M. Stravinsky involve himself in this disconcerting adventure. . . . Can M. Stravinsky imagine that a melody, because it is doubled a second higher or lower for fifty measures—or both at once—will gain a decisive and eloquent intensity? It seems so.[19]

But even if the music was inaudible at its premiere, audiences witnessed the overthrow of conventional ballet movement with the bound, spasmodic, grounded, in-turned action of the dancers. For the dancers, confronting the metrical irregularities and distortions of *Le Sacre* presented extraordinary challenges which required 120 rehearsals for only six performances (Propert 81).

Technically, *Le Sacre* was revolutionary with no dancing on *pointe*, no *pirouettes* or *entrechats*. Contorted limbs, inward toes, and heads stiffly bent sideways were the postures and movements. Instead of silent feet with dancers flying about the stage, feet were stamped or shuffled, constantly making noise. Arms were no longer rippling but awkwardly bent upward or rigidly pointing downward. Intricate group movements startled with polyrhythmic dancing. At the end of act 1, a circle of women moved to the notes of the main theme, while groups of men within the circle swung in smaller circles to a threefold counterpoint. Masterpiece or failure? At the time of its debut, the answer was unclear to some but evident to others.[20]

At the July 11 premiere in London, C. W. Beaumont, dance historian and critic, recalled that as a sign of the importance of the event, Diaghilev arranged for his friend, the music critic Edwin Evans, to address the audience before the performance to explain the music and intent of the new ballet. But the restive spectators, anticipating something unusual and exciting, almost booed him off the stage. Shortening his introduction, he retreated.[21]

Beaumont later explained that the choreography was

> startling, being a complete negation of those rare qualities of *élévation* and *ballon* [to appear lightweight while jumping] associated with Nijinsky. In the Sacre the dancers danced with their bodies seemingly weighted down, their movements often slow and heavy as though their feet were attached to the ground. The movements [were] made inwards, in complete opposition to academic tradition. . . . Everything possible seemed to have been done to make the poses as awkward, as uncouth, and as primitive as could be. (Beaumont 74)

Expecting light and graceful movements, the audience found, instead, "a maelstrom of rhythm, immensely vital and as dominating, as remorseless, and as irritating to the nervous system as the continuous thudding of a savage's tom-tom . . . " (Beaumont 75).

Ironically, in spite of its reputation as a revolutionary work, few actually heard the music and even fewer witnessed its first performance.[22] But the radical score and dancers' movements revolutionized what a ballet might be despite an audience that shouted, whistled, laughed, joked, and felt incredibly ill-at-ease but also mesmerized. And ironically, the work had lasting financial impact. The piano score was given to Diaghilev's patron Misia Sert the day after the premiere. She returned it to Diaghilev in 1920 before Massine's production of the work to be sold to make money for the new venture.[23] Finances could never be forgotten.

Parade, May 18, 1917, Théâtre du Châtelet. With designs by Picasso, music by Erik Satie, choreography by Massine, libretto by Cocteau, and program notes by Apollinaire, *Parade* became almost the epicenter of modernism, uniting a composer and artist whose contributions would re-direct modernist letters, music, and painting. Completing a triangle of modernism was Proust who was in the audience.

Massine's choreography visualized Cubism but it was not a smooth journey, beginning with Cocteau cajoling Picasso to collaborate. Cocteau, in fact, was the origin of the ballet and the link between the Cubists and the Ballets Russes who were uninformed about the movement. Cocteau's ideas, in fact, had a broad impact on Diaghilev and the company, less in the ballets themselves but more in the symphonic interludes introduced on a regular basis beginning in 1919.[24]

Cocteau had been writing pieces for the company since 1911 and designed a poster advertising their early Parisian season. In 1912, he developed a libretto for *Le Dieu bleu* and then received an invitation from Diaghilev to create a libretto for a new production. He settled on a parade or preview of circus acts on a Parisian street drawing from vaudeville designed to entice the audience to come in and see the entire show in the main tent. Circuses such as the *Cirque Médrano*, American silent films, and jazz were sources.

Picasso, who designed the costume of the Chinese Conjuror in the production, altered the structure, placing formerly off-stage Managers, used to introduce the acts, on-stage alongside the three main performers (a Chinese magician, a Little American Girl, and two acrobats). There was even to be a *cheval-jupon*, a horse played by two men. The finale would be a rapid ragtime dance where the entire cast attempts to entice the audience to see the show. The two Managers, one representing an American and the other a Frenchman, would be costumed in over-life-size cardboard Cubist constructions in contrast to the more realistic outfits of the other figures.[25] The idea was to create a work focused on ordinary, contemporary life, especially that of popular entertainment, but incorporate new technological inventions: the typewriter, airplane, and skyscraper, while using new avant-garde techniques, a departure for the Ballets Russes.

Applying such everyday material to ballet was a radical concept. But the goal was to transform popular art into a totally new form through certain elements of contemporary show-business as Massine outlined and Apollinaire explained. The music hall invaded art with Cocteau's aim of registering the widespread commercialism of modern life and entertainments in the art of the elite, ballet. Apollinaire, in particular, believed that common entertainment should inform high art, noted in his own poetry which included street signs, shouts, and sights. For *Parade*, this ranged from film to billboard advertising, the circus, and the music hall.

Celebrated in advance publicity, the mix of styles on stage resulted (again) in jeers and hoots. The geometric forms appeared to be mere constructions without meaning, distracting the audience. Cocteau tried to defend the forms in an essay shortly after the premiere, pointing out that in creating a false reality for the dancers they become puppets, artificial but artful. The three actual performers (not the two Managers who frame the action) are parallel to fragments in a Cubist collage or like "postcards pasted on a canvas," Cocteau wrote. The contrast between the two Cubist Managers and the other characters was to transform their real bodies into flat forms (Bellow 89–90).

Another feature was the painted front curtain and set both designed by Picasso. Ironically, it looked more like the decoration of a 19th-century fairground and gave no hint of the Cubist novelties to follow. The setting was a Cubist street with some objects even seen in reverse with contrasting light effects. Response to the surprising presentation was noisy, especially when Massine, the Chinese juggler, swallowed an egg and retrieved it from his foot while breathing fire. Other actions included starting a motorcar and taking a photograph, further signs of modernity. "Spectacle" best described the comic, discontinued logic of the events on stage.

Beginning with this production, Diaghilev commissioned contemporary artists to create a front curtain and sets, the curtain introducing the overall aesthetic of the performance. Picasso's curtain portrayed a group of entertainers in a simple style, while the orchestra played Satie's largely classical overture, but conventional expectations were overturned once the curtain was raised with the Cubist set, unusual music, and innovative choreography. However, the flooring and red curtains framing the painted scene made it uncertain if the viewer was in front, in the audience, or on the stage with the performers. The effect was disorienting, the impact on Diaghilev's budget distressing.

With its seven sections and three central dances within a dual frame, the ballet exposed the gap between the avant-garde and the public's ability or even willingness to comprehend the art of the everyday as art. But in its original incorporation of elements from popular culture, one might suggest a coming together of Left Bank bohemia with Right Bank conservatism.

Three forces were at work in the ballet: Satie's unusual music, Picasso's Cubist set and costumes, and Cocteau's obscure story. Making sense of any one part was no guarantee of understanding another and Satie's music didn't help: it was a mixture of ragtime, foghorns, the clatter of milk bottles, a pistol and a typewriter, modern sounds of the day added by Cocteau to the dismay of Satie. The costume of the American Manager included a skyscraper, top hat, trumpet-like instrument, and envelope, dramatic but in many ways unfathomable.[26] The two Managers were actually three-dimensional sculptures representing two cultures, the French carried a background of French chestnut trees, and the American, with his skyscraper, wore a red pleated shirt and cowboy chaps and carried a megaphone (Buckle 330–31). *Pirouettes* and *arabesques* competed with magic tricks with the finale a ragtime dance in which the figures attempted to lure the audience into the big tent.

The premiere occurred at the Théâtre du Châtelet but in their hostile reception, the audience duplicated that of the imaginary audience in the ballet itself. The press and audience felt the Cubist elements were a hoax, uncertain if the Cubist features were meaningful or a joke, as the lines between art and entertainment blurred. References to film, the circus, vaudeville, and even the music hall blended together in the ballet, intensified by the mingling of actual bodies and their virtual substitutes. The marionette-like Managers both alienated and reflected the condition of the audience. Apollinaire, in the program notes, predicted that *Parade* would upset many but their surprise will be agreeable and recognize the "grace of modern movement" (Buckle 331). The press was more negative, *Le Figaro* condescending: an interesting but failed experiment, they wrote. The box office suffered.

Parade is a series of vaudeville-style acts to lure people to a show that is never seen, an elaborate *entr'acte*. In his commentary on the ballet, Apollinaire coined the phrase "Surrealism." Perhaps no single work by the Ballets Russes, excluding *Le Sacre*, embodied modernism so forcefully on stage while creating estrangement in the audience. The human figures appeared both mechanical and real, hallucinatory and genuine. The proximity of Paris to the actual fighting of World War I and the appearance of so many wounded on the streets made connections between the ballet and the public vital. The body reconceived, disassembled, is what the audience saw on the streets and on the stage with fascination and repulsion.

A memorable public scandal, however, quickly followed: a court battle between Cocteau, Satie, and the music critic and composer Jean Poueigh, who gave *Parade* an unfavorable review. Satie had written a postcard to the critic which read, *"Monsieur et cher ami—vous êtes un cul, un cul sans musique! Signé Erik Satie"* ("Sir and dear friend—you are an ass, an ass without music! Signed, Erik Satie"). The critic sued Satie, and at the trial, Cocteau was arrested and supposedly beaten by the police for repeatedly yelling "ass" in the courtroom. Satie was given a sentence of eight days in jail, an event that only enhanced the public's interest in the revolutionary and influential *Parade* which altered the perception of modern ballet and even literature, from new stage movements and music to the shape of the poetic line.[27] And it permitted writers, composers, and artists to incorporate ordinary life and culture. Ballet became a billboard for popular experimentation.

Le Train bleu, June 20, 1924. This one-act ballet with music by Darius Milhaud based on a detailed libretto by Cocteau (his last for Diaghilev), with choreography by Bronisilava Nijinska, premiered at the Théâtre des Champs-Élysées. The setting is the Riviera with a sporting theme: swimmers, tennis players, golfers, and weightlifters populate the stage. A Picasso *gouache* done two years before the ballet became the startling drop curtain, the original copied by a scene painter. Picasso was so impressed he signed the enlarged work. Coco Chanel did the costumes in what became one of the most fashionable and contemporary productions of the Ballets Russes even if it was considered a farce and dropped from the repertoire within a year when Anton Dolin, the athletic and impressive male star (double backflips and cartwheels were done on-stage), left the company.

The ballet was composed for Diaghilev's Ballets Russes de Monte-Carlo, as it was then known, and parodied the fashionable and often frivolous characters who spent time on the Riviera. Diaghilev referred to it as an "opérette dansée." But Boris Kochno, dancer and librettist, who became Diaghilev's secretary and partial collaborator, had to explain to the company what the word "operetta" meant, what Milhaud's music was about, and how to handle the new, sports-inspired movements (Buckle 427). Cocteau's scenes were explicit: Scene 1: "Tarts, Gigolos, Sunbathing. Then gigolos run (*in place*) and do rapid physical exercise, while the tarts . . . assume the graceful poses of colored postcards" (Garafola, 1989: 109). Ironically, there are few references to dance and few dances in the work.

Nijinska and Cocteau did not get along and had conflicting ideas about the ballet. Rehearsals were tense. With handstands and body-tossing lifts, the dancers had the gymnastic flair Cocteau wanted but Nijinska changed the *pas de deux* of the tennis players from a flirtatious set of movements to a love duet. When he saw such changes, he became incensed and repeatedly interrupted rehearsals to replace dances Nijinska created with pantomime scenes. But Cocteau was not a choreographer; gesture and movement interested but did not captivate him. Nijinska, in turn, had no great love for male dancers and pursued her own vision (Garafola, 1989: 133–34).

At the rehearsal the day before the opening, Cocteau was upset with everything and Nijinska wept. The dress rehearsal the next morning, a frigid Paris day, occurred in a heatless theater and was a disaster. The dancers in bathing costumes shivered throughout. Witnessing the confusion, Diaghilev fled to the last row of the balcony and thought of a substitute ballet but in the hours that remained, Nijinska revised the choreography and Chanel made adjustments to the bathing outfits (Buckle 433). The ballet was an immediate, popular hit epitomizing how Diaghilev and company could, and did, use fashionable society to re-energize ballet attendance. But frictions persisted and Nijinska left the company after the production; Diaghilev did not stop her.

Nevertheless, *Le Train bleu* quickly became the essence of chic and premiered to great acclaim on June 20, 1924 in Paris with Nijinska as a tennis player based on the French champion Suzanne Lenglen. Lydia Sokolova, Anton Dolin, and Leon Woizikowski all had leading roles, Dolin, a golfer in plus-fours, modeled on the Prince of Wales.

But other than in fashion columns, the work was not well received. The production was considered too much like a musical hall variety sketch. André Levinson was especially harsh, claiming that the production showed how the Ballets Russes abdicated to the music hall, which ironically might become the last refuge of "the great tradition of theatrical dance" (Garafola, 1989: 113). It was thought a *jeu d'esprit* displaying recognized names rather than a serious work expanding the repertoire of the company. One paper referred to it as "Bathing Beach Ballet" but to promote the work in England, Diaghilev gave a lengthy, if mystifying, London interview beginning with the simple fact that no blue train appears in the work which is set on a beach in front of a casino. A plane flies overhead but is not seen and "the plot represents nothing," although as a result of its Paris premiere, the audience was animated to go to St. Tropez and Nice "and perform refreshing exercises" (Buckle 444).

He then adds that the ballet is actually not a ballet but an "*opérette dansée.*" A series of intriguing contradictions follow: the ballet is danced by the real Russian ballet, but yet has nothing to with the Russian ballet. Cocteau and Anton Dolin, a classical dancer, invented the work but Dolin is "a classical dancer who does nothing classical"; "the costumes are by the greatest arbiter of fashion, Chanel, who has never made a costume"; the curtain, based on a gouache by Picasso and serving as an introduction to the ballet, "was never painted for this purpose." He concludes that despite these contradictions, the ballet "is one of the most simple and the most delightful works imaginable."[28]

But like every new Ballets Russes work, criticism was unbounded. *Le Train bleu* was thought to be pandering to fashion, not art or dance, offering, in Lynn Garafola's phrase, "lifestyle modernism" (Garafola, 1989: 115).

The décor by the Cubist sculptor Henri Laurens was one of sloping planes and an irregular frame with lopsided bathing huts and two dancing dolphins. Disoriented space disoriented the audience. The bathing suits by Chanel were alternately risqué and fashionable with such props as cigarettes, wrist-watches, and sunglasses appearing on stage. In scene 5, Cocteau employed slow motion, while in section 6 he mimicked action photography which began to appear on the sports pages.[29] Nonetheless, the production and its popularity marks the company's response to contemporary if shallow values, initiating a more populist ballet practice which crossed from the classical and avant-garde to the contemporary.

With the Ballets Russes now residing in Monte Carlo and performing there and in Paris, publicity was continuous and it was Cocteau who epitomized, more than anyone else around Diaghilev, the connection between individual productions and merchandising. He constantly promoted the company. But there was also anxiety as Diaghilev realized his growing separation from younger generations; to compensate, he increasingly relied on younger com-posers, dancers, and lovers, notwithstanding his dyed hair and false teeth. The young also came cheap (Garafola, 1989: 255).

Apollo or *Apollon musagète*, April 27, 1928. With music by Stravinsky and choreographed by Adolph Bolm at its Washington, DC premiere, and then on June 12 that year by the twenty-four-year-old George Balanchine at its Paris opening, *Apollon Musagète* ("Apollo, Leader of the Muses") marked the Ballets Russes's renewal of a neoclassical style, returning full circle to its earliest programming which balanced experimental work with a classical rep-ertoire. For Balanchine, it was a turning point in his own artistic life because of his ability to match his dancer's movements with Stravinsky's restrained, disciplined style.[30]

Balanchine and Stravinsky had earlier worked together on a production of *The Song of the Nightingale* in Paris in 1925 but without the creative freedom afforded to him by *Apollo*. *Apollo* was similarly momentous for Stravinsky who faced personal issues at the time, struggling between loyalty to his wife and desire to be with his companion, Vera de Bosset. It was also his first new ballet in five years. Apollo's maturation in the ballet mirrors Stravinsky's own transformation as circumstances in his personal life began to influence his music.[31]

Diaghilev, however, was less welcoming, annoyed with Stravinsky for accepting the commission from an American, no less, Elizabeth Sprague Coolidge. Stravinsky, intent on provoking Diaghilev, happily received the $500 advance but Diaghilev, in turn, provoked Stravinsky by (a) asking for the work to be retitled and (b) later supposedly cutting certain passages in the opening Terpsichore section because it was too similar to the Calliope sec-tion (Joseph, 2001: 41–42; Walsh 469).[32] However, Stravinsky was so pleased with the ballet, first known as *Apollon musagète*, later shortened to *Apollo* by Balanchine (although some claim it was Diaghilev's doing [Walsh 467]), that he decided to conduct the entire Paris run himself.

The work itself is a short dance essay presented in a series of tableaux: Apollo's birth, education by the muses, and his reascent to Parnassus. The move is from uneducated to civilized embodying art and dance. Lifar was the original Apollo. Balanchine's movements are both classical and modern, "bent and off balance with flexed feet, jutting hips and concave backs sunk in contraction" (Homans 2010: 337). Movement is nonetheless lyrical, although lunges, not positions, structure the dance. The effect is spare, purifying the dancer's movements.

Not all critics felt the same, however, and many were uncomfortable with the new musical style asking, why did it imitate older genres? Even the composer Nicolas Nabokov admitted difficulty with the work, complaining that in comparison with Stravinsky's earlier compositions "it seemed to me too artificially restrained and stylistically quotational" (Walsh 467). The arts critic Helen Fetter, who attended the Washington premiere, complained that the music "seemed flat, [and] insufficient to the aloof possibilities." Furthermore, "the traditional steps of the ballet seemed oddly at variance with the music," while the lack of rehearsal practice was evident in the "fumbling in a reverse pirouette" (in Joseph 2001: 60).

Elizabeth Coolidge's offer of the commission redirected Stravinsky to composition from his flourishing career as a pianist and conductor. Yet he did not celebrate her as he did his European patronesses: Misia Sert, Gabrielle "Coco" Chanel, and Winnaretta Singer, better known as Princesse de Poilgnac.[33] He also did not attend the American premiere conducted by Hans Kindler but would soon conduct the Paris debut held at the Théâtre Sarah-Bernhardt on June 12, 1928.[34] Bolm danced Apollo in Washington, Lifar in Paris. The American audience, however, might have been confused: there were no program notes, nor was there a dress rehearsal for the dancers and musicians who had to be imported from Philadelphia. The performance was broadcast live on the radio (Joseph 2001: 55, 56, 58).

The musical discipline, partly the result of its premiere as a chamber ballet in the limited space of the Coolidge Auditorium at the Library of Congress, Balanchine transferred to Paris where his refined ballet movements, emphasizing simplification and control, ruled.[35] The power of the ballet derives partly from the opening birth of the Terpsichore figure, who combines within her the rhythm of poetry and the revelation of dance to the world. Stravinsky would, himself, consider *Apollo* a unified and pure score, eliminating contrast partly by paring down the composition to only strings and relying on a diatonic harmony. Stravinsky understood the musical and spatial constraints as liberating. Balanchine's abstract choreography matched such discipline.

The saga of *Apollo* began in July 1927 and the Stravinsky archive has more than a hundred pages of compositional sketches, the beginning of his first entirely new work since *The Firebird*. But there was a change: the music would forego the abrasiveness and violence of his early work and express a new calmness despite a period of anxiety and conflict both legal and personal (Walsh 452). But disruptions did not deter him from his goal, Diaghilev misrepresenting the piece in a garbled interview of October 1927 in the *Excelsior*. Stravinsky countered with his own explanatory interview in *L'Intransigeant* three months later (Walsh 453). But in many ways, *Apollo*, at this late date and with Diaghilev ill, reinvented the Ballets Russes yet again. Diaghilev recognized that the way forward, from a business point of view, was to turn back to a classical style.

Stravinsky's shift to Bach and a more pristine, pure sound relates to his return to the Orthodox Russian Church and the teachings of Jacques Maritain, a Catholic philosopher. Maritain argued for an impersonal and detached aesthetic and a renewal of classical ideals. The goal was to eliminate ornaments, musically and balletically. Stravinsky began work on the piece in July 1927; Lifar was to be the principal dancer. Diaghilev, when he heard the music, referred to it as "a filigree counterpoint around transparent, clear-cut themes all in the major key . . . without any intentional Russianizing" (in Homans, *Mr. B* 137). Balanchine would call it "white music, in places as white on white" (Homans, *Mr. B* 137).

The challenge for Balanchine was to match movement with the music but he did it uniquely in his turn to pure classicism. Versification was important in the process: Stravinsky folded the strict rhythmic patterns of alexandrines (the favored French measure, an iambic line of 12 syllables with major stresses on the 6th and last) into the musical structure, mapping the story of the ballet in the music (Homans, *Mr. B* 137). Stravinsky made it clear that in the classical he saw "the perfect expression of the Apollonian principle," rules overtaking the haphazard (Homans, *Mr. B* 138). Balanchine reflected this inversely, his early sketches emphasizing a powerful woman with legs wide apart seated on a high platform, a form more expressive than controlled. Buddha-like, she gives birth to Apollo. Opening on an island that seems to float in a single spotlight, what follows is a ceremonial birth and presentation of Apollo's lyre. Apollo then staggers about, spurning any classical postures. Even the finale—with Apollo dancing with Terpsichore—is performed with simple gestures with walking moving towards dance as balance and form reassert themselves. The figures (Terpsichore and Apollo) end by bending together with their arms open to the sky, although the music now becomes almost fatalistic. In the final moment, Apollo ascends to his mother's platform and grows from a boy to a god and an artist (Homans, *Mr. B* 140–41).

Balanchine achieved a new classicism, not of the Greeks, but of something stripped down and pure. He would eventually perform the ballet in white practice clothes on an empty stage. It was a performance of elimination, matching Stravinsky's pristine score. It placed dance, Homans writes, "in the realm of formal poetic gesture and painting reaching back to the Renaissance" (Homans, *Mr. B* 141). Personally for Balanchine, it seemed the renunciation of Petipa, Diaghilev, and even his own Russian past. Abstracted gesture was the result, equaling Stravinsky's pure sound.

But there was the inevitable conflict: Diaghilev acquiesced to a request by Lord Rothermere, supporting the company at this point, that his lover Nikitina would dance the role of Terpsichore (Rothermere had an affection for Ballets Russes dancers having previously pursued Komarova; he also made advances to Sokolova, followed by Nikitina who was eventually replaced by Vadimova [Buckle 463]). Balanchine objected to allowing Nikitina to dance but compromised, giving her only some of the performances. Diaghilev then decided he did not like the Terpsichore variation and cut it. Stravinsky, when he learned of this, threatened to pull all the music. Diaghilev backed down, restoring the variation and the principal dancer Danilova. But that very year, Balanchine's knee gave way while dancing and he needed an emergency operation. It was a success but the stiffness meant limited motion and, to his delight, he no longer had to dance. He stopped performing and began to create ballets (Homans, *Mr. B* 142).

In sum, *Apollo* consists of two tableaux, composed in 1927 and 1928. The subject was Apollo visited by three muses, that of dance, mime, and poetry. Its technique and emphasis restarted neo-classicism anticipated by Nijinska's *Les Noces* and *Les Biches* of 1923 and 1924. But Balanchine's choreography compresses the classical myth: the birth of Apollo, the discovery of his creative powers, and his instruction of the three Muses in their arts, ascending with them at the climax to Parnassus.[36] The theme is creativity itself mixed with artistic purity and renewal externally matched by the needs of the Ballets Russes at this time. But not all of it was new: a false Hellenism emerged with Apollo costumed as if a god epitomized by a chariot at the end to take all to Parnassus, evoking an 18th-century sense of glory (Garafola 1989: 139–41). Such "retrospective classicism" brought mixed reviews but box office success (Garafola 1989: 141).

Apollo displays an international character: conceived and written in Nice in 1927, its world premiere was a single performance in Washington followed by its Paris opening six weeks later with Balanchine's choreography, Stravinsky conducting, and Lifar dancing. In 1951, it returned to America restaged under Balanchine's direction at the New York City Ballet rising to almost legendary status in the repertoire of the company, culminating an odyssey almost equal to its Greek origins (Joseph 2001: 62).[37]

The success of the work relates to Stravinsky's effort to write a ballet freed of Russian folklore, turning for the first time to Ancient Greek material with Apollo the god of music, poetry, light, and truth. Musically, he went French, writing music for strings infused with the rhythms of classical French poetry and French baroque dances. It develops diatonic harmony with no chromaticism, called by Stravinsky a "ballet blanc," meaning 19th-century ballet scenes where the principal ballerina wore white. The first performances had six dancers in monochrome costumes without any elaborate scenery. The movement was restrained, the staging reflecting the clarity and calm of the music. Unlike his earlier ballets, the work was more of a meditation on classical themes than a narrative. For the Paris performances of 1929, Lifar danced Apollo and Chanel redesigned the costumes. With its restraint and discipline, a new, formal modernism appeared in the music and movement. Stravinsky, with Diaghilev's hesitant support, reconfirmed a classical past for the present age.

The box office responded positively but the critics were cautious, one complaining that there was nothing inventive or picturesque; there was also no abandon or frenzy. The critic from *Le Figaro*, watching Stravinsky conduct, imagined him smiling and saying to himself that "I have written this noble Greek imposition, in praise of everything I have burnt!"[38] The piece is frequently performed partly because it reveals the transformation of Apollo into a god moving from the earthly to the divine expressed by the heroic key of D major, although there is an undercurrent of regret noted by triads of G major and B minor which conclude the ballet.[39] Nevertheless, performances of the work implicitly recalled and renewed the stature of the Ballets Russes. It was a triumph.

What this survey of these seven disparate ballets, ranging in time from 1910 to 1928, reveals is that despite the "backstage" financial chaos that accompanied Diaghilev each step of his artistic career, Ballets Russes productions at "front of house" were often box office successes even if receipts never matched expenses. But despite the lack of funds, disputes, and resignations, the public supported the company's programming. The Ballets Russes was a phenomenon not to be missed whether in Paris, London, Monte Carlo, or Berlin. Critics and fans may have disagreed but fans still flocked to the productions, eager to see the newest, if complex, presentations. Standing between these two poles was Diaghilev with a sometimes impromptu, sometimes confused management style which despite numerous setbacks, promoted and encouraged remarkable artistic innovations. He may have needed funds to travel from Paris to Venice but he never lacked the will to finance, at any expense, the music for *The Firebird* or costumes for *Schéhérazade*.

NOTES

1. Stephen Walsh, *Stravinsky: A Creative Spring: Russia and France, 1882–1934* (New York: Knopf, 1999) 141.

2. The choreographers themselves often starred: Fokine danced in the first *Firebird*; Massine created the role of Pulcinella; Nijinsky danced the Fox in *Renard* and danced in *Petruska* and Balanchine appeared in his production of *Chant*.

3. On this topic see Sally Banes, "Firebird and the Idea of Russianness," *The Ballets Russes and Its World*, ed. Lynn Garafola and Nancy Van Norman Baer (New Haven: Yale Univ. Press, 1999) 117–34.

4. Stravinsky from *Chronicle of My Life*, in Alexander Schouvaloff and Victor Borovsky, *Stravinsky on Stage* (London: Stainer & Bell, 1982) 16.

5. The list includes *The Firebird, Le Sacre du printemps, Le Chant du Rossignol, Le Renard, Les Noces*, plus the operas *Mavra* and *Rossignol* and a symphonic tableau, *Feu d'artifice.*

6. For Fokine on suggesting the breakdown of Stravinsky's themes, see Michel Fokine, *Memoirs of a Ballet Master*, trans. Vitale Fokine, ed. Anatole Chujoy (Boston: Little, Brown, 1961) 161. On Diaghilev's dictum, sometimes restated as "the essence of art is omission," see Diaghilev in Serge Lifar, *Serge Diaghilev, His Life, His Work, His Legend* (London: Putnam, 1940) 186.

7. Thomas Forrest Kelly, *First Nights: Five Musical Premieres* (New Haven: Yale Univ. Press, 2000) 276.

8. There is much literature on *Petrushka.* Useful sources are Joan Lawson, *A History of the Ballet and Its Makers* (New York: Pitman Publishing, 1964); Stephen Walsh, *Stravinsky: A Creative Spring, Russia and France 1882–1934* (New York: Knopf, 1999); Lynn Garafola, *Diaghilev's Ballets Russes* (New York: Oxford, 1989); and Juliet Bellow, *Modernism on Stage* (Burlington, VT: Ashgate, 2013).

9. Levinson, "The 'Saison Russe' and the Grand Opéra," *Ballet Old and New*, 20.

10. The *Observer* in Macdonald, *Diaghilev Observed* 76. Also see Mengyang Wu, "Dance with *Petrushka*: The Ballets Russes, Russia and Modernity," *Open Journal of Social Sciences* 7.8 (August 2019), https://www.scirp.org/journal/paperinformation.aspx?paperid=94297.

11. Auguste Rodin in Serge Lifar, *Serge Diaghilev, His Life, His Work, His Legend: An Intimate Biography* (London: Putnam, 1940) 271–73.

12. Diaghilev in *Daily Mail*, June 18, 1912 in Nesta Macdonald, *Diaghilev Observed* 78.

13. T. S. Eliot, "London Letter," *The Dial* LXXI (October 1921): 453.

14. Peter Hill, *Stravinsky: The Rite of Spring* (Cambridge: Cambridge Univ. Press, 2000) 39. Hereafter Hill.

15. Dame Marie Rambert in "For Art's Sake—The Story of the Ballets Russes," BBC 4 DVD. 2019. At Diaghilev's request, Rambert assisted the dancers in learning their steps in *Le Sacre du printemps.*

16. On these and other production matters, plus the limited productions of the work, see Thomas Goss, "Musings on Le Sacre's 100th Birthday," Orchestration

Online, May 29, 2013. https://orchestrationonline.com/musings-on-le-sacres-100th
-birthday-2/.

17. Eksteins, 14–15; Stein, *Autobiography of Alice B. Toklas* (1933; London: Penguin Books, 2001) 149–50. Stein's reporting mixes fiction with fact. She attended on June 2, 1913 and at this performance she met Carl van Vechten, who would eventually become her literary executor. The subtitle of the ballet is "Scenes of Pagan Rus."

18. In 2006, a highly publicized television dramatization was shown on BBC 2, March 11. The title was *Riot at the Rite*.

19. Quoted in James Keller, "Le Sacre du printemps," Program Notes, San Francisco Symphony Orchestra, September 2018. Keller also points out that a press release, reprinted in several Paris newspapers the day of the premiere, referred to the "stammerings of a semi-savage humanity" while "frenetic human clusters wrenched incessantly by the most astonishing polyrhythm ever to come from the mind of a musician." https://www.sfsymphony.org/Data/Event-Data/Program-Notes /S/Stravinsky-le-sacre-du-printemps.

20. Propert 81. The distinguished Russian/French dance critic André Levinson, recognizing the work as a *succès de scandale*, also called it "a genuine catastrophe." Levinson, "The Ballets Russes at the Théâtre des Champ-Élysées (1913)," *Ballet Old and New*, trans. Susan Cook Summer, 51.

21. Cyril W. Beaumont, *The Diaghilev Ballet in London: A Personal Record* (London: Putnam, 1940) 72.

22. For a list of all productions of *Le Sacre* up to 1991, see Joan Acoccella, Lynn Garafola, and Jonnie Green, "Catalogue Rasisonne," *Ballet Review*, 20/2 (Summer 1992): 68–100.

23. Stephanie Jordan, *Stravinsky Dances: Re-Visions across a Century* (Alton, Hampshire: Dance Books, 2007) 421.

24. Lynn Garafola, "In His Own Voice: Diaghilev in the British Press," *The Ballets Russes and the Art of Design,* ed. Alston Purvis, et al. (New York: Monacelli Press, 2009) 135. She also points out that by 1921 the programming had become much more adventurous, possibly a result of Cocteau's influence.

25. For additional details, see John Richardson, "Parade," *A Life of Picasso*, Vol. II: 1907–1917 (New York: Random House, 1996) 419–33. Richardson notes that after *Parade*, classical motifs returned to Picasso's paintings but with a difference, parallel to Diaghilev's return to the classical in his late productions where "classical subjects or themes are not necessarily treated classically" (Richardson 432). This "return," or recurrence, matches Michael North's argument concerning the new in *Novelty: A History of the New* (2013) echoed by Juliet Bellow in *Modernism on Stage*, 239.

26. For an image see Judi Freeman, "Fernand Léger and the Ballets Russes," *The Ballets Russes and Its World*, ed. Lynn Garafola and Nancy Van Norman Baer (New Haven: Yale Univ. Press, 1999) 151.

27. On the literary impact of *Parade,* see Nancy Hargrove, "The Great Parade: Cocteau, Picasso, Satie, Massine, Diaghilev—and T.S. Eliot," *Mosaic: Journal for the Interdisciplinary Study of Literature*, 31.1 (1998): 83–106.

28. Diaghilev in the *Observer*, November 23, 1924, quoted in Buckle 444–45.

29. For details from Cocteau's script, see Garafola, *Diaghilev's Ballets Russes*, 109–10.

30. For Balanchine's remark see Charles M. Joseph, *Stravinsky & Balanchine*, 74. Balanchine especially admired the "sustained oneness of tone and feeling." ("Apollo," New York City Ballet, https://www.nycballet.com/discover/ballet -repertory/apollo/.) The ballet is 28 minutes long and premiered with Balanchine's own New York City Ballet in November 1951.

31. Charles M. Joseph, *Stravinsky Inside Out* (New Haven: Yale Univ. Press, 2001) 38. In addition to comments on Stravinsky's personal life, Joseph offers some important remarks on the American premiere of the work (39–41). Hereafter Joseph 2001.

For a compositional timeline, see Vera Stravinsky and Robert Craft, *Stravinsky in Pictures and Documents* (New York: Simon and Schuster, 1978) 275–77.

32. If that did occur, it was in performances following the Paris and then London premieres, likely on the company's autumn tour triggered by Diaghilev's vengeful attitude towards the piece and Stravinsky (Walsh 469, 478, 482–83).

33. Walsh 42, 46. For a useful account of Winnaretta Singer and her relationship with Diaghilev and Stravinsky, see Sylvia Kahan, *Music's Modern Muse: A Life of Winnaretta Singer, Princesse de Polignac* (Rochester: University of Rochester Press, 2003).

34. Marking his eightieth birthday, he again conducted *Apollo* at the Staatsoper in Hamburg on June 18, 1962. The New York City Ballet participated.

35. On the development of *Apollo* and Stravinsky's collaboration with Balanchine, see Charles M. Joseph, "A New Approach—a New Collaboration, the Pathway to Apollo," *Stravinsky's Ballets* (New Haven: Yale Univ. Press, 2011) 102–33.

36. For a description of the Paris production, see Buckle 501–2.

37. The New York City Ballet performed it again in October 2022.

38. In Walsh, *Stravinsky* 468.

39. For a musical analysis of *Apollo*, see Jonathan Cross, "Stravinsky in Exile," *Stravinsky and His World*, ed. Tamara Levitz (Princeton: Princeton Univ. Press, 2013) 13–16.

Conclusion

Dancing for Diaghilev

"To dance is to take part in the cosmic control of the world."

Havelock Ellis, "The Philosophy of Dancing,"
The Atlantic (February 1914)[1]

"The task is to astonish Europe," Diaghilev announced to five young students, including a young Serge Lifar, in Warsaw auditioning to join his company.[2] The goal was not as outlandish as it might have seemed given the accomplishments of the Ballets Russes between 1909 and 1923 (the audition year) but more ambitious than his 1912 challenge to Cocteau: "Astonish me!" The reputation of the Ballets Russes had been fixed as a provocative, experimental company, although questions emerged postwar over Diaghilev's vision: Was it truly avant-garde or simply neo-classicism in modern dress?

Diaghilev partially answered the question himself when speaking of American skyscrapers, noting that they possess their own classicism exhibited through their formally based lines, scale, and proportions; nonetheless, they represent palaces of the modern age. So, too, he believed, did the Ballets Russes with its music and choreography, which mixed the traditional with the modern: "Our plastic and dynamic structure must have the same foundation as the classical work which enables us to seek new forms," he wrote. A classical foundation allows for the new, something Eliot, Joyce, and even Pound acknowledged.[3] Diaghilev's insight and artistic vision ensured an almost continuous set of aesthetic triumphs which engaged audiences throughout Europe, America, and South America.

But the astonishment was financial as well as artistic. Without consistent funding from governments, institutions or individuals, Diaghilev, nevertheless, sustained a revolutionary private theatrical enterprise partly by vision, partly by personality. He was able to attract and maintain working relationships with Europe's elite and emerging modernist innovators from Stravinsky and Picasso to Satie and Balanchine. What he could not supply in practical

173

terms (adequate wages, proper contracts, job security), he made up for in charisma and belief that his work would startle and remain in repertoires worldwide. Innovation and novelty became his *imprimatur,* coupled with an ability to spot young talent and capitalize on it. His idea of repertoire tested but expanded the vision of his audiences *and* his patrons.

Diaghilev managed to create a desire for the new, captivating audiences even when they had no understanding of the work. This sense of the difficult, allied with the new, was as absorbing as it was perplexing.[4] The business of ballet was a constant adventure for Diaghilev but he rarely failed, except when the bills came due, which sent him off to find new backers. His reputation, and that of the company, for original productions never faltered and against all odds, he managed to discover new patrons and new bookings drawn to the allure of ballet and the magnetism of Diaghilev. Matching his talent for artistic creativity was that for business often conducted in an unconventional, unorthodox manner. But he succeeded, leaving a lasting imprint on European artistic enterprises and venues. He became his own "brand" and one that could not be overlooked, nor forgotten. After his death, the company faltered but then reformed in 1932 under a new director, Col. Wassily de Basil, with René Blume artistic director. Monte Carlo, not Paris, became its home. But it lasted, showing that artistic success can sometimes triumph over financial failure.

In a 1914 letter to the *Times of London*, Fokine essentially presented the Ballets Russes manifesto. He outlined five new principles beginning with the need to eliminate combinations of ready-made dance steps. New forms must be created to correspond with the subject; movement and gesture must serve to express the ballet's dramatic action, not entertainment; replace gestures of the hands by the "mimetic of the whole body"; as to groups, expressiveness must expand from the face to the body and then from the individual to groups of bodies and eventually to the crowd. Dance must align itself with the other arts but avoid specific "ballet music" to accompany the dancers. It must now accept every form of music provided that it is expressive. Dance imposes no specific "ballet" conditions on the composer or decorative artist but gives "complete liberty to their creative powers."[5]

One of Diaghilev's goals was to resurrect Russian culture outside the physical space of the country, an expression of émigré cultural aspirations. This was often articulated in his remounting, with alterations, earlier works in the Russian ballet tradition such as *The Sleeping Princess*. But his belief in the modernity of Russian music and ballet as quintessentially Russia never wavered. In 1926, for example, in response to harsh criticism of *Les Noces* (1921) by Stravinsky and Nijinska, he explained that it is the "unrealized dream of Mussorgsky":

If you want anything Russian, I believe that nothing represents Russia more completely than this work. After all, I am a Russian myself and I know what I am saying: And it is possibly not for nothing that the work is dedicated to me.[6]

Never did he, or the ballet company, lose their Russian identity, even when exiled by the Revolution. Asked in 1919 if he ever hoped to return to Russia in the future, Diaghilev replied, "I would not be a Russian if I did not hope" (in Garafola V. 136).

Diaghilev's dancers felt a similar commitment to his art and to their country. Lydia Sokolova, who spent sixteen years on-and-off with the company, records her sense of privilege in working with Diaghilev and in a community devoted to producing outstanding works of art. To have a part "in their creation was intoxicating," she wrote. No other way of life could exist for her other than "dancing for Diaghilev."[7] Serge Lifar, in his account of Diaghilev, was equally praiseworthy but also critical. Diaghilev loved his friends and mankind, he explained, but "individuals were purely *episodes* in his creative activity, *necessary* at one moment but *nuisances* when new horizons . . . opened before him." But Lifar never lost his admiration for Diaghilev's creative will and energy.[8] Nor did most of his dancers who somehow felt relaxed and encouraged in his company, even his star and one-time lover, Nijinsky. When asked how he managed to soar so high, he offered a clear, "Diaghilevish" answer—confident, uncomplicated, direct: "It's very simple; you jump and just stop in the air for a moment" (Lifar, *Diaghilev* 198).

But Diaghilev never just stopped in mid-air: he was constantly looking for new ideas, acknowledging that at first they may seem threatening. In a 1929 letter to the *Times*, he noted that when new artistic movements occur "people seem to be more frightened of being run over by them than by a motor-car in the street. . . . Society will have to recognize that my experiments, which appear dangerous to-day, become indispensable to-morrow" (Garafola V. 139). Diaghilev never lost faith in this belief summarized in his one-sentence history of ballet: "The birthplace of classical dance was France; it grew up in Italy and has only been conserved in Russia" where it progressed not in the classical style but in the "national or character dance which has given the evolution of the Russian ballet" (Garafola V. 140). Diaghilev was inescapable as an artistic impresario of unparalleled ability and imagination. Hence the lasting fascination with his dancers, his company, and his art.

The social and cultural impact of the Ballets Russes was incomparable. They performed to a sold-out matinee audience in London on Gold Cup Day at Ascot. London celebrated them with art and photography shows. After a Covent Garden performance, the poet Rupert Brooke, a devoted follower, told the actress Cathleen Nesbitt that seeing Nijinsky was seeing a miracle: "Nijinsky actually stopped still in the air" (Buckle 236).

Russian dancers were soon in demand at parties: Lady Ripon had a dinner for fifty after which Karsavina and Nijinsky performed; Nijinsky and others danced for the Aga Khan at the Ritz. But they also danced at galas, one for the Red Cross in Paris held at the Grands Magasins du Printemps department store (Buckle 235, 429). Younger artists like Alexander Calder in Paris in the late twenties were thoroughly taken with the company, partly because the artistic air at the time was saturated by the "collaborative, cross-disciplinary spirit of the Ballets Russes."[9] Lynn Garafola, in her masterful account *La Nijinska* writes that it was the choreographer's time with the Ballets Russes, beginning in 1909, where she "experienced the artistic awaking to which she owed her future as a choreographer" (Garafola, *La Nijinska* xvi). In her new book on the life of Balanchine, Jennifer Homans states that "his work on Diaghilev's new ballets was its own vast education in music and art." Diaghilev gave Balanchine a chance to work and invent. Both were at low points in their careers, Diaghilev needing new Russian ballets and Balanchine needing a place to create them. They found it in each other. "If it wouldn't be for him, I wouldn't be here," Balanchine later admitted (Homans, *Mr. B.* 121, 122).

Virgil Thomson later said that the Ballets Russes was "the choreographic stage that made the epoch shine" and wondered if it was not so much the stock market crash of 1929 as the death of Diaghilev that year that ended a great era in the arts. The artistic and cultural effect of the company was so great that Robert McAlmon jested in his memoir *Being Geniuses Together* that "everybody felt called upon to become ballet dancers."[10] The same year Diaghilev died, McAlmon published an essay entitled "Mr. Joyce Directs an Irish Word Ballet."[11] And in a strange twist, a large, bulky American stumbled upon the burial service for Diaghilev at the Greek Orthodox church San Giorgio dei Greci before burial at the island of San Michele. The observer was Lincoln Kirstein who would himself become a co-founder of the School of American Ballet and later the New York City Ballet and one of Balanchine's closest friends and supporter.

Years later, Jacqueline Lee Bouvier, Mrs. John F. Kennedy, began her 1951 award-winning "Prix de Paris" essay for *Vogue*, "People I wish I had known," by declaring that the three men she most wanted to know were Baudelaire, Wilde, and Diaghilev. What she admired most about Diaghilev was the way he established "an interaction of the arts, an interaction of the cultures of East and West." She then highlights his work with Rimsky-Korsakov, Bakst, Fokine, and Nijinsky which makes him "for me an alchemist unique in art history." "If I could be a sort of Overall Art Director of the Twentieth Century," she continues, "watching everything from a chair hanging in space," it is his artistic theories that she would apply to her time.[12]

Not only did artists, dancers, critics, writers, and the public respond but they soon incorporated elements and references to the Ballets Russes in their work, especially their writing. Virginia Woolf refers to them in both her first novel, *The Voyage Out*, and her last, *Between the Acts,* where she writes that swallows darting in the air seemed "by the regularity of the trees, to make a pattern, dancing, like the Russians, only not to music but to the unheard rhythm of their own wild hearts."[13]

Zelda Fitzgerald, in her novel *Save Me the Waltz*, contrasts the worldliness of the Ballets Russes with the cloistered existence of a dancer. At one point, a character exclaims, "I don't want to live—I want to love first, and live incidentally," a phrase easily attached to the world of the Ballets Russes. And in the novel, the studio ruled over by "Madame" is actually the studio school of the retired Mariinsky dancer Lubov Egorova.[14] Both Zelda and Lucia Joyce studied with her in Paris. Joyce was aware of the Ballets Russes and at one point sought to collaborate with Virgil Thomson on a ballet based on the Children's Games chapter of *Finnegans Wake*, the proposal to include designs by Picasso and choreography by Massine with a production at the Paris Opéra, replicating elements of Diaghilev's productions.[15]

Gerald Murphy, who with his wife Sara were American devotees of the Ballets Russes, attended rehearsals for *Les Noces* and at one point helped to paint Goncharova's sets in Paris. They later explained to the writer Calvin Tompkins that the "Diaghilev ballet was a kind of movement in itself." The company was the "focal center of the whole modern movement in the arts" Murphy claimed (Garafola 1989: 351). Writers like John Dos Passos and e. e., cummings soon appeared at performances, dragged there by the Murphys. Following the premiere of *Les Noces*, the Murphys hired a barge and had a champagne after-party with Picasso, Cocteau, Stravinsky, Gontcharova, Diaghilev (despite his fear of water), and others attending.

At the center, of course, was the imposing Diaghilev, labeled by Matisse "Louis XIV" (Homans *Mr. B* 113). He identified his role in the Ballets Russes in a conversation with King Alfonso of Spain before whom the company performed several times in 1916. The puzzled king declared, "You don't conduct. You don't dance. You don't play the piano. What *do* you do?" The imperturbable Diaghilev replied, "Your Majesty, I'm like you. I don't work. I do nothing, but I am indispensable" (Buckle 313). This confirmed Diaghilev's role as the essential force of the enterprise, the impresario who established "new fronts for the avant-garde using old Russian forms" (Homans, *Mr. B* 114). But it wasn't merely the old Russia Diaghilev recaptured but a new Russia he largely invented.[16] When asked about his own obsession with Diaghilev, the producer John Drummond, who prepared two hour-long documentaries on the Ballets Russes for the BBC, answered that he "is for me almost a synonym for artistic authority." It had nothing to do with democracy or accountability, he added, but the "judicious exercise of limited tyranny."[17]

Not everyone agreed with such power, however, despite his constant pursuit of artistic and even (to the degree it was possible) financial security. In his notebook for 1926–1929, inherited by Lifar, Diaghilev occupied himself with noting "available dates for performances, probable outlays, the names of singers . . . the whereabouts of scores and piano parts, and even managing to keep an eye on doors needing to be painted, velvet for the boxes."[18] Diaghilev was forming his own legend, although some found it unsatisfactory and exhibitionist: "In his avid search for modernity of subject and form, M. Diaghilev becomes more and more the tributary of the circus and the music hall," wrote André Levinson in 1926.[19]

But the story of the Ballets Russes is fundamentally economic. Without the support of patrons, committees, government, promoters, and early 20th-century social media, including posters, magazine articles, and publicity photos, the company would not have survived. He disguised his understanding of money through his relentless social quests, acting as if he had little sense of expenses, budgets, or contracts. But the situation was quite the opposite. His avoidance of bankruptcy was as much an art as his productions and echoes his family's rejection of their early financial collapse through new loans and borrowings. And almost immediately he understood that for the success of the company, Parisian salons were as essential as Russian princes and industrial magnates. Diaghilev relentlessly promoted his dancers, composers, and artists, emphasizing the originality and notoriety of the company. Early on he understood the value of publicity and certainly flattery, encouraging and welcoming the socially elite, especially, but not only, in Paris. As Garafola summarizes, "For Diaghilev and other entrepreneurs of modernism, these crossroads of Right Bank fashion and contemporary art defined the narrow world of their ventures: here, reputations were launched, commissions awarded and audiences mustered for a theatrical debut" (Garafola V. 356). But this was also true of his social circles in London, New York, Rome, and Monte Carlo.[20]

Yet, he died penniless, an ironic testament to the relentless economic demands upon his personal and professional life, something dancers, producers, and choreographers also suffered. Bronislava Nijinska went to Hollywood in 1934 to work on a Warner Brothers production of *A Midsummer Night's Dream* directed by Max Reinhart because she needed the money to pay off debts accumulated while running a ballet company in Paris, supporting a family, and dealing with other hangers-on.[21] Diaghilev did not have such opportunities and it is unclear if he would have seized them.

Shortly after his death, Diaghilev's close confidants (including Lifar, according to his autobiography *Ma Vie*) entered his Paris apartment and took material from his private collection of letters, books, musical manuscripts, and artworks.[22] They left by the tradesmen's entrance with suitcases stuffed with items, justifying their actions because Diaghilev left no will. Lifar was able to buy additional literary works from the French government and made a general plea to keep Diaghilev's legacy intact. Some additional material appeared. But following Diaghilev, and his preference for the good life, Lifar (who was at Diaghilev's bedside when he died) began to sell a fair portion of the items as early as 1933. In 1975, he consigned to Sotheby's in Monte Carlo Diaghilev's library of over 800 works including books printed in 1564 by Ivan Fedorov, the Gutenberg of Russia, as well as first editions of Pushkin, Lermontov, Gogol, and Dostoevsky.[23]

Yet money continued to plague his heirs. In 1933, Lifar took company dancers and a collection of Ballets Russes set and costume designs on a tour of the U.S. Attendance, however, was poor and he needed money to return the company to France. Only by selling his collection to the director of the Wadsworth Atheneum in Hartford, Connecticut, for $10,000 was he able to return. Ironically, Lifar had to borrow the collection back for his exhibition at the Louvre in 1939 to commemorate the tenth anniversary of Diaghilev's death.[24]

A later auction of May 1984 contained sketches of Diaghilev's career, including a working notebook detailing plans for lighting, costumes, and sets in several ballets acquired by the Library of Congress for more than $60,000. Photo albums, ballet manuscripts, letters, and costumes reinforced the sense of the impresario's continued presence. An orange-and-red satin jacket Picasso designed for Léonide Massine for the 1917 production of *Parade*, marking the debut of Picasso as a designer for the stage, went to the Victoria and Albert Museum. Other items included the manuscript of *Jeux*, a ballet by Debussy containing annotations by the composer and Nijinsky; a letter from Diaghilev to Mata Hari, the dancer who became a spy, about a job possibility; and several letters from Prokofiev. The full tally of the Sotheby's sale was $1.1 million.

The loss of Diaghilev and his vision was severe, his vanity and willfulness gone. He had reigned almost supreme in modernist theatrical culture leading to satiric reactions beginning with Cocteau who created backstage caricatures of Diaghilev and his courtiers published in 1923. Cartoons appeared regularly. But Diaghilev's achievement was the legibility of his *imprimatur*, his input assuring the "artistic legitimacy" of his productions as the creator of their value. His authority over the music, dance, design, and art of the Ballets Russes was unquestioned by the public or professionals. It was also essential to maintain their integrity and authenticity. It is why he knew he had to be in total control: exerting his artistic authority insured their validity. In many ways he was a visionary, foreseeing what would surprise and delight audiences, summarized by Ezra Pound's statement "my eyes are geared for the horizon."[25] He also found young avant-garde artists eager for exposure and excellently trained young dancers often from the Mariinsky Theater and promoted both. He recognized talent.

Ballet historian C.W. Beaumont wrote that when Diaghilev died his company "melted away like an army seized with doubt and misgiving at the loss of a tried and trusted leader." But during his period, ballet, once thought of as an exotic form of entertainment, "became an established cult with an ever-increasing band of worshippers drawn from all classes of society."[26] Part of the reason was Diaghilev's masterminding an artistic policy that saw modernism displace symbolism, free choreographic movement replace rigid rules. The released body had aesthetic consequences for all the arts. Musically, he took the old and made it new, constantly pruning bars and musical passages, changing chords, keys, and tempi while making notations for conductors, choreographers, and musicians. But he also incorporated tradition through his pastiche ballets, blending music, perhaps by Pergolesi or Rossini, with new sounds and movements, occurring simultaneously with T. S. Eliot's ideas in "Tradition and the Individual Talent" and concepts formed by Pound beginning with "Make It New."[27] Diaghilev was a contradiction, summarized by the editors of *The Ballets Russes and Its World*: "a revolutionary with the habits—and top hat—of an oligarch."[28]

The influence of the Ballets Russes ranged widely affecting European art, fashion, and behavior, its impact on international ballet expressed through Russian dance, 20th-century music, and culture. Jennifer Homans, in her omnibus history of ballet, writes that the Ballets Russes did no less than place "dance at the center of European culture for the first time since Louis XIV" (Homans 2010: 339). And our fascination continues: celebrations of the 100th anniversary of their founding resulted in worldwide festivals. "I can't see a ballet, or a fashion show, or an art installation, or a frieze, without thinking of Diaghilev and the connections he made possible," wrote the writer/critic Andrew O'Hagan in 2010. He also credits the Ballets Russes with "the development of choreographic art in the entire world."[29] Beyond that, the Ballets Russes and Diaghilev demonstrated the vitality of artistic interchange, uniting visual, musical, dance, and literary arts marked by numerous reinterpretations of their work.[30]

René Blum, who aided their resurrection in Monte Carlo, wrote of Diaghilev that he showed him the "resources of modern ballet as an eclectic art, how it synthesizes harmoniously dance, music, poetry, architecture and painting."[31] This is a useful summary statement of his unmeasured accomplishments but not as sharp as some of Diaghilev's own aphorisms: "the greatest virtue of an artist is infidelity"; "every new composer may inspire a new school of dancing" (Garafola V. 146). But Diaghilev himself may have been his own greatest artist, combining the skills of an entrepreneur with that of a showman. Whether it was his artistic knowledge, ability as a director, or talent for publicity, marketing, and promotion, his mix of creativity and charisma worked. But the business of ballet never left him, whether on-or-off the stage.

After his death, Prokofiev recalled that Diaghilev never left a theatre or a room without making a vivid impression. He was, he added, one whose dimensions actually increased "the more he recedes into the distance," a marvelous gesture for the instigator of avant-garde dance at a time of artistic revolution (Scheijen 441).

NOTES

1. Havelock Ellis, "The Philosophy of Dancing," *The Atlantic,* February 1914: 98.

2. Diaghilev in Serge Lifar, *Ma Vie* (London: Hutchinson, 1970) 24. Lifar debuted with the company in 1923.

3. Diaghilev in Scheijen 429. This is from a 1928 interview he gave in *Vozrozhdeniye,* December 18, 1928. Eliot's *Waste Land*, Joyce's *Ulysses*, and sections of Pound's *Cantos* all incorporate classical sources and allusions but in modernist forms.

4. See Leonard Diepeveen, *The Difficulties of Modernism* (London: Routledge, 2003).

5. Fokine, "Five Principles," *London Times*, 1914, Fokine Estate Archive. http://www.michelfokine.com/id63.html.

6. Diaghilev in Garafola, "In His Own Voice: Diaghilev in the British Press," *The Ballets Russes and the Art of Design,* ed. Alston Purvis, 136. Hereafter Garafola V.

7. Lydia Sokolova, *Dancing for Diaghilev: The Memoirs of Lydia Sokolova,* ed. Richard Buckle (London: John Murray, 1960) 272.

8. Serge Lifar, *Serge Diaghilev, His Life, His Work, His Legend: An Intimate Biography* (London: Putnam, 1940) x.

9. Jed Perl, *Calder: The Conquest of Time: The Early Years, 1898–1940* (New York: Knopf, 2017) 477, 476. Calder would, himself, soon reach out to Léonid Massine for a possible collaboration.

10. Robert McAlmon, *Being Geniuses Together, 1920–1930,* rev. Kay Boyle (London: Hogarth Press, 1984) 275.

11. McAlmon in *Our Exagmination* 105–16.

12. Jacqueline Lee Bouvier, "People I wish I had known," *Vogue*, 1951, in *The World in Vogue,* ed. Bryan Holm and Katherine Tweed (New York: Viking, 1963) 301. She was twenty-one years old.

13. Virginia Woolf, *Between the Acts,* ed. Frank Kermode (Oxford: Oxford World's Classics, 2000) 59–60. For more on Woolf, the Ballets Russes, and Russia, see Ira Nadel, "The Russian Woolf," *Modernist Cultures*, Vol. 13.4 (2018): 546–67.

14. Zelda Fitzgerald to F. Scott Fitzgerald, March 1919, *Dear Scott, Dearest Zelda: The Love Letters of F. Scott and Zelda Fitzgerald*, ed. Jackson R. Bryer and Cathy W. Barks (New York: St. Martin's Press, 2002) 15–16.

In Ch. 3 of *Save Me the Waltz*, the hero Alabama says to the Madame that she has been "to the Russian ballet . . . and it seemed to me—Oh, I don't know! As if it held all the things I've always tried to find in everything else." She saw *La Chatte.* Zelda Fitzgerald, *Save Me the Waltz* (Carbondale, IL: Southern Illinois Univ. Press, 1967) 121.

15. It is perhaps no surprise that even a mystery exists: David Dickinson's *Death Comes to the Ballets Russes* (London: Constable, 2015). Set in 1912 London, it involves a prince stabbed to death in the orchestra pit, although the victim is not a dancer in the program but his understudy.

16. Balanchine had little patience with the old Russia. He found it suffocating and suffering from its historical past. For him, all must be new (Homans, *Mr. B* 120).

17. John Drummond, *Speaking of Diaghilev* (London: Faber and Faber, 1997) ix.

18. Serge Lifar, *Diaghilev* (London: Gollancz, 1945) 326.

19. André Levinson, "A Crisis in the Ballets Russes," *André Levinson on Dance* 66.

20. A curious postscript to the question of magic and money, of dance and economics, is that when Sotheby's London held its auction of Ballets Russes material in London in May 1984 from the collection of Serge Lifar, which had as its centerpiece scrapbooks that once belonged to Lady Juliet Duff, and the price for the books went to £135,000, the ballet world gasped. Dealers, collectors, librarians, and connoisseurs of ballet were dazzled, but the auction was only the beginning of extravagant prices for Ballets Russes material. Many of the additional items displayed Diaghilev's generosity to those he loved, whether showering art on his protégés or Savile Row suits. The existence and fate of this material is, itself, a story.

21. See Lynn Garafola, *La Nijinska,* passim, and Harold Robinson, *Russians in Hollywood, Hollywood's Russians* (Boston: Northeastern Univ. Press, 2007).

22. At the end of his biography of Diaghilev, Lifar includes a two-page summary of the rare editions and manuscripts owned by Diaghilev beginning with only the third copy of the eighth-century *Book of Hours* and ending with unpublished mss. and letters by Pushkin, Lermontov, and Tolstoy. See Lifar, *Diaghilev* 534–35.

23. See Lynn Garafola, "Price-Tagging Diaghilev," *Legends of Twentieth Century Dance* (Middletown, CT: Wesleyan Univ. Press, 2005) 377–78. Also useful is Jon Nordheimer, "Diaghilev Memorabilia is sold for $1.1 Million," *New York Times*, May 10, 1984. https://www.nytimes.com/1984/05/10/arts/diaghilev-memorabilia-is-sold -for-1.1-million.html.

24. Alexandre Schouvaloff, "The Diaghilev Legend," *A Feast of Wonders, Sergei Diaghilev and the Ballets Russes,* ed. John Bowlt, et al. (Milan: Skira, 2009) 97.

25. Ezra Pound, *Guide to Kulchur* (1938; New York: New Directions, 1970) 55.

26. Cyril Beaumont, *The Monte-Carlo Russian Ballet: Les Ballets Russes de Col. W. de Basil* (London: C.W. Beaumont, 1934) 7.

27. Ezra Pound, *Make It New* (London: Faber and Faber, 1934) passim. Pound also uses the phrase in "Canto LIII," *The Cantos of Ezra Pound* (New York: New

Directions, 1995) 265. "Canto LIII" originally appeared in 1940, the first of the so-called "Chinese Cantos."

28. Lynn Garafola and Nancy Van Norman Baer, eds., "Tradition and Innovation," *Ballets Russes and Its World,* 95.

29. Andrew O'Hagan, "Diaghilev: Lord of the Dance," *Guardian* October 9, 2010. https://www.theguardian.com/culture/2010/oct/09/diaghilev-ballets-russes -victoria-albert. Also see Stravinsky, "The Diaghilev I Knew," *Atlantic Monthly* 192.5 (November 1952) 33–36.

30. For an unusual re-staging of *Le Sacre de printemps* retitled as *The Sacrifice* and choreographed by the South African Dada Masilo using the techniques of tswana, a movement style native to Botswana, see Emily May, "Death and rebirth, The Sacrifice," *Times Literary Supplement,* No. 6259 (March 17, 2023): 14.

31. Quoted in Judith Chazin-Bennahum, *René Blum and The Ballets Russes* (New York: Oxford, 2011) 78.

Bibliography

Acocella, Joan. "The Showman: How Diaghilev Came to Dance," *New Yorker* Sept. 13, 2010. https://www.newyorker.com/magazine/2010/09/20/the-showman.

Acocella, Joan, with Lynn Garafola and Jonnie Green. "Catalogue Raisonnés," *Ballet Review* 20/2 (Summer 1992): 68–100. Full listing of *Le Sacre* productions up to 1992.

Amazons of the Avant-garde, ed. John E. Bowlt and Matthew Drutt. New York: Guggenheim Museum, 2000.

Anon. "The Sitter Out," *Dancing Times* (August 1927): 296.

Aragon, Louis and André Breton. "Surrealist Manifesto," in Serge Lifar, *Serge Diaghilev, His Life, His Work, His Legend: An Intimate Biography.* London: Putnam, 1940.

Astruc, Gabriel. "Papers," Dance Collection of the New York Public Library for the Performing Arts, Lincoln Center, New York. Call number: (S) *MGZMC-Res. 1. The collection number is *ZBD-161. Reels 1 & 2.

———. *Le Pavillon des Fantômes: Souvenirs*, preface by Pierre Lebaillif. Paris: Pierre Belfond, 1983, 1987.

Ballets Russes and Its World, ed. Lynn Garafola and Nancy Van Norman Baer. New Haven: Yale Univ. Press, 1999.

Ballets Russes and the Art of Design, ed. Alston Purvis, Peter Rand, and Anna Ulinestein. New York: Monacelli Press, 2009.

Banes, Sally. "Firebird and the Idea of Russianness," *The Ballets Russes and Its World*, ed. Lynn Garafola and Nancy Van Norman Baer. New Haven: Yale Univ. Press, 1999. 117–34.

Banni-Viñas, Vanessa. "Correcting a Ballerina's Story: The Truth Behind Makletzova v. Diaghileff," *American Journal of Legal History* 53.3 (July 2013): 353–61.

Baumol, William J. and William G. Bowen, *The Performing Arts: The Economic Dilemma.* New York: The Twentieth Century Fund, 1966.

Beaumont, Cyril W. *The Diaghilev Ballet in London: A Personal Record.* London: Putnam, 1940.

———. *The Monte-Carlo Russian Ballet: Les Ballets Russes de Col. W. de Basil.* London: C.W. Beaumont, 1934.

Bellow, Juliet. *Modernism on Stage: The Ballets Russes and the Parisian Avant-garde.* Burlington, VT: Ashgate, 2013.

Benois, Alexandre. *Reminiscences of the Russian Ballet*, trans. Mary Britnieva. London: Putnam, 1941.

Berrett, Jessica L. and Bradley S. Holliday. "The Effect of Revenue Diversification on Output Creation in Nonprofit Organizations: A Resource Dependence Perspective," *Voluntas: International Journal of Voluntary and Nonprofit Organizations*, Vol. 29. 6 (2018): 1190–1201.

Blackwood, Brian. "The Black Notebook of Serge Diaghilev," *Bulletin of the New York Public Library*, 75.8 (October 1971): 345–56.

Bourdieu, Pierre. *The Field of Cultural Production*, ed. Randal Johnson. New York: Columbia Univ. Press, 1993.

Bouvier, Jacqueline Lee. "People I wish I had known," *Vogue*, August 13, 1951, repr. in *The World in Vogue*, ed. Bryan Holm and Katharine Tweed. New York: Viking, 1963.

Bowlt, John. *Moscow & St. Petersburg 1900-1920: Art, Life & Culture of the Russian Silver Age.* New York: Vendome Press, 2008.

———. "Sergei Diaghilev and Stravinsky: From World of Art to Ballets Russes," *Stravinsky in Context*, ed. Graham Griffiths. Cambridge: Cambridge Univ. Press, 2021. 61–70.

———. *The Silver Age: Russian Art of the Early Twentieth Century and the "World of Art" Group.* Newtonville, MA: Oriental Research Partners, 1979.

———. "Stage Design and the Ballets Russes," *Journal of Decorative and Propaganda Arts* 5 (1987): 28–45.

Brezgin, Oleg. "Sergei Diaghilev: A Centennial Bibliography," trans. Olge Minin. *Experiment* 17 (2011): 459–687.

Bridgman, Elena. "Mir Iskusstva, Origins of the Ballets Russes," *The Art of Enchantment: Diaghilev's Ballets Russes, 1909-1929*, ed. Nancy Van Norman Baer. New York: Universe Books with the Fine Arts Museum of San Francisco, 1988.

Bromberg, C. S. "Dance as Commodity," *Dance Scope* Vol. 15. 3 (1981).

Buckle, Richard. *Diaghilev.* London: Weidenfeld and Nicolson, 1979.

———, with John Taras. *George Balanchine, Ballet Master: A Biography.* New York: Random House, 1988.

Bürger, Peter. *Theory of the Avant-Garde*, trans. Michael Shaw. Minneapolis: Univ. of Minnesota Press, 1984.

Burliuk, David. "Cubism (Surface-Plane), 1912," *The Russian Avant-garde and Radical Modernism: An Introductory Reader*, ed. Dennis G. Ioffe and Frederick H. White (Boston: Academic Studies Press, 2012) 93–101.

Caddy, Davinia. *The Ballets Russes and Beyond: Music and Dance in Belle-Époque Paris.* Cambridge: Cambridge Univ. Press, 2012.

Chang, Cyril F. and Howard P. Tuckman. "Revenue Diversification among Non-Profits." *Voluntas*, Vol. 5. 3 (1994): 273–90.

Chazin-Bennahum, Judith. *René Blum and The Ballets Russes.* New York: Oxford, 2011.

Christiansen, Rupert. *Diaghilev's Empire: How the Ballets Russes Enthralled the World.* London: Faber and Faber, 2022.

Cross, Jonathan. "Stravinsky in Exile," *Stravinsky and His World*, ed. Tamara Levitz. Princeton: Princeton Univ. Press, 2013. 13–16. Musical analysis of *Apollo.*

Davenport-Hines, Richard. *Proust at the Majestic.* London: Bloomsbury, 2006.

Diaghilev, Serge. "The Eternal Conflict," in Joan Acocella, "Diaghilev's 'Complicated Questions," *The Ballets Russes and Its World,* ed. Lynn Garafola and Nancy Van Norman Baer. New Haven: Yale Univ. Press, 1999. 72–73.

Diaghilev and the Golden Age of the Ballets Russes 1909-1929. Ed. Jane Pritchard. London: V&A Publishing, 2010.

Diaghilev Observed by Critics in England and the United States 1911-1929. Ed. Nesta MacDonald. New York: Dance Horizons, 1975.

Diaghilev and the Ballets Russes, 1909-1929: When Art Danced with Music. DVD. Dir. Carroll Moore. National Gallery of Art, Washington, DC. 2013.

Dianina, Katia. *When Art Makes News: Writing Culture and Identity in Imperial Russia.* DeKalb, IL: NIU Press 2013.

Dickinson, David. *Death Comes to the Ballets Russes.* London: Constable, 2015.

Diepeveen, Leonard. *The Difficulties of Modernism.* London: Routledge, 2003.

Di Virgilio, Stella. "Igor Stravinsky and the Salon of Winnaretta Singer," https: //parisianmusicsalon.wordpress.com/igor-stravinsky-and-the-salon-of-winnaretta -singer/.

Dodd, Nigel. *The Social Life of Money.* Princeton: Princeton Univ. Press, 2014.

Doyle, K. O. "Toward a psychology of money," *American Behavioral Scientist* 35 (1992) 708–24.

Drummond, John. *Speaking of Diaghilev.* London: Faber and Faber, 1997.

Drutt, Matthew. "Introduction," *Amazons of the Avant-garde*, ed. John Bolt and Matthew Drutt. New York: Guggenheim Museum, 2000. 13–19.

Eksteins, Modris. *Rites of Spring: The Great War and the Birth of the Modern Age.* Toronto: Lester & Orpen Dennys, 1989.

"Ekstrom Collection," Diaghilev and Stravinsky Foundation, Victoria and Albert Museum, London. https://archiveshub.jisc.ac.uk/search/archives/c446cbf1-8ec3 -3183-9464-60a32727c9e4.

Eliot, T. S. "London Letter," *The Dial* LXXI (October 1921): 453.

Eliot, T. S. "London Letter," in Nancy D. Hargrove, "Eliot and Dance," *Journal of Modern Literature* 21.1 (1997) 61–88.

Ellis, Havelock. "The Philosophy of Dancing," *The Atlantic*, February 1914: 197–207.

Elyot, Kevin. *Riot at the Rite*. Dir. Andy Wilson, BBC 2, March 11, 2006.

"The Fairy's Kiss," *The Cambridge Stravinsky Encyclopedia*, ed. Edward Campbell and Peter O'Hagan. Cambridge: Cambridge Univ. Press, 2012. 151–83.

Ferguson, Drue. "Bringing *Les Noces* to the Stage," *The Ballets Russes and Its World*, ed. Lynn Garafola and Nancy Van Norman Baer. London: British Library, 1999. 167–87.

Figes, Orlando. *Natasha's Dance: A Cultural History of Russia.* London: Allen Lane, 2002.

Fitzgerald, Zelda, in *Dear Scott, Dearest Zelda: The Love Letters of F. Scott and Zelda Fitzgerald*, ed. Jackson R. Bryer and Cathy W. Barks. New York: St. Martin's Press, 2002.

————. *Save Me the Waltz.* Carbondale, IL: Southern Illinois Univ. Press, 1967.

Fokine, Michel. "Five Principles," *London Times,* 1914, Fokine Estate Archive. http://www.michelfokine.com/id63.html.

————. *Memoirs of a Ballet Master,* trans. Vitale Fokine, ed. Anatole Chujoy. Boston: Little, Brown, 1961.

For Art's Sake: The Story of the Ballets Russses. DVD. BBC 4, 2019.

Freeman, Judi. "Fernand Léger and the Ballets Russes," *The Ballets Russes and Its World,* ed. Lynn Garafola and Nancy Van Norman Baer. New Haven: Yale Univ. Press, 1999. 151.

Froelich, Karen A. "Diversification of Revenue Strategies: Evolving Resource Dependence in Nonprofit Organizations." *Nonprofit and Voluntary Sector Quarterly,* Vol. 28. 3 (1999): 246–68.

Fry, Roger. "M. Larionow and the Russian Ballet," *A Roger Fry Reader,* ed. Christopher Reed. Chicago: Univ. of Chicago Press, 1996. 290–96.

Furnham, Adrian and M. Argyle. *The Psychology of Money.* London: Routledge, 1998.

Garafola, Lynn. "The Ballets Russes in America," *The Art of Enchantment: Diaghilev's Ballets Russes 1909-1929,* ed. Nancy Van Norman Baer. San Francisco: Fine Arts Museums of San Francisco, 1988. 122–37.

————. "Choreography by Nijinska," *Legacies of Twentieth-Century Dance.* Middletown, CT: Wesleyan Univ. Press, 2005.

————. *Diaghilev's Ballets Russes.* New York: Oxford, 1989.

————. "In His Own Voice: Diaghilev in the British Press," *The Ballets Russes and the Art of Design,* ed. Alston Purvis, et al. New York: Monacelli Press, 2009. 135.

————. "The Making of Ballet Modernism," *Dance Research Journal,* Vol. 20. 2 (1988) 23–32.

————. "Price-Tagging Diaghilev," *Legends of Twentieth Century Dance.* Middletown, CT: Wesleyan Univ. Press, 2005.

————. *La Nijinska: Choreographer of the Modern.* New York: Oxford Univ. Press, 2022.

————. "Reconfiguring the Sexes," *The Ballets Russes and Its World,* ed. Lynn Garafola and Nancy Van Norman Baer. New Haven: Yale Univ. Press, 1999. 245–68.

————, and Nancy Van Norman Baer, eds. "Tradition and Innovation," *Ballets Russes and Its World.* New Haven: Yale Univ. Press, 1999.

Garrigues, Manon. "Edgar Degas and the dancer: The artist's most beautiful representations," *Vogue* (French) March 7, 2021. https://www.vogue.fr/fashion-culture/article/edgar-degas-and-the-dancer-the-artists-most-beautiful-representations.

Georges-Michel, Michel. "A New Work by a Great Musician of Today: *Apollon Musagète,*" *Excelsior,* October 27, 1927, in Charles M. Joseph, *Stravinsky's Ballets.* New Haven: Yale Univ. Press, 2011.

Gombrich, Ernst. *The Sense of Order* 1979; New York: Phaidon Press, 1984.

Goss, Thomas. "Musings on Le Sacre's 100th Birthday," Orchestration Online, May 29, 2013. https://orchestrationonline.com/musings-on-le-sacres-100th-birthday-2/.

"Great Figures of Russian Ballet," *The Great History of Russian Ballet: Its Art and Choreography,* ed. R. Coalson. Bournemouth: Parkstone Press, 1998.

The Great History of Russian Ballet: Its Art and Choreography, ed. R. Coalson. Bournemouth: Parkstone Publishers, 1998. An illustrated survey.

Grieg, Valerie. *Inside Ballet Technique.* Hightstown, NJ: Princeton Book Publishers, 1994.

Grigoriev, S.L. *The Diaghilev Ballet, 1909-1929,* trans. Vera Bowen. 1953; Alton, Hampshire: Dance Books, 2009.

Haldey, Olga. "Savva Mamontov, Serge Diaghilev and a Rocky Path to Modernism," *Journal of Musicology* 22.4 (2005): 559–603.

———. *Mamontov's Private Opera: The Search for Modernism in Russian Theater.* Bloomington: Indiana Univ. Press, 2010.

Hargrove, Nancy. "The Great Parade: Cocteau, Picasso, Satie, Massine, Diaghilev— and T.S. Eliot," *Mosaic: Journal for the Interdisciplinary Study of Literature*, 31.1 (1998): 83–106.

Haskell, Arnold. *Balletomania Then & Now.* New York: Knopf, 1977.

Hatfield, Henry Rand. "Some Variations in Accounting Practice in England, France, Germany and the United States," *Journal of Accounting Research* Vol. 4. 2 (1966): 169–72.

Hill, Peter. *Stravinsky: The Rite of Spring.* Cambridge: Cambridge Univ. Press, 2000.

Homans, Jennifer. *Apollo's Angels: A History of Ballet.* New York: Random House, 2010.

———. "Fluidity," *The New Yorker*, February 27, 2023. https://www.newyorker.com /magazine/2023/02/27/ballet-review-copland-dance-episodes-justin-peck.

———. *Mr. B: George Balanchine's 20th Century.* New York: Random House, 2022.

Horowitz, Andy. "Untenable Economics of Dancing," *Culturebot* (March 27, 2014). https://www.culturebot.org/2014/03/21361/the-untenable-economics-of-dancing/.

"Igor Stravinsky: An 'Inirentor of Music' Whose Works Created a Revolution," *New York Times* April 7, 1971. https://www.nytimes.com/1971/04/07/archives/igor -stravinsky-an-inventor-of-music-whose-works-created-a.html.

Järvinen, Hanna. "Failed Impressions: Diaghilev's Ballets Russes in America, 1916," *Dance Research Journal* 42.2 (2010): 77–108.

Jensen, Robert. *Marketing Modernism in Fin-de-Siècle Europe.* Princeton: Princeton Univ. Press, 1994.

Jones, Susan. *Literature, Modernism, and Dance.* Oxford: Oxford Univ. Press, 2013.

Jordan, Stephanie. *Stravinsky Dances: Re-Visions across a Century.* Alton, Hampshire: Dance Books, 2007.

———. "Igor Stravinsky and Ballet as Modernism," *Stravinsky in Context*, ed. Graham Griffiths. Cambridge: Cambridge Univ. Press, 2021. 161–69.

Joseph, Charles M. "A New Approach—a New Collaboration, the Pathway to Apollo," *Stravinsky's Ballets* (New Haven: Yale Univ. Press, 2011) 102–33.

———. "Diaghilev and Stravinsky," *The Ballets Russes and Its World,* ed. Lynn Garafola and Nancy Van Norman Baer. New Haven: Yale Univ. Press, 1999.

———. *Stravinsky & Balanchine: A Journey of Invention.* New Haven: Yale Univ. Press, 2002.

———. *Stravinsky Inside Out.* New Haven: Yale Univ. Press, 2001.

Joyce, James. *Finnegans Wake.* New York: Viking, 1966.

Kahan, Sylvia. *Music's Modern Muse: A life of Winnaretta Singer, Princess de Polignac.* Rochester, NY: University of Rochester Press 2009, 203.

Karthas, Ilyana. *When Ballet Became French: Modern Ballet and the Cultural Politics of France, 1909-1939.* Montreal: McGill-Queens Univ. Press, 2015.

Kaufman, Sarah. "Ballets Russes, and the enduring dancing man," *Washington Post,* May 10, 2013. https://www.washingtonpost.com/entertainment/museums/ballets -russes-and-the-enduring-dancing-man/2013/05/09/0d367e1c-b7ef-11e2-b94c -b684dda07add_story.html.

Keller, James. "Le Sacre du Printemps," Program Notes, San Francisco Symphony Orchestra, September 2018. https://www.sfsymphony.org/Data/Event-Data/ Program-Notes/S/Stravinsky-le-sacre-du-printemps.

Kelly, Thomas. *First Nights: Five Musical Premieres.* New Haven: Yale Univ. Press, 2000.

Kendall, Elizabeth. *Balanchine and the Lost Muse: Revolution and the Making of a Choreographer.* New York: Oxford Univ. Press, 2013.

Kochno, Boris. *Diaghilev and the Ballets Russes,* trans. Adrienne Foulke. New York: Harper & Row, 1970.

Krueger, D. W. "Money, success and success phobia," *The Last Taboo: Money as a symbol and reality in psychotherapy and psychoanalysis.* New York: Brunner/ Mazel, 1986.

Lambert, Constant. *Music Ho! A study of music in decline.* London: Faber and Faber, 1966.

Larionov, Mikhail. "Rayonist Paintings," along with "Rayonists and Futurists: A Manifesto, 1913," in *Russian Art of the Avant-garde: Theory and Criticism, 1902-1934,* ed. John E. Bowlt. New York: Viking, 1976. 91–100, 87–91.

Larkin, Áine. "Theatre and Dance," *Marcel Proust in Context,* ed. Adam Watt. Cambridge: Cambridge Univ. Press, 2013. 97–104.

Lawson, Joan. *A History of Ballet and Its Makers.* New York: Pitman Publishing, 1964.

LeBere, Kathryn. "Red Swans: The Transformation of Ballet after the Russian Cultural Revolution (1924-1937)," honours thesis, University of Victoria, April 2019. https://www.uvic.ca/humanities/history/assets/docs/honours-thesis---kate -lebere-2019.pdf.

Legat, Nicolas. *The Story of the Russian School,* trans. Sir Paul Dukes. London: British Continental Press, 1932.

Les Ballets Russes a Paris, Representations exceptionnelles (Program), Library of Congress, Washington, DC, 35. https://tile.loc.gov/storage-services/service/music /vaultscan.2/200181871/200181871.pdf.

Levinson, André. "A Crisis in the Ballets Russes," *André Levinson on Dance: Writings from Paris in the Twenties,* ed. Joan Acocella and Lynn Garafola. Hanover, NH: Wesleyan Univ. Press, 1991. 66–72.

———. "The Ballets Russes at the Théâtre des Champ-Élysées (1913)," *Ballet Old and New,* trans. Susan Cook Summer. New York: Dance Horizons, 1982. 51.

———. "The Fairy's Kiss," *The Cambridge Stravinsky Encyclopedia,* ed. Edward Campbell and Peter O'Hagan. Cambridge: Cambridge Univ. Press, 2021. 151–53.

————. "The 'Saison Russe' and the Grand Opéra," *Ballet Old and New*, trans. Susan Cook Summer. New York: Dance Horizons, 1982. 17–24.

————. "Two Aesthetics," *Ballet Old and New*, trans. Susan Cook Summer. New York: Dance Horizons, 1982. 37–44.

Lieven, Prince Peter. *The Birth of the Ballets Russes*, trans. L. Zarine. London: George Allen & Unwin, 1956.

Lifar, Serge. *Ma Vie from Kiev to Kiev: An Autobiography*, trans. James Holman Mason. London: Hutchinson, 1970.

Lobanov-Rostovsky, Nina. "Diaghilev's Death," *Diaghilev and the Golden Age of the Ballets Russes 1909-1929*, ed. Jane Pritchard. London: V&A Publishing, 2010. 206–7.

Lopokova, Lydia. *Lydia and Maynard Letters*, ed. Polly Hill and Richard Keynes. London: Andre Deutsch, 1989.

Macdonald, Nesta. *Diaghilev Observed by Critics in England and the United States, 1911-1929.* New York: Dance Horizons, 1975.

Malevich, Kazimir. "Suprematism," *Russian Art of the Avant-Garde: Theory and Criticism, 1902-1934*, rev. ed., trans. John E. Bowlt (London: Thames and Hudson, 1988) 143–45.

Margit, Rowell. *Art of the Avant-garde in Russia: Selections from the George Costakis Collection* (1981).

Marinetti, F. T. "The Futurist Manifesto," *Critical Writings*, ed. Günter Berghaus, trans. Doug Thompson. New York: Farrar, Straus and Giroux, 2006. 11–17.

Marinetti, F. T., in Lynn Garafola, "The Making of Ballet Modernism," *Dance Research Journal* 20.2 (Winter 1988): 23–32.

Marinetti, F. T., in Galina Yelshevskaya, "Russian Avant Garde," https://arzamas .academy/materials/1231.

Marks, Steven G. *How Russia Shaped the Modern World.* Princeton: Princeton Univ. Press, 2003.

Marsh, Geoffrey. "Serge Diaghilev and the Strange Birth of the Ballet Russes," *Diaghilev and the Golden Age of the Ballets Russes 1909-1929*, ed. Jane Pritchard. London: V&A Publishing, 2010.

Mason, Francis. "Introduction," *I Remember Balanchine: Recollections of the Ballet Master by Those Who Knew Him.* New York: Doubleday, 1991. vii–xvi.

Matich, Olga. "Gender Trouble in the Amazonian Kingdom: Turn-of-the-Century Representations of Women in Russia," *Amazons of the Avant-garde*, ed. John E. Bowlt and Matthew Drutt. London: Royal Academy of Arts, 1999. 81–87.

May, Emily. "Death and rebirth, The Sacrifice," *Times Literary Supplement*, No. 6259 (March 17, 2023): 14.

McAlmon, Robert. *Being Geniuses Together, 1920-1930*, rev. Kay Boyle. London: Hogarth Press, 1984.

————. "Mr. Joyce Directs an Irish Word Ballet," *Our Exagmination Round his Factification.* 1929; New York: New Directions, 1972. 103–16.

Melville, Joy. *Diaghilev and Friends.* London: Haus Publishing, 2009.

Misler, Nicoletta. "Dressing Up and Dressing Down: The Body of the Avant-garde," *Amazons of the Avant-garde,* ed. John Bowlt and Matthew Drutt. New York: Guggenheim Museum, 2000.

———. *The Russian Art of Movement: 1920-1930.* London: Allemandi & Co., 2017.

Mitchell, Terence R. and Amy E. Mickel. "The Meaning of Money: An Individual-Difference Perspective," *The Academy of Management Review,* Vol. 24. 3 (1999) 568–78.

Moore, Gillian. *The Right of Spring: The Music of Modernity.* London: Head of Zeus Publishers, 2019.

Nadel, Ira. "The Russian Woolf," *Modernist Cultures*, Vol. 13. 4 (2018): 546–67.

Nelson, Karen. "The Evolution of the Financing of Ballet Companies in the United States," *Journal of Cultural Economics* Vol. 7. 1 (1983): 43–62.

———. "How Diaghilev Did It (Without the NEA)," *Dance Scope* Vol. 15. 3 (1981).

Newman, Ernest in *Sunday Times* Nov. 6, 1921, in *Diaghilev Observed,* ed. Nesta MacDonald. New York: Dance Horizons, 1975. 276.

Nice, David. *Prokofiev: From Russia to the West, 1891-1935.* New Haven: Yale Univ. Press, 2003.

Nijinska, Bronislava. *Early Memories*, trans. Irina Nijinska and Jean Rawlinson. New York: Holt, Rinehart and Winston, 1981.

Nordheimer, Jon. "Diaghilev Memorabilia is sold for $1.1 Million," *New York Times*, May 10, 1984. https://www.nytimes.com/1984/05/10/arts/diaghilev-memorabilia -is-sold-for-1.1-million.html.

North, Michael. *Novelty: A History of the New.* Chicago: Univ. of Chicago Press, 2013.

O'Hagan, Andrew. "Diaghilev: Lord of the Dance," *Guardian* October 9, 2010. https:// www.theguardian.com/culture/2010/oct/09/diaghilev-ballets-russes-victoria-albert.

Pasticci, Susanna. "Futurism," *The Cambridge Stravinsky Encyclopedia*, ed. Edward Campbell and Peter O'Hagan. Cambridge: Cambridge Univ. Press, 2021. 181–83.

Perl, Jed. *Calder: The Conquest of Time: The Early Years, 1898-1940.* New York: Knopf, 2017.

Phillips, Deasee. "Let's get to the Pointe: Ballet and Business," *Business Today,* August 24, 2017. https://journal.businesstoday.org/bt-online/2017/lets-get-to-the -pointe-ballet-and-business.

Poggioli, Renato. *The Theory of the Avant-Garde*, trans. Gerald Fitzgerald. Cambridge, MA: Belknap, 1968.

Pouncy, Caroline. "Dancing Up a Storm: The 1917 Revolution and Russian Ballet," *Culture Matters*, March 19, 2017. https://www.culturematters.org.uk/index.php/ arts/theatre/item/2484-dancing-up-a-storm-the-1917-revolution-and-russian-ballet.

Pound, Ezra. "Canto LIII," *The Cantos of Ezra Pound.* New York: New Directions, 1995. 262–74.

———. *Guide to Kulchur.* 1938; New York: New Directions, 1970.

———. *Make It New.* London: Faber and Faber, 1934.

Press, Stephen D. *Prokofiev's Ballets for Diaghilev.* Burlington, VT: Ashgate, 2006.

Priest, Douglas M. "The Bolshoi Meets Bolshevism: Moving Bodies and Body Politics, 1917-1934," PhD thesis, Univ. of Michigan, 2016. file:///C:/Users/ Ira/AppData/Local/Temp/Priest_grad.msu_0128D_14463.pdf.

Prince, M. "Self-concept, money beliefs and values," *Journal of Economic Psychology* 14 (1993): 161–73.

Pritchard, Jane. "Creating Productions," *Diaghilev and the Golden Age of the Ballets Russes 1909-1929*, ed. Jane Pritchard. London: V&A Publishing, 2010. 71–88.

———. "From the Russian avant-garde to Serge Diaghilev's Ballets Russes," *Studies in Theater and Performance* 36.3 (2016): 219–29.

Propert, W. A. *Russian Ballet in Western Europe, 1909–1920*. London: John Lane, 1921.

Proust, Marcel. "The Captive," *Remembrance of Things Past*, trans. C. K. Scott Moncrieff, Terence Kilmartin, and Andreas Mayor, Vol. III. New York: Random House, 1981.

———. "Cities of the Plain," *Remembrance of Things Past*, trans. C. K. Scott Moncrieff and Terence Kilmartin, Vol. II. New York: Random House, 1981.

———. *Sodom and Gomorrah*, trans. C. Scott Moncrieff and Terence Kilmartin, rev. D. J. Enright. New York: Modern Library, 2003.

Pushkin, Alexander. *Eugene Onegin,* trans. Henry Spalding. London: Macmillan, 1881. Project Gutenberg, http://www.gutenberg.org/files/23997/23997-h/23997-h.htm.

Raeff, Marc. *Russia Abroad: A Cultural History of the Russian Emigration, 1919-1939.* New York: Oxford Univ. Press, 1990.

Raev, Ada. "Working for Diaghilev: An Introduction," *Working for Diaghilev*, ed. Sjeng Scheijen. Netherlands: Groninger Museum, 2004. 8–13.

Rambert, Dame Marie, in "For Art's Sake – The Story of the Ballets Russes," BBC 4 DVD, 2019.

Ramuz, C. F. *Souvenirs sur Igor Strawinsky.* Paris: NRF, 1929.

Rappaport, Helen. *After the Romanovs: Russian Exiles in Paris from the Belle Époque through Revolution and War.* New York: St. Martin's Press, 2022.

Richardson, Ben J. "'A Conversation with Spectres': Russian Ballet and the Politics of Voice in T.S. Eliot," *Journal of Modern Literature* 37.1 (2013) 158–77.

Richardson, John. "Parade," *A Life of Picasso*, Vol. II: 1907-1917. New York: Random House, 1996. 419–33.

Richardson, Philip. "No English Need Apply," *Dancing Times* (December 1923): 347–49.

Robinson, Harold. *Russians in Hollywood, Hollywood's Russians.* Boston: Northeastern Univ. Press, 2007.

Roslavleva, Natalia. *Era of Russian Ballet, 1760-1965.* New York: E. P. Dutton, 1966.

Rumnev, Alexander, in Nicoletta Misler. "Precarious Bodies: Performing Constructivism," *Russian Avant-Garde Theatre: War, Revolution & Design.* London: Nick Hern Books, 2014.

Russian Art of the Avant-Garde: Theory and Criticism, 1902-1934, ed. and trans. John E. Bowlt. New York: Viking, 1976.

"The Russian Ballet as Presented by Diaghilev," *The World in Vogue*, ed. Bryan Holme and Katherine Tweed. New York: Viking, 1963.

Scheijen, Sjeng. *Diaghilev: A Life,* trans. Jane Hedley-Prôle and S. J. Leinbach. New York: Oxford, 2009.

Schimmelpfenning, Jörg. "Ballet," *A Handbook of Cultural Economics*, ed. Roth Towse. Northampton, MA: Elgar Publishing, 2003. https://core.ac.uk/download/pdf/18507441.pdf.

Schirn Kunstalle Frankfurt. *The Great Utopia: The Russian and Soviet Avant-Garde, 1915-1932*. New York: Guggenheim Museum, 1992.

Schmid, Marion. "Proust at the Ballet: Literature and Dance in Dialogue," *French Studies* 67.2 (2013): 184–98.

———. "Proust's Choreographies of Writing: *À la recherche du temps perdu* and the Modern Dance Revolution," *Marcel Proust Aujourd'hui, Swann at 100*, Vol. 12 (2015): 91–108.

Schmidt, Paul. "Pushkin and Istomina: Ballet in Nineteenth-Century Russia," *Dance Research Journal* 20.2 (1988): 3–8.

Scholl, Tim. *From Petipa to Balanchine: Classical Revival and the Modernization of Ballet.* London: Routledge, 1994.

Schouvaloff, Alexandre. "The Diaghilev Legend," *A Feast of Wonders: Sergei Diaghilev and the Ballets Russes*, ed. John Bowlt, *et al.* Milan: Skira, 2009.

Schumpeter, Joseph. *Capitalism, Socialism and Democracy.* New York: Harper, 1950.

Semenova, Natalya, *et al. The Collector: The Story of Sergei Shchukin and His Lost Masterpieces.* New Haven: Yale Univ. Press, 2018.

Sharp, Jane Ashton. *Russian Modernism between East and West: Natal'ia Goncharova and the Moscow Avant-Garde.* Cambridge: Cambridge Univ. Press, 2006, 2018.

Simmel, Georg. *The Philosophy of Money*, 3rd ed., ed. David Frisby, trans. Tom Bottomore and David Frisby. London: Routledge, 2005.

Sixsmith, Martin. "The story of art in the Russian Revolution," Royal Academy Post, December 20, 2016. https://www.royalacademy.org.uk/article/art-and-the-russian-revolution.

Slonimsky, Yuri. "Balanchine: The Early Years," trans. John Andrews, *Ballet Review* Vol. 5. 3 (1976): 1–64; repr. in *I Remember Balanchine: Recollections of the Ballet Master by Those Who Knew Him*, ed. Francis Mason. New York: Doubleday, 1991. 19–78.

Smith, Thomas. *Raising the Barre: The Geographic, Financial, and Economic Trends of Nonprofit Dance Companies.* Washington, DC: National Endowment for the Arts, 2003. https://www.arts.gov/sites/default/files/RaisingtheBarre.pdf.

Sokolova, Lydia. *Dancing for Diaghilev: The Memoirs of Lydia Sokolova*, ed. Richard Buckle. London: John Murray, 1960.

Sonner, Sarah. "Sponsorship and Funding for the Ballets Russes," *Diaghilev and the Golden Age of the Ballets Russes 1909-1929*, ed. Jane Pritchard. London: V&A Publishing, 2010. 94–95.

Souritz, Elizabeth, in Robert Gottlieb, *George Balanchine: The Ballet Maker.* New York: Atlas Books, 2004.

———. *Soviet Choreographers in the 1920s*, trans. Lynn Visson, additional trans. and ed. Sally Banes. Durham, NC: Duke Univ. Press, 1990.

Spicer, Graham. "Picasso in Rome, with Diaghilev, Cocteau and Massine: The Ballets Russes and Parade," Gramilano, March 22, 2017. https://www.gramilano.com

/2017/03/picasso-in-rome-with-diaghilev-cocteau-and-massine-the-ballets-russes
-and-parade/.

Starostina, Natalia. "On Nostalgia and Courage: Russian Émigré Experience in
Interwar Paris through the Eyes of Nadezhda Teffi," *Diasporas* Vol. 22 (2013).
https://journals.openedition.org/diasporas/213.

Stauffer, George B. "Foreword," in Charles M. Joseph, *Stravinsky's Ballets*. New
Haven: Yale Univ. Press, 2011.

Stein, Gertrude. *Autobiography of Alice B. Toklas.* 1933; London: Penguin
Books, 2001.

Stravinsky, Igor. From *Chronicle of My Life,* in Alexander Schouvaloff and Victor
Borovsky, *Stravinsky on Stage.* London: Stainer & Bell, 1982.

———. "The Diaghilev I Knew," *Atlantic Monthly* 192.5 (November 1952): 33–36.

———, and Robert Craft. "Some Painters of the Russian Ballet," *The Atlantic*
(August 1958). https://www.theatlantic.com/magazine/archive/1958/08/some
-painters-of-the-russian-ballet/641640/.

Stravinsky, Vera and Robert Craft. *Stravinsky in Pictures and Documents.* New
York: Simon and Schuster, 1978.

Strutinskaia, Elena. "Paris 1925: The European Premiere of the Russian Theatrical
Avant-Garde," *Russian Avant-Garde Theatre: War Revolution and Design,* edited
by John Bowlt. London: Nick Hern Books, 2014. 71–91.

Taruskin, Richard. "The Antiliterary Man: Diaghilev and Music," *On Russian Music*.
Berkeley: Univ. of California Press, 2009.

Tolstoy, Leo. *War and Peace,* trans. Louise and Aylmer Maude, ed. George Gibian.
New York: Norton, 1996.

Toorn, Pieter C. van den and John McGinness. *Stravinsky and the Russian
Period: Sound and Legacy of a Musical Idiom.* Cambridge: Cambridge Univ.
Press, 2012.

Toorn, Pieter van den, *Stravinsky and The Rite of Spring.* Berkeley: Univ. of
California Press, 1987.

Unwin, Stephen. *The Complete Brecht Toolkit.* London: Nick Hern Books, 2014.

Walsh, Stephen. *Stravinsky*: *A Creative Spring: Russia and France, 1882-1934*. New
York: Knopf, 1999.

———. *Stravinsky: The Second Exile: France and America, 1934-1971*. New
York: Knopf, 2006.

Wasserman, Max J. "Accounting Practice in France during the Period of Monetary
Inflation (1919-1927)," *The Accounting Review* Vol. 6. 1 (March 1931) 1–32.

Wellman, Daniel J. "Ballet Revenue Structures: What's Working and What's
Not in Ballet Companies in the USA," Master's thesis, Drexel University,
2022. https://drexel.esploro.exlibrisgroup.com/esploro/outputs/graduate/Ballet
-Revenue-Structures-Whats-Working-and/991019104705904721?institution
=01DRXU_INST.

White, Eric Walter. *Stravinsky: The Composer and His Works*, 2nd ed. Berkeley: Univ.
of California Press, 1979.

Wolfman, Ursula Rehn. "Misia Sert – Muse and Patron to Poets, Painters and Musicians (II)," *Interlude,* July 10, 2016. https://interlude.hk/misia-sert-muse -patron-poets-painters-musicians-ii/.

Woolf, Virginia. *Between the Acts,* ed. Frank Kermode. Oxford: Oxford World's Classics, 2000.

Wu, Mengyang. "Dance with *Petrushka:* The Ballets Russes, Russia and Modernity," *Open Journal of Social Sciences* 7.8 (August 2019). https://www.scirp.org/journal /paperinformation.aspx?paperid=94297.

Zeitlin, Solomon. "Dr. Zeitlin Describes Status of Archives," *The Jewish News* (Detroit), July 27, 1956: 1. https://digital.bentley.umich.edu/djnews/djn.1956.07 .27.001/1.

Zelizer, V. A. *The Social Meaning of Money.* New York: Basic Books, 1994.

Index

About the Author

Ira Nadel is Professor of English Emeritus at the University of British Columbia, Vancouver, and a Fellow of the Royal Society of Canada. His published works include biographies of Leonard Cohen, Tom Stoppard, David Mamet, and Philip Roth. He has also authored *Biography: Fiction, Fact & Form*, *Joyce and the Jews*, and *Modernism's Second Act*. Forthcoming is *Love and Russian Literature: From Benjamin to Woolf*.

Milton Keynes UK
Ingram Content Group UK Ltd.
UKHW011406230124
436547UK00006B/59

SAS GREAT ESCAPES FOUR

Damien Lewis
SAS
GREAT ESCAPES FOUR

DARING ESCAPE STORIES EXECUTED BY SECOND WORLD WAR HEROES

QUERCUS

First published in Great Britain in 2025 by

QUERCUS

Quercus Editions Limited
Carmelite House
50 Victoria Embankment
London EC4Y 0DZ

An Hachette UK company

The authorised representative in the EEA is Hachette Ireland,
8 Castlecourt Centre, Dublin 15, D15 XTP3, Ireland (email: info@hbgi.ie)

A CIP catalogue record for this book is available
from the British Library

HB ISBN 978 1 5 2944 109 3
TPB ISBN 978 1 5 2944 110 9
EBOOK ISBN 978 1 52944 112 3

1

Typeset by CC Book Production
Printed and bound in Great Britain by Clays Ltd, Elcograf S.p.A.

Papers used by Quercus Editions Ltd are from well-managed forests and other responsible sources.

For the Great Escapees
as depicted in these pages.